PRAISE FOR *NEUROSCIENCE FOR CHANGE AT WORK*

The guidance for leaders who are championing change in their organizations will enable you to avoid common pitfalls and achieve early and significant return on investment.

Richard Pharro, CEO, APMG-International

Tibisay and Melanie are at the cutting edge of business change, and this book will give you the insights from neuroscience and the tools to plan and embed positive change, enabling your business to adapt at pace and thrive. We will wonder one day how organizations in the past survived without this knowledge.

Jo Stanford, CEO, Healthcare Project and Change Association

Too busy to celebrate? *Neuroscience for Change at Work* reveals how to combat demotivation, chronic stress, and lack of creativity in a century of instant gratification and constant change. By fostering psychological safety and using the innovative PEPE© model, this scientifically grounded book shows how to boost productivity and innovation during times of change. A must-read for any 21st-century leader.

Nieves Pérez, CEO, ANE International – Academy of Neuroscience and Education

Neuroscience for Change at Work

*Practical insights to overcome workforce
resistance to organizational change*

Tibisay Vera and Melanie Franklin

KoganPage

Publisher's note
Every possible effort has been made to ensure that the information contained in this book is accurate at the time of going to press, and the publishers and authors cannot accept responsibility for any errors or omissions, however caused. No responsibility for loss or damage occasioned to any person acting, or refraining from action, as a result of the material in this publication can be accepted by the editor, the publisher or the author.

First published in Great Britain and the United States in 2024 by Kogan Page Limited

2nd Floor, 45 Gee Street
London
EC1V 3RS
United Kingdom

8 W 38th Street, Suite 902
New York, NY 10018
USA

www.koganpage.com

Kogan Page books are printed on paper from sustainable forests.

ISBNs
Hardback   978 1 3986 1442 0
Paperback   978 1 3986 1440 6
Ebook   978 1 3986 1441 3

British Library Cataloguing-in-Publication Data
A CIP record for this book is available from the British Library.

Library of Congress Cataloging-in-Publication Data
Names: Vera, Tibisay, author. | Franklin, Melanie, author.
Title: Neuroscience for change at work : practical insights to overcome
    workforce resistance to organizational change / Tibisay Vera and Melanie
    Franklin.
Description: London ; New York, NY : Kogan Page, 2024. | Includes
    bibliographical references and index.
Identifiers: LCCN 2024026041 | ISBN 9781398614406 (paperback) | ISBN
    9781398614420 (hardback) | ISBN 9781398614413 (ebook)
Subjects: LCSH: Organizational change.
Classification: LCC HD58.8 .V464 2024 | DDC 658.4/06019–dc23/eng/20240701
LC record available at https://lccn.loc.gov/2024026041

Typeset by Integra Software Services, Pondicherry
Print production managed by Jellyfish
Printed and bound by CPI Group (UK) Ltd, Croydon, CR0 4YY

CONTENTS

FOREWORD

It is with great pleasure and a profound sense of professional camaraderie that I pen this foreword for *Neuroscience for Change at Work*, a seminal work by my esteemed colleague and friend Tibisay Vera and change management expert Melanie Franklin. Having shared the enriching journey of academic exploration at Roehampton University in 2014, where we were both mature students immersed in the transformative world of neuroscience, I have witnessed first-hand Tibisay's dedication to applying scientific insights to practical, real-world challenges developed over the years.

Neuroscience for Change at Work is an extraordinary guide that stands at the intersection of neuroscience and organizational change. It navigates the complex terrain of brain science with clarity and applicability that only those with Tibisay's and Melanie's unique backgrounds could offer. Having transitioned from corporate careers to neuroscience, Tibisay and I understand the critical importance of grounding lofty scientific concepts in the concrete realities of workplace dynamics. This is not just a book about the brain's workings. It's a practical guide that demystifies the intricate processes of the brain with respect to change. Whether adapting to new corporate policies, shifting organizational cultures or implementing new technologies, this book offers actionable change management strategies. Tibisay and Melanie weave together a rich tapestry of insights from diverse neuroscientific areas, making the science accessible and relevant.

What sets *Neuroscience for Change at Work* apart is its profound understanding that at the heart of all organizational change are people, individuals with unique brain functions that determine how they perceive and react to change. Therefore, their approach is one of empathy and precision, aiming to foster productive but also nurturing and inclusive environments.

The book is meticulously structured, guiding readers through the complexities of neurological responses to change and offering strategies to manage these responses effectively. It is replete with practical examples and real-life applications, making the science accessible and relevant. This relevance is crucial, especially in today's diverse work environments, where inclusivity is not just a moral imperative but a competitive advantage. The passion for promoting neurodiversity in the workplace is evident throughout the book, championing the idea that understanding and leveraging neurological differences among employees can lead to more innovative, resilient and successful organizations.

In writing this book, Tibisay and Melanie have provided a valuable resource for leaders, HR professionals, change managers, people facing change and anyone interested in understanding neuroscience's profound impact on organizational change. It is a testament to the power of science to transform our approaches to leadership, management and collaboration. As someone who has walked a similar path, I am delighted and proud to see how Tibisay and Melanie encapsulate such complex, vital knowledge in a format that is both accessible and engaging.

Neuroscience for Change at Work is more than just a book; it is a road-map for building more adaptive, innovative and human-centred organizations. I wholeheartedly recommend this book to anyone eager to explore how neuroscience can revolutionize our understanding of change, enhance organizational health and elevate human potential in the work-place.

Miguel Toribio-Mateas, Clinical Neuroscientist
Honorary Research Fellow, School of Psychology, Cardiff University

PREFACE

We all have brains, and that simple fact is the cornerstone of why neuroscience is so exciting, especially when it comes to understanding and managing change at work. In a world where change is constant and inevitable, neuroscience offers us powerful tools to feel empowered and in control. This book will show you how to unlock the mysteries of the brain and harness its potential to foster resilience, positive adaptability and sustainable high performance during times of change.

As co-authors, we bring together complementary expertise. Tibisay Vera, a neuroscientist and business change expert, explores how the human brain influences behaviour, decision-making and our capacity to adapt to new situations. Melanie Franklin, with extensive experience in change management, translates these scientific insights into practical strategies that can be applied in real-world organizational settings.

Our collaboration has allowed us to combine cutting-edge scientific research with hands-on strategies for times of change. Our goal is to make the complex subject of neuroscience accessible and relevant to everyone, from leaders aiming to inspire their teams to HR professionals developing training programs, from coaches and consultants to individuals who want to enhance their own adaptability.

Neuroscience for Change at Work is the culmination of years of research, practical application and personal experiences. Neuroscience is complex. Tibisay Vera has simplified it through a practical but very powerful model – PEPE© – which will be accessible to any reader.

We think it is vital to create a culture that embeds change in the day-to-day, by creating habits, routines, processes and brain-friendly strategies. By understanding the neurological basis of behaviours and emotions, you can develop strategies that not only mitigate resistance but also promote a positive and proactive approach to change. This involves fostering an environment where employees feel safe and valued and empowered to take risks and innovate.

The book covers a wide range of topics, from how to maintain productivity to well-being during times of change. Each chapter blends scientific explanations with real-world examples and actionable strategies, making the content both theoretically sound and practically applicable.

We believe that by leveraging the power of neuroscience, organizations can unlock new potentials, drive meaningful change and create workplaces that are not only successful but also dynamic and fulfilling, so that individuals will thrive through change.

HOW TO USE THIS BOOK

This book is a practical guide to using neuroscience to create a brain-friendly experience of change at work. It has four objectives:

1 You will appreciate how the brain works.

2 You will understand how the brain responds to events and situations at work.

3 You will understand how to adapt positively to change based on how the brain works.

4 You will have a compendium of techniques and examples to create the brain responses that will help you manage yourself and your team through change at work

Part One

To help you appreciate how the brain works, the first two chapters explain the structure of the brain, how the brain processes information and the challenges created by change at work.

In the rest of Part One we explain how to use the PEPE© neuroscience model to create brain friendly ways of coping and thriving during change. The model looks at four fundamental principles that drive resistance to change from the brain perspective:

- pain
- energy
- peaks and valleys
- error detection

We refer to each of these as a *domain*, and each one has its own chapter (Chapters 4 to 7). We explain the reactions in the brain and provide practical ways to reduce our natural resistance to change.

Each domain has two dimensions, positive and negative, and we describe the brain reactions and techniques connected to each one. There are real-life examples from our extensive consulting experience to explain each technique, so you can understand how they work and their effect. Activities are not restricted to one dimension. The brain does not work in a linear pattern, so actions that help reduce resistance to change in one dimension will also support the creation of motivation for change in another dimension.

This gives you a rich toolkit, enabling you to select relevant activities depending on the type of change you are involved in, the complexity of your change and the culture of your organization.

We conclude each of the activities with a table explaining how the approach discussed supports other brain friendly activities in the other dimensions. For example, in this table we describe how the activities and techniques for altruistic giving and volunteering apply to promoting valleys dimension and the releasing energy dimension of the PEPE© model:

TABLE 0.1

Dimension	Activity	Contribution
Promote valleys	Balance anticipation and pleasure	By engaging in altruistic giving, we are helping to provide pleasure to our brain in order to balance the pressure of being all the time "on the go"
Releasing energy	Implement a culture of bravery and risk taking	When there are opportunities to volunteer to participate in the change, people are more likely to stretch themselves and take risks

Part Two

In Part Two we explain how to use the PEPE© model to enable you to manage continuous change at work. Specifically, we help you build resilience and reduce cynicism, and to flex your approach to support neurodiversity.

The majority of this book provides techniques suitable for anyone experiencing change at work. If you are sponsoring this effort, you have additional responsibilities, and we have provided a wide range of techniques and practical guidance to support you in your role.

Finally, to help you use everything you have learnt from this book, we have created a template to create your own Change Plan and example content to bring it to life and act as a guide for your own ideas.

PART ONE

Applying neuroscience to change

01

Introduction

The human brain

The human brain, boasting an astounding 100 billion neurons and a complex network of 100 trillion connections (equivalent to over 100,000 kilometres of interconnections), is one of Earth's most complex systems. It is the product of millions of years of evolution. Throughout human history, our ancestors exhibited an unwavering curiosity about comprehending the enigma of the brain. Despite academics' enduring efforts over centuries to decipher its codes and functions, our understanding remains in its infancy.

Nonetheless, the relentless march of technology, the influence of culture, and the insistent pursuit of scientific knowledge have propelled us from the rudimentary notions of the past. Ancient thinkers, such as the Greek philosopher Aristotle, speculated that the brain merely acted as a radiator, shielding the 'all-important' heart from overheating.

Today, our comprehension has evolved significantly, revealing the brain's multifaceted role in shaping our understanding of the world around us. It orchestrates a symphony of functions, giving meaning to our experiences, governing thoughts, preserving memories, facilitating speech, orchestrating movements and intricately regulating various organs within the body.

Furthermore, we now know that the brain and its intricate network of connections play a pivotal role in shaping human behaviour and responses to:

- stressful situations (e.g. navigating challenging exams, coping with job loss, confronting significant life changes);
- threat (e.g. danger of survival, social exclusion); and
- reward (e.g. excitement, pleasure, contentment).

In the 21st century, neuroscientists have come to recognize that emotions play a pivotal role in the brain's decision-making processes. While the brain makes decisions and is responsible for 'the thinking process' overall, it is crucial to recognize that 'we are not thinking machines; we are feeling machines that think'.[1] Together with the nervous system, the brain figures out our emotions, both consciously and unconsciously, to inform our choices.

With conviction, we can assert that the nervous system serves as a vital conduit, sending messages between the brain and the body, driven by the fundamental purpose of ensuring the survival and perpetuation of the human species.

Our brain represents our most precious asset, having navigated countless challenges throughout human history, from contending with predators and harsh climates to securing sustenance in the wilds of natural selection. Yet never before has it been subjected to the demanding rigours of the modern age, characterized by technology, globalization, social media and unceasing change.

Today, science has not yet succeeded in uncovering all the secrets of the human brain, but while it may never fully unlock all its mysteries, each passing day brings new revelations and astonishing progress.

To fully grasp the untapped potential at our disposal, we need to learn how we can control, guide and even 'artificially' prepare the brain to confront the novel challenges of our modern world. This concept is what we call 'hacking' our brain purposely. The PEPE© model further in this book provides a framework to help with 'hacking' our brain to facilitate change and positive adaptation, foster engagement and enhance overall well-being in today's ever-evolving landscape.

The brain's evolutionary challenge of the 21st century

Scientific consensus suggests that the human brain, as we understand it today, likely reached its current state of development approximately 40,000 years ago, often referred to as the 'great leap forward'[2] in human history. It is important to recognize that evolution is a gradual process that unfolds over an extended timeframe, spanning roughly 1.5 million years. In fact, many of the brain's functions can trace their origins back to the Ice Age. Nevertheless, within the realm of academia, there exists a robust debate regarding the most recent substantial evolutionary change in the human brain. Current discourse indicates that these noteworthy transformations occurred relatively recently, ranging from 3,000 to 10,000 years ago.

Subsequently, the most notable evolutionary shift since that 'great leap forward' has been a rather intriguing one: the average size of the human brain in proportion to our bodies has reduced by approximately 3 or 4 per cent. This reduction is a consequence of more efficient neural wiring, as well as a reflection of a subtle decline in our overall mental faculties. This decline can be attributed to the complexities of modern societies, where those with lesser cognitive abilities can survive and thrive thanks to the support and resources provided by their more intelligent peers. In contrast, in ancient times, they might have not fared as well.[3] In essence, intelligence has become a collective endeavour, with human beings increasingly choosing to live in groups and societies.

Despite the ongoing nature of evolution, contemporary scholars hold the conviction that we currently inhabit a modern society where natural selection no longer reigns as the sole driving force behind future evolution and adaptation. Instead, the artificial environment we've created – characterized by technology, urban landscapes and economic pursuits – presents new and distinct selective challenges very different to the trials of the Ice or Stone Ages. In terms of brain evolution,[4] our ancestral brain is not well equipped to navigate this modern terrain yet.

Let's not even mention the impact of the huge amount of overwhelming information we will be able to get instantly by using artificial intelligence (AI), which further exacerbates the challenges posed by our Stone Age neural architecture. Our ancient brain struggles with concepts such as instant gratification and the ceaseless pursuit of one objective after another without pause. This inclination is deeply rooted in our evolutionary history, where ensuring safe 'hunting' for sustenance and future procreation were paramount.

Extensive research indicates that repeated instances of gratification are closely linked to unhealthy behaviours and impulsive decision-making, heightening the risk of addiction, obesity, demotivation and disengagement from more meaningful life experiences.

Neuroscientists have now uncovered the neural underpinnings of delayed gratification, highlighting the importance of striking a balance between immediate rewards and those deferred over time to optimize survival and reproduction. Prolonged exposure to instant gratification disrupts this crucial equilibrium.

Essentially, when we persist in our pursuit of immediate gratification, our brains unleash a surge of dopamine long before we even attain the actual achievement. This premature dopamine release diminishes the intrinsic reward of the accomplishment, ultimately diminishing its quality.[5] This phenomenon often leads to demotivation and a disconnection from more profound and meaningful objectives, as we become ensnared by potent cravings and distractions.

> **Dopamine** is a neurotransmitter in the brain that plays a crucial role in motivation, reward and excitement. It helps regulate movement, emotions and cognitive processes, and is involved in reinforcing behaviours that are linked to positive experiences and outcomes.

To illustrate some of the challenges our brains have struggled with in the 21st century, consider the arrival and proliferation of the internet and social media, a relatively recent phenomenon that emerged 15 to 35 years ago.

In the context of social media, each time someone interacts with your tweet, post or message on platforms such as Facebook, Instagram, TikTok, WhatsApp and others, it triggers a substantial surge of dopamine. Over time, if the levels of this neurotransmitter do not normalize or follow a healthy pattern of highs and lows, the brain becomes conditioned to crave the fleeting excitement these interactions offer, even without accomplishing tangible goals. This craving can lead to a host of issues, including anxiety, addiction, demotivation and other mental health challenges.

> A **neurotransmitter** is a chemical substance that transmits signals across a synapse, which is a gap between two nerve cells (neurons), or between a neuron and a muscle cell or gland cell. They play a crucial role in communication within the nervous system and are involved in various physiological processes, including cognition, behaviour, emotion, sensation, movement and autonomic functions. Examples of neurotransmitters include dopamine, serotonin, acetylcholine and gamma-aminobutyric acid (GABA). Each of these neurotransmitters can have different effects.

COMPLEXITIES OF INSTANT GRATIFICATION

I remember my early years at secondary school when academic research was introduced to me. I can still remember the excitement I felt going from my local school library to the town hall library and then to the main national library in Caracas, Venezuela, where I was born and lived in my teenage years, in order to read and compile information for my assignments.

The 'hunt' and the 'wait' for more information to come over a period of two weeks made me so excited and motivated. What a pleasure I felt at the end of each trip to the library! Not to mention the celebration I had after having found eight or ten articles and books that talked about the Big Bang theory in only two weeks!

In contrast, early this year, I was helping my son, who is eight years old, to do a little research for an assignment he had from school about the universe. It was a great opportunity to visit the British Library so he could see and get a sense of all the books and articles he could find in this library and how it could help him with research; we then planned to go over the weekend.

What a surprise I got the following evening after our conversation and before we went to the library when my son showed me more than 10 articles and references he had found during the day by spending no more than an hour in front of my laptop and also by asking 'Alexa' to talk about the universe... My immediate reaction was to smile and feel proud about his achievement and his independence in finding the information he needed even before we went to the library, but the situation left me thinking and questioning overnight how much 'hunt' and effort he could have put into his research and what quick gratification he'd got in less than one hour by asking 'Alexa' for an answer.

I could not help going back 30 years in my memories, thinking how long it took me to get much less information than he had in less than one hour. Straight away my concern was:

Did he even build up excitement? Did he celebrate each of his findings before engaging in the next quest?

Another formidable challenge confronting our brains in the modern era is the relentless and unceasing exposure to change, be it at the individual or organizational level. It is this very challenge that inspired us to write this book, aiming to unveil the constraints that change imposes on our ancient brain and, more importantly, to provide practical strategies for mitigating its impact on our mental and physical well-being.

Our intention is to facilitate the process of adaptation to change, preventing adverse outcomes such as withdrawal, diminished motivation, compromised well-being, cynicism and other unfavourable responses. This becomes more important as we recognize the ever-increasing volume of planned and emergent changes taking place in organizations. Recent surveys indicate this volume of change has grown exponentially over the last few years and shows no signs of slowing down.

Change and the brain

Change disrupts the established wiring of our brain,[6] challenging the fundamental role it plays in our survival and reward systems.

The fundamental role of the brain: to help the species (in our case, the human species) to perpetuate through time and to pass genes on to future generations. Hence, it controls all the functions of the body and makes decisions based on the principles of threat and reward.

We are inherently wired to resist change initially, rather than embrace it. The good news is our wiring also equips us to adapt and display resilience in the face of change. Even though our instinct may be to resist, our brains possess an inherent capacity to adapt due to a property of the brain called brain plasticity.

However, the price of this adaptation can be very high, resulting in maladaptation, stress, development of unhealthy behaviours such as addiction, or even illness, both for the brain and the body. From an organizational perspective, such poor adaptation can lead to a lack of innovation and motivation, disengagement, financial losses as a result of poor performance or low productivity, and failure to achieve desired outcomes during a period of change.

Understanding the underlying reasons why people often find it challenging to change, even when substantial rewards await them, has been a significant focus of research by psychologists, organizational leaders, change managers and experts from various disciplines over the past few decades. Their aim has been to unearth insights that can aid the change process.

In our ever-evolving world marked by constant change and increasing uncertainty, there is a pressing need to comprehend how we can best facilitate adaptation to change and behavioural transformation, and offer support to individuals and organizations navigating profound transformations.

The study of the brain in real time and in action – thanks to cutting-edge scanner technology, electroencephalography (a technique to record the electrical activity of the brain) and innovative developments in laboratory research – is beginning to provide us with a comprehensive understanding of how the brain resists and eventually adapts to change. Importantly, it offers us a fresh approach to managing change and navigating uncertainty. Advances in neurobiology hold the potential to unlock novel strategies for behavioural change.

Neurobiology is a branch of biology that integrates knowledge and techniques from multiple disciplines, including neuroscience, molecular biology, genetics, physiology, anatomy, pharmacology and computational biology, to understand how the nervous system works at both the cellular and systems levels.

What is change?

Organizational change is the transformation of what an organization does and how it does it. It spans various dimensions, including alterations to culture, systems and processes, restructuring, mergers, expansions into new markets and the development of new products and services.

These changes vary in scale from improvements originated by a single team, to changes identified as part of continuous improvement initiatives and multiple workstreams forming a strategic transformation programme.

As the scope of the change increases, so does the number of those affected by the change. The change is initiated in one part of the organization but will change the outputs delivered to internal teams, departments and business functions or external customers. It can alter the content, format and frequency of the inputs created by others inside the organization or what is required from external suppliers.

This means that everyone in an organization is impacted by change they have some control over, and indirect changes originated elsewhere that they cannot control but must incorporate into their ways of working. The level of interconnectedness in our organizations, especially as we move towards

FIGURE 1.1 Scope and scale of change

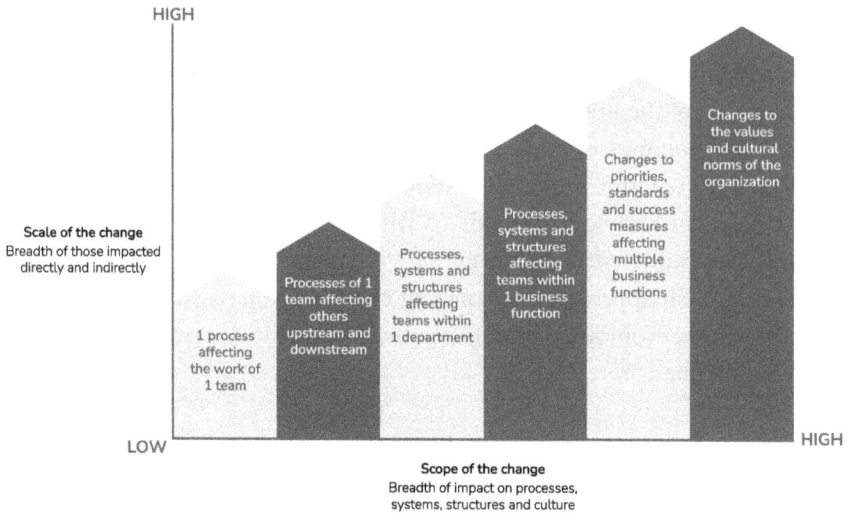

common platforms, systems and standards, means the volume of indirect change continues to increase.

Crucially, all these instances of organizational change have a profound impact on individuals. It is the individuals within and associated with the organization who must adapt and alter their work patterns. At the individual level, change entails learning to approach tasks differently, experiencing shifts in emotions, adjusting priorities as aspects of our roles become more or less significant, and adopting new behaviours to establish fresh routines and relationships.

Each of these changes disrupts existing patterns. As we explained earlier, our brains are naturally wired to resist change, but they also possess a remarkable capacity to adapt and display resilience. To ensure change takes hold, we must overcome this initial resistance by addressing both our emotions and our rational thought processes.

Recognizing that our brains are inherently 'feeling machines that think', we must cultivate a sense of desire to change, backed by compelling reasons that underscore the wisdom of the decision to change. This process entails 'hacking' our brains at both the conscious and the unconscious levels.

Our initial response to change is to view it as a threat. Change initially creates fear and anxiety, often triggered by a lack of understanding of the effects of the change on how we work. As the change is explained to us in terms of the likely benefits and improvements that it will create, we can see the change as an opportunity, so we become energized and motivated to make the change happen.

However, as we discover more about the impact of the change, we become overwhelmed by the considerable effort involved in achieving it, along with the potential for embarrassment in front of colleagues. Embarrassment comes from the unfamiliarity of the new ways of working. We ask 'inexperienced' questions and potentially make mistakes as we acquire the necessary skills. These apprehensions trigger feelings of threat, fuelling our desire to avoid change, to resist it.

To successfully adapt to the multitude of changes we encounter in our professional lives, we must find a balance between these feelings of threat and reward. This involves savouring the rewards of change through the anticipation of the improvements it will bring, while at the same time using the energy from our threat response to motivate us, and not dwelling too much on the threats as this will inhibit us from getting involved.

Throughout this book, we will offer brain-friendly activities designed to help you achieve this balance.

The phases of change

To understand the experience of change, we use a six-step, cyclical lifecycle of change to explain how we move from current to new ways of working. The intention is not to oversimplify the complex emotional and psychological journey involved in adopting new ways of working. This model is a tool to provide insights into the experiences of individuals affected by change.

For each step in the lifecycle, we describe the activities and experiences of those commissioning the change, those managing its implementation and those who must adopt the new ways of working. Specifically, we examine three areas of responsibility:

1 Senior leaders sponsoring the change

2 People managers planning the implementation and motivating their teams to change

3 Team members who must change how they work

As we can see, the steps do not necessarily flow from one to the other in a straight line. Change is an emotional experience, and at any point we can refuse to move forward because we do not have the energy or motivation.

FIGURE 1.2 Lifecycle of change

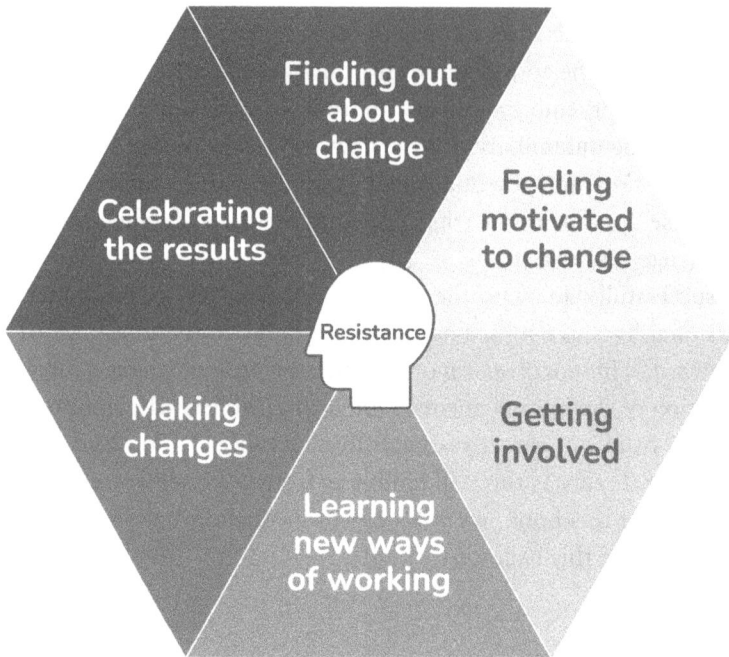

We can move backward because we have experienced problems that have reduced our positivity, which reduces our resilience for change.

This resistance to change is experienced in every lifecycle step:

Finding out about the change – our brain interprets the new information about the change, the move from the status quo as a risk to our survival, so we trigger pain. These changes to the status quo can trigger fears about a loss of personal status or unfairness that others are benefiting whilst we suffer losses including more complicated work or higher workloads. To avoid this pain, we attempt to ignore the change. Our brains might experience feelings of cynicism, doubting that the change will make any real difference. Our brains will display resistance by not believing or trusting in the information provided.

Feeling motivated to change – insufficient pleasure associated with the change will encourage our brains to resist the change. Our brains recognize that the change needs high levels of energy. Our brains fear how much work is involved and will try to avoid this extra effort.

Getting involved – our brains might resist the change because as we understand more about the change, the chances to become involved and the work we will be doing do not match our expectations. We might discover it requires more energy and effort than we are prepared to give, so our brains refuse to get involved. In addition, our brains may experience cynicism when remembering previous change initiatives and how much effort was involved, how hard this was and how little reward was gained.

Learning new ways of working – resistance is triggered by the feeling that we are out of our comfort zone. We need high levels of curiosity and to challenge the status quo. This requires a lot of energy and positive reinforcement about our achievements during the learning process. If our brains do not receive this feedback, or we have insufficient energy to process all the new information needed to learn about the change, then we will resist it.

Making changes – it is painful to give up old habits and routines. This loss of certainty generates a desire to resist change. This is compounded by a lack of psychological safety as we fear making mistakes and being criticized.

Celebrating the results – the resistance comes from the temptation to keep achieving, keep learning and having achievements. Effectively, we are too busy to celebrate and enjoy the results. Our brains resist achievement as much as they resist change.

Any change is a series of changes, where the lifecycle is triggered multiple times. This is because as we adapt to one aspect of the change, we discover more information that pushes us back to earlier steps. This is especially true when we first find out about a change as we need to hear the explanation of what is changing and why numerous times before we fully comprehend it.

If we are adopting an agile approach to change, then the iterative nature of the change means that as we complete one element of the change, we re-enter this lifecycle model at 'finding out' and move through each of the steps again and again.

Finding out about change

This is the starting point for any change. The scope of the change and the reason why the change is needed must be communicated to all those involved. With the increase in the volume of change taking place simultaneously in our organizations, it is also important to explain why the change is needed now, and cannot wait until a quieter, less busy time.

Ideally, these formal announcements of the change are the starting point. However, in some cases, informal rumours and gossip have created an awareness that change is coming, although this type of message may not

FIGURE 1.3 Lifecycle of change repeating throughout an iterative plan

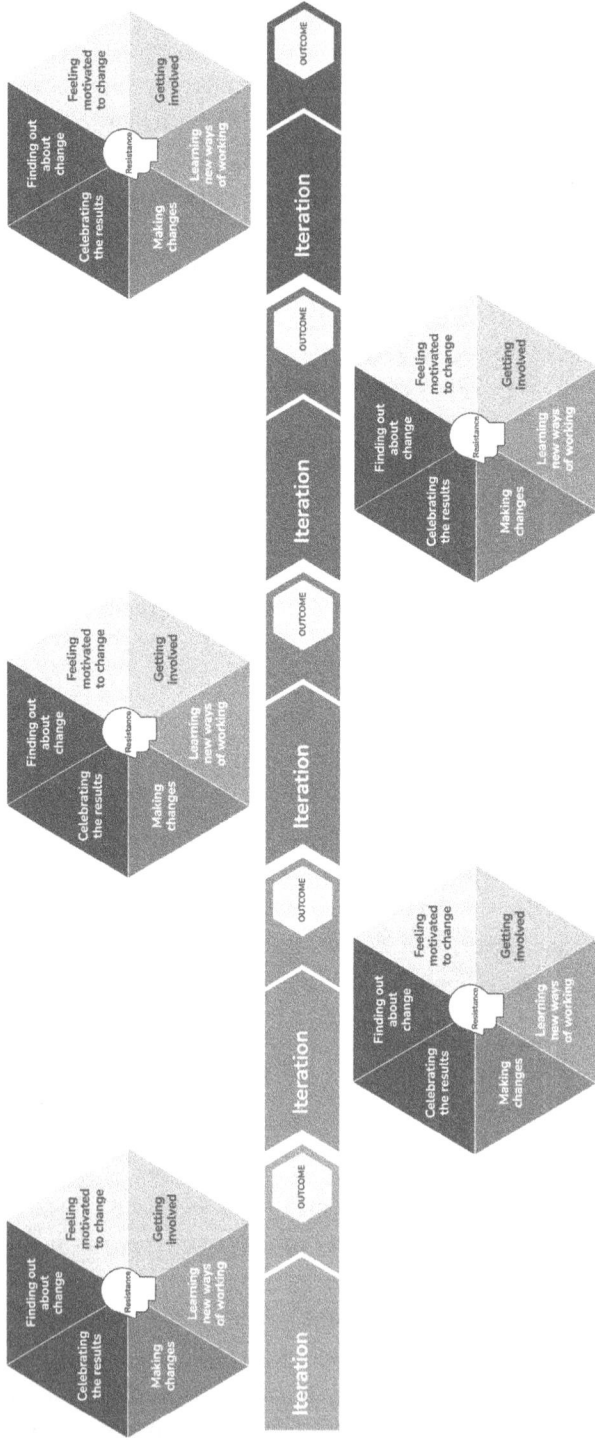

FIGURE 1.4 Finding out about change

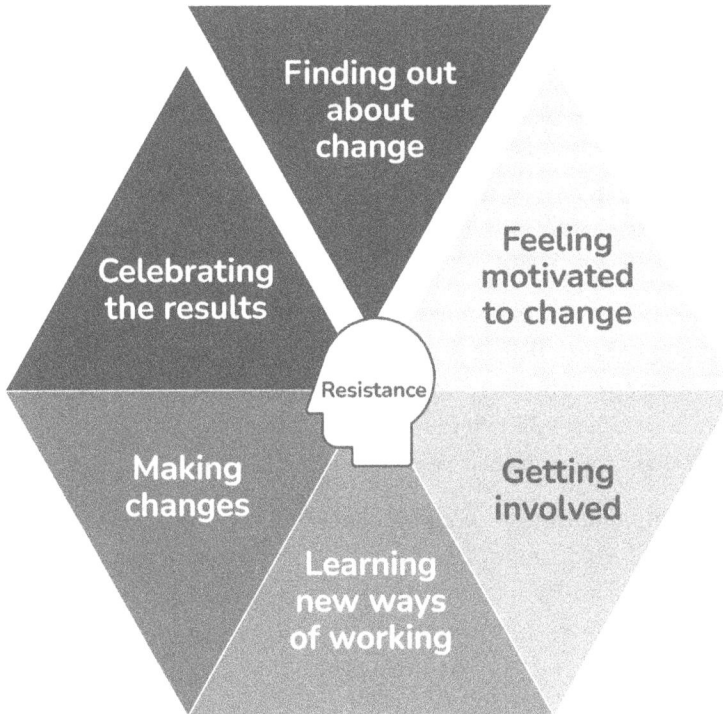

accurately reflect the actual change, but may be a negative perception based on early and incomplete information.

Information at this point in the lifecycle needs to be factual, explaining what will change and what remains the same. Explaining what will remain unchanged is an effective way of reducing the mismatch between what people assume will be affected by the change and what is really affected. This is because our brains 'catastrophize' when we hear the initial announcement, immediately identifying the change as a threat to aspects of our work that might be affected.

We also need to understand the forces that have created the need for the change. These forces are often a mixture of an internal desire for improvements and a response to external factors including customer demand, economic and regulatory changes:

- Senior leaders – describe the origins of the change so that everyone feels part of the decision. For example, explain what triggered the original ideas for the change, who has been involved in the process and what sources of information were used to decide on the change. Explain not only what is expected to change, but what will remain unchanged and why. Set the change in the context of changes taking place societally, technologically and from the perspective of customer expectations and competitor performance.

- People managers – to increase understanding of the change, managers should describe the change in their local context, explaining how it will impact the work, skills, priorities and relationships of the team.

- Team members – it is important that those who are directly affected by the change realize that they are impacted and that this is not something they can ignore. They need to think through the personal implications for what, how, when and where they work, to understand, at least at a high level, what aspects of their role will need to change.

This early communication about the change must generate enough energy to move us into the next stage of the lifecycle. It is unlikely that initial announcements will achieve this outcome, so there is an internal arrow in the diagram to demonstrate the need for repeated communications.

If there is an air of passivity, or a sense that those impacted think the change can safely be ignored, or have decided it is not important right now, then work is needed, repeating the information using different communication channels until the message has been heard.

To assess progress, managers and senior leaders need to assess if there is any 'buzz' about the change:

- Are people asking questions about the intended impact, the expected benefits, the scope or timing of the change?

- Are people checking their understanding by playing back what they have heard to assess its accuracy?

- Are they requesting more information?

- What proportion of the audience are asking for more information?

- Is there involvement from all those affected or just pockets of interest?

The outcome from this first step in the lifecycle is an acceptance that change is happening. No one can move to the next step and begin to feel motivated about something that they do not believe is really going to happen.

FIGURE 1.5 Feeling motivated to change

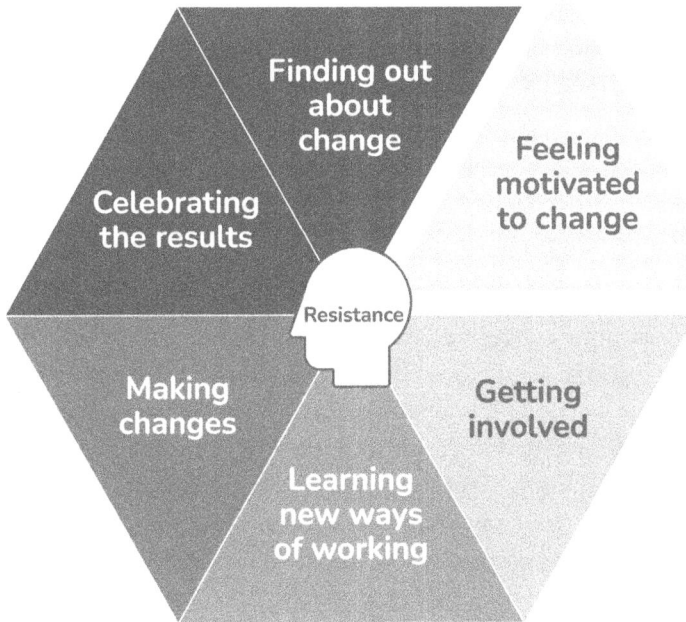

Feeling motivated to change

The purpose of this step is to ensure that all those who need to commit effort and energy to making the change happen are motivated to do so. We need to create an internal passion and drive, generating a belief in its value, its relevance and its necessity.

Everyone must find their own motivation for making the change a success. It is unlikely that these reasons will be the same as the 'official' strategic reasons why the organization will benefit from the change. Sharing these reasons can be a useful starting point, but the main focus in this step of the lifecycle is to encourage everyone to find their own motivation.

This happens when there is the chance for discussion. People need to ask questions, have these questions acknowledged, answered credibly and with enough detail. There should be opportunities to ask further questions, share feedback and discuss different perspectives:

- Senior leaders – to generate support for the change, it must feel necessary and meaningful. Those affected need to hear the reasons for the change from someone senior in their organization, as this gives the change credibility and importance. At this point, there may be few details to share about what will change, so the emphasis should be on explaining why the change is needed.

- People managers – facilitate discussions on how work will change, and what these changes mean for the individuals involved. Encourage discussion about how the change fixes current problems and how it enables improvements to current processes and methods. Emphasize the opportunities for learning new skills and applying the latest techniques.

- Team members – identify aspects of your work that you find frustrating or confusing, and consider how the changes will remove or improve these. Ask questions and share your views. Describing how you feel and hearing how others are feeling will help you see possibilities and opportunities that you may not have thought about.

The initial reaction to change is often negative as those affected calculate the cost to themselves of losing their comfortable routines. Even if current ways of working are unpopular, when threatened with change they become far more attractive compared to the effort needed to learn something different.

One of the most important factors in changing perception is to listen, and to let the other person know that their concerns and objections have been heard. Once these are expressed, especially to someone senior, individuals are free to think past their initial reaction, and will often become less negative.

Silence is not an indicator of support. It masks various types of resistance to the change, from anger to boredom or a belief that the change will not really happen. Those affected may hope that by staying quiet the change will melt away. If there is no discussion at this point, then senior leaders and managers must ask for opinions, concerns and ideas.

The outcome from this step is the identification of reasons why the change will provide benefits and/or is an opportunity for those who must change how they work. Without these benefits, there will be no willingness to participate. If those affected believe the change is harmful to their career, the quality of the work they provide, or does not lead to an improvement in their current situation then they will sit on the sidelines (at best) or actively campaign against it (at worst).

Getting involved

This step marks a shift from providing information to generating involvement. A key challenge is to find the time to create new ways of working, at the same time as operating the current processes.

FIGURE 1.6 Getting involved

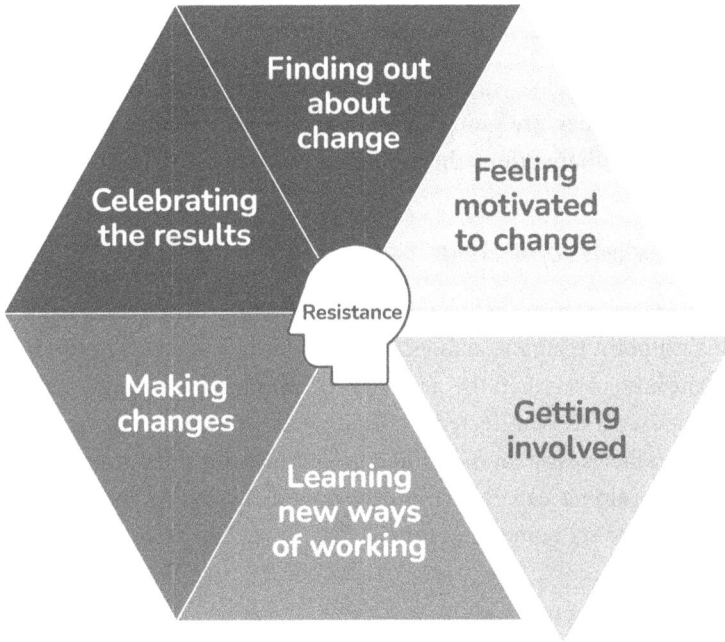

Change requires additional effort, which is powered by the motivation to achieve the change. This motivation can be boosted by offering choices in what to do, how and when to do it and who to work with:

- Senior leaders – work with people managers to streamline current workload to create capacity for the change activities. Demonstrate commitment to the change by talking about your own involvement in the change. Describe your activities including any training you will have, and the adjustments you are going to make to your processes and your measures of success.

- People managers – provide practical support for balancing effort between change activities and current workload. Encourage team members to partner with others within their team and with other parts of the organization also affected by the change. This team spirit makes it harder for individuals to withdraw their effort.

- Team members – encourage individuals to identify activities they enjoy and find easy to do. Volunteering for these activities reduces the probability of giving up even when the work turns out to be more difficult than expected. When deciding how to contribute to the change, individuals may return to 'finding out' or 'feeling motivated' as they have insights into what the change really means for them.

The outcome from this step is voluntary action. This requires those affected to identify how they are going to include change activities in their current workload, and what actions they are going to take.

Learning new ways of working

This is a logical step to achieving change because it avoids wasted effort. There is no point trying to make changes to how you work if you have not first learnt how to work in the new way. Understanding the new 'rules of the game' empowers those affected to design new processes, taking account of new rules, policies, system functionality and measures of success.

Effective training can reduce mistakes and the dip in performance that occurs when we try something for the first time. This training might not be

FIGURE 1.7 Learning new ways of working

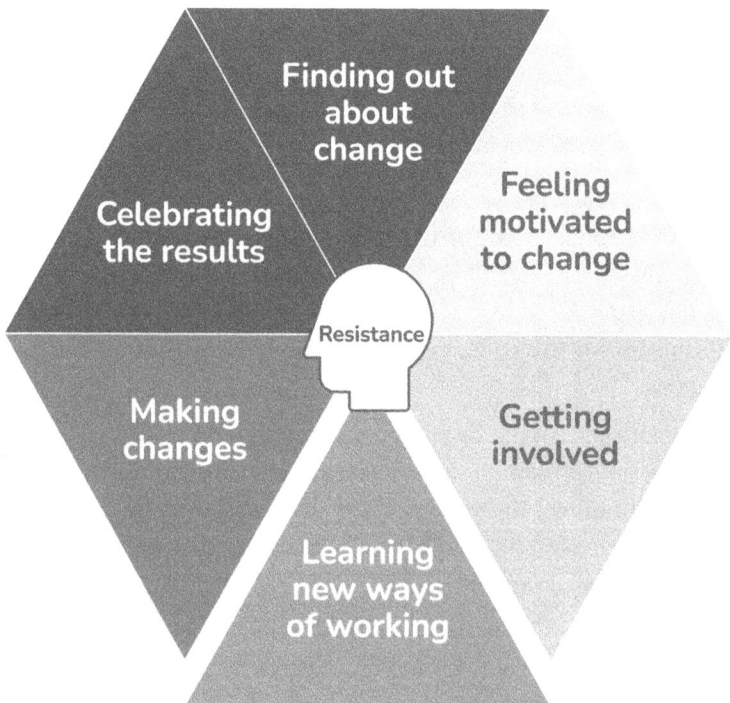

formal courses. Instead, learning new ways of working can occur through collective discovery, challenge and design in workshops where team members come together to create their new approach:

- Senior leader – ensure that the resources needed for training in the new ways of working are available. This will include helping people managers balance the team workload so that individuals can spend time in training activities. Your seniority may be required to ensure those involved in creating the tangible changes (developing and configuring new systems; building new operating models and structures; building new products and services) are willing to give their time to demonstrating their work and training those affected. For more explanation of tangible and behavioural change, please refer to Chapter 11, 'Sponsoring Change', specifically the section on understanding the sponsor role.

- People managers – ensure team members feel able to attend training by reducing their workload. Facilitate discussions about what has been learnt so far, what the implications are for this learning and what other information is needed.

- Team members – take an active part in your own learning and help others to learn what you know. Learning new ways of working is a process of discovery that may trigger the need for more 'official' information about the change from senior leaders or managers. The hard work of learning new ways of working may require more motivation so there is a need to return to the activities in 'feeling motivated'. Understanding what is involved in the change might affect the contribution that individuals want to make, changing what they are prepared to volunteer for, so they return to the 'getting involved' step.

As we learn, we seek out more information to create greater insight. Learning stimulates our motivation for change, as we enjoy the pleasure of acquiring new knowledge and skills. As we learn, we feel more able to contribute to the change, so we may revisit our original offer to become involved and increase the number of activities we volunteer for.

The outcome of this step in the lifecycle is to understand the new procedures, standards and rules for working in the new way and start to build the necessary skills.

FIGURE 1.8 Making changes

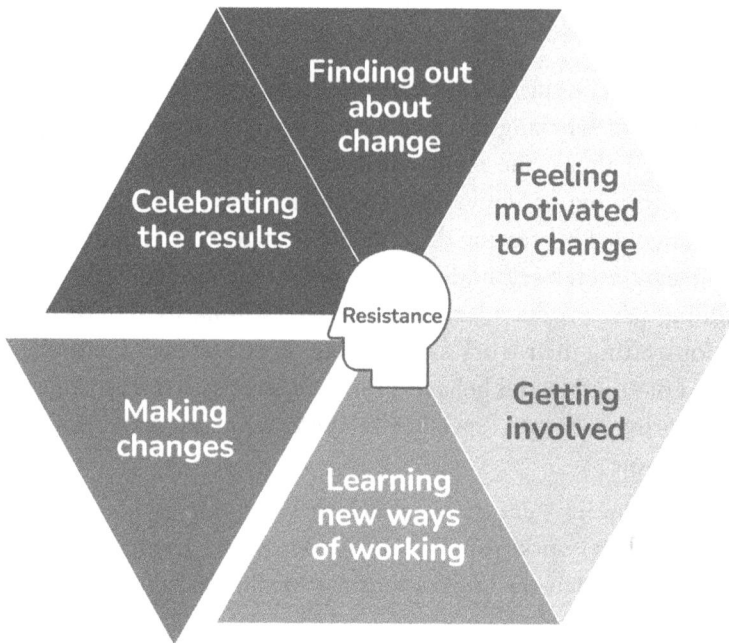

Making changes

In this step, those impacted by the change consistently apply these new ways of working, and with repeated use enable the situation to shift from being a change to being normal:

- Senior leaders – encourage everyone affected by the change to identify improvements and benefits. Showing interest in the impact of the change and its results demonstrates your involvement and commitment to it. At this point, your seniority may be needed to arbitrate on decisions. Often, when specific changes are made, unexpected side effects and consequences are discovered. Other teams are impacted and may want to reject the changes or make changes of their own. This will require senior-level approval to ensure that the end-to-end impact on how the organization works is acceptable.

- People managers – there is a need to boost energy, motivation and resilience during this step of the lifecycle. By this point, change will have been taking place for some time and people are getting tired. They will be making extra effort alongside their current workload but not necessarily feeling any of the benefits yet. Take time for team members to share their frustrations and their fears with you. Provide reassurance that their hard work is appreciated and point out improvements and positive impacts that you see. Facilitate sharing of experiences so that team members can learn from each other.

- Team members – keep making the changes to how you work. Use the support of your colleagues and your managers to remain motivated. Share your experiences so that others affected by the change can learn from you. Making detailed changes to how work is done is not always a smooth process. One change can trigger other unexpected changes that cause problems and are seen as a disadvantage. This means individuals may return to earlier steps in the lifecycle to find out more about the change, or to feel motivated to make the change happen. Discovery of this additional work may affect the activities they are prepared to volunteer for and the skills they need to learn.

As we begin to change how we work, we seek out more information to validate our experiences and help us decide what other aspects of our work to change. The outcome of this step is the adoption of new ways of working. Adoption means that individuals have used their understanding of new procedures, systems, policies and priorities and are applying their new skills to create new habits and routines.

Celebrating the results

Throughout this book we recognize the importance of celebration in creating positive brain chemistry. Celebration should be repeated for every achievement to generate the energy and motivation for further changes.

Whilst this appears to be the last step in the lifecycle, it is often an interim step because of the iterative nature of change. If our experience of change is positive and leads to achievement, we want to celebrate it. This inspires us to find out about more changes, and creates more motivation for change and a willingness to make more change happen:

- Senior leaders – acknowledge the effort that has been made and talk openly and frequently about the improvements. Use your understanding of the wider context to explain how the change is making other things possible and how this change is part of a bigger improvement agenda.

FIGURE 1.9 Celebrating the results

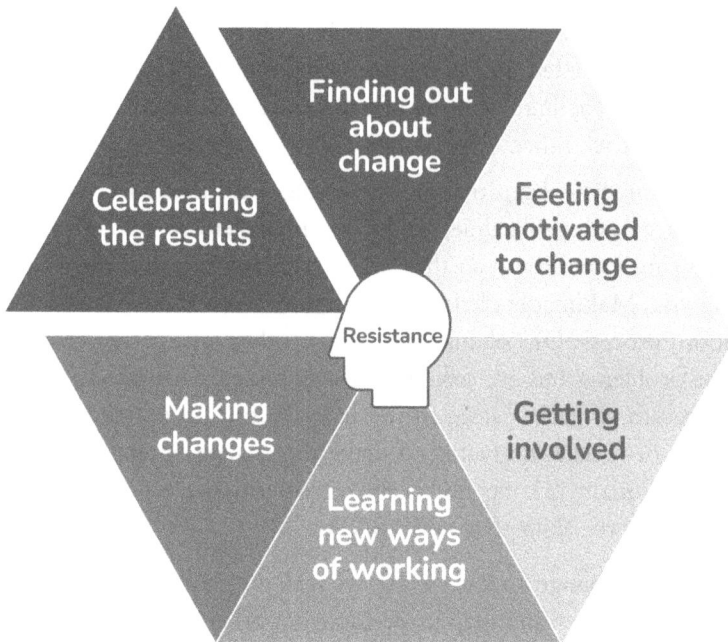

- People manager – help your team to reflect on what has changed so that everyone has a clear understanding of the new ways of working. Compare this to how things were before, emphasizing the improvements and benefits that have been achieved.
- Team members – feel proud of your achievements. Reflect on what you have learnt and the skills you have developed. Find ways to celebrate and share these celebrations with colleagues to reinforce the feelings of positivity.

The outcome of this step is the motivation to continue to change. This celebration generates the resilience to keep making more change happen.

Relationship with agile approaches

Neuroscience for Change at Work equips you with the tools to effectively 'hack your brain', enabling you to not only navigate but also thrive in an ever-changing environment. To achieve many of the brain-friendly activities described within the PEPE© model, consider adopting an agile approach to implement your desired changes.

Agile approaches deliver change in an incremental way, to prevent the need to define the complete scope of the change at the start. As the initial elements of the change are implemented, more becomes known about what else needs to change. This confirms what else needs to change and triggers the next iteration of the change. This iterative, incremental approach enables flexibility and responsiveness as circumstances change and the required outcomes from the change evolve. For more guidance on creating an iterative plan, refer to Chapter 5, 'Energy and the Brain', specifically the section headed 'Small but frequent deadlines'.

Individuals experience the agile approach as a series of changes, each triggering threat and reward responses.

The fundamental principles captured in numerous agile methodologies support the achievement of the sweet spot between threat and reward. These principles are:

- Delivering early and frequent *value* to the business – creation of value reduces the pain of change, because individuals feel that their work is important, helpful and respected.

- An *iterative approach* that prioritizes delivering to agreed deadlines. The high-level end-to-end plan reduces pain by providing certainty about what will be delivered and when; the frequent deliverables increase pleasure by enabling frequent celebrations.

- *Openness and transparency* of progress and goals, often via the use of visual planning techniques to enable everyone to see what is happening.

- Seeking out and *welcoming new ideas* – releasing the energy for change by encouraging continued anticipation of new achievements, and providing opportunities for people to contribute their insights, managing the peaks of effort by encouraging curiosity and willingness to challenge the status quo.

- Experimentation, piloting and prototyping as early as possible – this releases energy for the change by recognizing that solutions are discovered through trying things out and that all activities offer the *chance to learn* and develop.

- *Collaboration* increases pleasure because it increases a sense of belonging, creates common goals and objectives and increases positive signals by encouraging the exchange of positive feedback between team members.

- *Decentralizing decision-making* reduces the pain associated with change by increasing the autonomy of those involved in the change, creating an expectation of personal responsibility for results.

TABLE 1.1

Agile principle	Dimension	Activity
Value	Release positive signals	Manage expectations from the beginning and at every stage
Iterative approach	Releasing energy	Small but frequent deadlines
	Reducing the mismatch between reality and expectation	Focus on incremental (iterative) changes
	Reducing the mismatch between reality and expectation	Move from big to small
	Managing peaks	Focus on small cycles of change
Openness and transparency	Reducing the perception of pain	Certainty and assurance
	Saving energy	Promote visualization – reduce listening time
Welcoming new ideas	Managing peaks	Challenge the status quo
	Managing peaks	Promote curiosity
	Release energy	Provide opportunities for people to come up with their own insights
Chance to learn	Saving energy	Provide the right amount of information at the right time
Collaboration	Reduce perception of pain	Being valued and respected
	Increase pleasure	Common goals and objectives
Decentralizing decision-making	Promoting valleys	Balance anticipation and pleasure

These agile principles are incorporated into the model described in this book. In Table 1.1 we have identified some dimensions and activities that in our view align to the agile principles, but use your interpretation of the agile principles to find your own connections to the PEPE$^{©}$ model.

Table 1.1 shows that an agile approach has a positive impact on the brain as agility triggers all four domains of the PEPE$^{©}$ model.

There is a further explanation of the agile approach in Chapter 5, which explains the benefits to the brain of using small but frequent deadlines.

The nervous system

Neuroscience is the study of the nervous system, which comprises the brain, spinal cord and a complex network of nerves. This network sends messages back and forth between the brain and the rest of the body. Its fundamental purpose is to ensure the survival and perpetuation of the species, with two core imperatives: to protect us from threats (survive) and to propel us to seek rewards (fostering social connections and facilitating the passage of our genes to future generations).

In vertebrates, including humans, the nervous system consists of two main parts:

1 **The Central Nervous System (CNS):** Comprising the brain and spinal cord, the CNS serves as the epicentre of information encoding, integration and processing. It adeptly handles input from the environment through sensory channels, devising adaptive responses to threats and rewards. Notably, scientists also recognize that the brain can synthesize insights derived from thoughts and memories, not limited to external stimuli.

2 **The Peripheral Nervous System (PNS):** The PNS extends from the central nervous system (CNS) to the organs, limbs and skin. This system allows the brain and spinal cord to receive and send information to and from other areas of the body, which allows us to react to stimuli from the environment. These transmissions enable coordination between organs, arms, legs, fingers, toes and more. The PNS is further subdivided into:

   a. The somatic system, which is responsible for carrying information to and from the central nervous system.

   b. The autonomic nervous system: regulating involuntary physiologic processes such as heart rate, blood pressure, breathing, digestion or stimulation. The autonomic nervous system is the primary mechanism in control of the regulation of the flight and fight response. The automatic nervous system is further divided into:

   – b.1) *The Sympathetic Nervous System:* This system takes the reins during emergency 'fight or flight' responses and periods of physical exertion. Its overarching goal is to prepare the body for rigorous activity, drawing from an evolutionary perspective. It accomplishes this by bolstering the flow of well-oxygenated, nutrient-rich blood to tissues requiring an energy boost. This process involves the release and signalling of adrenaline and noradrenaline. Adrenaline prompts a rapid spike in blood glucose levels, providing a sharp and short-lived burst of energy essential for coping with demanding activities.

During demanding times, such as those marked by transformation and change, the sympathetic system provides the essential surge of energy needed to meet heightened demands. However, if overstimulated or not reset, it increases the risk of anger issues, disengagement, or freeze-type response, in addition to potential blood pressure disorders, heart failure and chronic stress.

- b.2) *The Parasympathetic Nervous System:* Primarily overseeing the body's 'rest and digest' functions, this system helps in restoring equilibrium during periods of rest. It counterbalances the 'fight or flight' response, preventing the body from overexertion and returning to a calm and composed state. Its actions encompass a reduction in heart rate, dilation of blood vessels, muscle relaxation and energy conservation.

- The main component responsible for signalling this information is the 'vagus' nerve. The vagus nerve makes up 75 per cent of the parasympathetic system and plays a prominent role in

FIGURE 1.10 A simplified illustration of the nervous system and its relationship with threat and reward

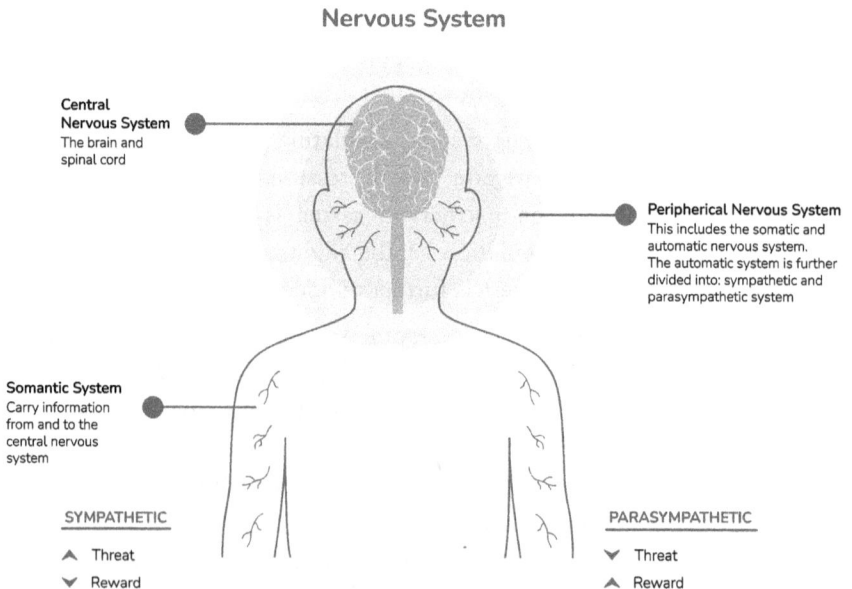

Nervous System

Central Nervous System
The brain and spinal cord

Peripherical Nervous System
This includes the somatic and automatic nervous system. The automatic system is further divided into: sympathetic and parasympathetic system

Somantic System
Carry information from and to the central nervous system

SYMPATHETIC

⋀ Threat

⋁ Reward

PARASYMPATHETIC

⋁ Threat

⋀ Reward

connecting the heart, lungs and vital organs. Acetylcholine, along with some GABA, are the main neurotransmitters released during parasympathetic activation, facilitating the body's restorative and maintenance function; they induce relaxation, digestion and calm.

– During times of change and transformation, the parasympathetic system assumes a crucial role by moderating heightened levels of denial and anger at the outset of the change cycle. As change progresses, it promotes acceptance and curiosity. Acetylcholine also plays a fundamental role in facilitating the learning necessary to adapt to new operating models.

– The latest research has also demonstrated that the parasympathetic system has a paramount role in preserving optimal health, immunity and well-being during disruption periods and when changing the status quo.

Notes

1 A Damasio (2006) *Descartes' Error*, Vintage
2 S Neubauer, JJ Hublin and P Gunz. The evolution of modern human brain shape, *Science Advances*, 2018, 4 (1) eaao5961
3 JM DeSilva et al. (2021) When and why did human brains decrease in size? A new change-point analysis and insights from brain evolution in ants, *Frontiers in Ecology and Evolution*, 2021, 9
4 N Longrich. Future evolution: from looks to brains and personality, how will humans change in the next 10,000 years? The Conversation, 1 March 2022, https://theconversation.com/future-evolution-from-looks-to-brains-and-personality-how-will-humans-change-in-the-next-10-000-years-176997 (archived at https://perma.cc/YT54-HJ6Q)
5 Z Gao et al. The neural basis of delayed gratification, *Science Advances*, 2021, 7:49
6 Wired in this context refers to the way our brain operates, is connected and the functionalities it has.

02

The sweet spots of the brain

As we mentioned earlier, the nervous system serves two primary objectives to facilitate the perpetuation of the human species over time: a) protecting us from threats (survival) and b) seeking rewards (passing on our genes and connecting socially).

The threat and reward sweet spot of the brain

Therefore, the brain's main priority is to strike a balance between threat and reward, providing us with an evolutionary advantage in safeguarding the species. The threat and reward systems harmoniously interact, influencing and regulating each other.

The brain's 'sweet spot' between the threat and reward systems refers to an optimal state activation of each other where an individual experiences peak performance, engagement and motivation.

Unfortunately, these systems can fall out of synchrony and disrupt the balance, giving rise to maladaptive changes within the nervous system. This dis-regulation can manifest as chronic stress, addiction, demotivation, resistance, compulsive behaviour or even depression. It occurs when the threat system becomes overly responsive or the reward system becomes hyperactive, a phenomenon known in neuroscience as maladaptation or 'malplasticity'.

One of the primary factors contributing to the dis-regulation is the mismatch between the speed at which the brain has evolved and the speed at which our environment and society have evolved. The accelerated speed of change in our modern surroundings, coupled with the increased frequency of constant change to the status quo, significantly contribute to brain maladaptation.

Furthermore, it is essential to acknowledge that the human brain has evolved to conjure imaginary threats and fabricate scenarios that trigger the same biological response as genuine dangers. This capacity to contemplate the past, envision the future, and ruminate on 'what if' scenarios can lead to an excessive exposure to threat responses or the compulsive pursuit of rewards.

During periods of change and transformation, it is common to see a surge in emotions like anger, demotivation, chronic stress, compulsive behaviour, a decline in creativity, cynicism and decreased performance among those involved in the change, regardless of whether they perceive the change as beneficial or detrimental. This surge stems from the dis-regulation and imbalance within the threat and reward systems.

Before exploring deeper into the intricacies of balancing the threat and reward systems, let's take a closer look at Table 2.1 on the next page.

Imagine this scenario: You arrive early at work one morning and your boss calls you to his office to share some exciting news. He tells you that you have been promoted to a new senior position that you have been hoping to get for the last year. As if that wasn't enough good news, the promotion comes with a major salary increase. Your boss mentions that the board of directors will be making an important announcement the next day and he would like you to do a public presentation in front of shareholders and investors about the results of the programme you have been in charge of for the past year.

After hardly taking in the unexpected positive news, you realize that the results of the programme are not as good as you had hoped. You know you would need a lot of effort and time to prepare the presentation and make it sound positive for tomorrow. On top of that, you start thinking about how nervous you were the last time you made a public presentation and how badly it all went. You're not comfortable with public speaking, and the thought of tomorrow's presentation makes you anxious.

Mixed emotions of excitement and fear course through you, and you tell your boss that you'd rather wait until next month's announcement to make the presentation. However, he is convinced that tomorrow is the best opportunity to do it, leaving you with no option but to prepare for it.

What happens to your brain, emotions and behaviours in this scenario? Firstly, receiving unexpected good news sets off a remarkable chain of events in your brain. It unleashes a substantial surge of dopamine, flooding

TABLE 2.1

THREAT SYSTEM	REWARD SYSTEM
Brain structures	Brain structures
– Mediated by the amygdala (subcortical brain network in the limbic system)	– Mediated by basal ganglia, striatum and nucleus accumbent
– When conditions allow conscious processing anterior cingulate cortex and insula (cortical network) are involved	– Two major phases of reward: 'wanting' (incentive salience or motivational system) and 'liking' (hedonic pleasure system)
– Thalamus signals other areas of the brain	Neurotransmitters and hormones
– Sympathetic nervous system is engaged	– Dopamine modulates the 'wanting'
– Parasympathetic system regulates threat response when danger is gone	– Opioids such as endorphins modulate 'liking'
Neurotransmitters and hormones	– Oxytocin (strictly speaking not part of the brain reward system, however it does enhance the system)
– Adrenaline, noradrenaline and stress hormones, such as cortisol to confront danger	Physical and behavioural responses
Physical and behavioural responses	– Dopamine plays a key role in promoting motivation, engagement and learning
– Fight and flight response is triggered	– Endorphins play a key role in promoting well-being and positive mood
– Glucose, blood pressure, blood flow increases to confront danger	– Both reward systems could lead to addiction and compulsion seeking
– Attention, fast movement and hypervigilance increase	– Promote risk-taking and creativity
– Trigger a sharp narrow focus	– Promote new ideas, open mind and approaching behaviours
– Adrenaline raises sugar levels to provide energy	

your system with feelings of exhilaration, excitement, heightened energy and newfound motivation. You might even notice physical manifestations such as trembling, a fluttering sensation in your stomach, or an infectious, ear-to-ear smile spreading across your face. This delightful cascade of sensations emerges from the activation of your brain's reward system, specifically a component known as 'incentive salience' or the 'wanting' part of the reward system.

Dopamine is a neurotransmitter in the brain that plays a crucial role in motivation, reward and excitement. It helps regulate movement, emotions and cognitive processes, and is involved in reinforcing behaviours that are linked to positive experiences and outcomes.

Secondly, the moment your boss mentions the public presentation and the announcement of the results, your amygdala swiftly detects a potential 'threat'. In response, your thalamus promptly dispatches signals to various regions of your brain, triggering the activation of your sympathetic nervous system. This activation prompts the release of adrenaline and noradrenaline, propelling your heart into a rapid rhythm. You might sense a heightened state of vigilance and alertness, teetering on the edge of hypervigilance, with an increased awareness of what could go wrong yet sharply focused on what needs to be done. This vivid experience is the result of the threat system being activated.

The amygdala is a small almond-shaped structure located deep within the brain. It plays a vital role in processing and regulating emotions, particularly fear and aggression. The amygdala is involved in the formation of emotional memories and the detection of potential threats in the environment, triggering the body's threat response, which involves adrenaline, noradrenaline and cortisol.

The thalamus is a key structure located in the centre of the brain. It plays a crucial role in processing and transmitting sensory signals from the body to the brain and the other way around. It is also involved in regulating sleep, consciousness and attention.

Adrenaline and noradrenaline: These are both neurotransmitters and hormones produced in response to a challenge or stress. They are both part of the brain threat system. Adrenaline provides energy to confront the threat, preparing the body to 'fight'. Noradrenaline increases arousal and attention. They both increase heart rate, blood pressure and blood flow.

After leaving your boss's office, the sequence of events primarily depends on what you do next and how your conscious, rational mind processes the information available. It's at this juncture that your parasympathetic system may come into play, modulating your perception of danger. The heightened state of hypervigilance you experienced might either gradually decrease or remain high. Should it persist, the body may initiate the release of stress hormones, including cortisol, designed to fortify your readiness for confronting the perceived 'danger.'

> **Cortisol** is a steroid hormone that gets released in response to stress, both physical and psychological. It helps the body respond to stress by increasing blood sugar levels, providing an energy source for the 'fight or flight' response. Cortisol also suppresses the immune system's activity temporarily to prioritize immediate survival needs. Chronic or prolonged exposure to cortisol can have negative effects on health and well-being.

On the other hand, your response to the situation, whether you choose to celebrate your promotion or take a moment to bask in the achievement and enjoy the news before embarking on your new role's challenges, can trigger the activation of the pleasure reward system. This activation leads to the release of endorphins, enhancing the enjoyment of the moment and enabling you to fully savour the present. In neuroscience terms, this corresponds to the 'liking' or pleasure part of the brain reward system.

The endorphins may induce feelings of euphoria or relaxation, depending on how your conscious processing unfolds. Furthermore, the release of endorphins can help alleviate any 'pain' associated with the substantial effort and changes that lie ahead in the next 24 hours.

> **Endorphins** are neurotransmitters produced by the central nervous system (part of a group of neurotransmitters called opioids). They act as natural painkillers and are often referred to as 'feel-good' chemicals. The primary role of endorphins is to reduce pain and promote feelings of well-being and euphoria. They create a sense of pleasure and happiness.

The scenario outlined above sheds light on the intricate workings of the threat and reward systems in the brain, and what it takes for the brain to trigger one system or the other. Equally, it is important to reflect on 'what you can do' when you have the choices to engage the rational brain to help to balance the threat and reward systems and to create what we call 'the sweet spot of the brain', a state that optimizes efficiency while minimizing detrimental effects on performance and well-being.

During times of change, it's a common tendency to remain in a state of hypervigilant threat perception unless proactive steps are taken to activate the parasympathetic system and move towards a reward-oriented mindset.

Naturally, the initiation of the threat system offers considerable advantages, as it will give us the energy, attention and narrow focus required to meet deadlines, and perform at our peak during brief periods of heightened demand, as illustrated in the earlier scenario.

However, should the threat system remain unchecked by the parasympathetic nervous system, and the hypervigilant state persists for an extended duration, the release of chronic nocturnal cortisol under these circumstances can undermine sustained high performance and the behaviours necessary to function effectively under pressure and changing conditions. Additionally, it can impede the ability to make creative and assertive decisions, as responses become dominated by the brain's 'emergency control command'. Furthermore, overall well-being and positive moods may deteriorate, and undesirable behaviours such as anger, irritability and narrow-mindedness may emerge.

There are situations where even brief periods of heightened threat may not be beneficial, necessitating the activation of the brain's reward system instead. For example, to maintain motivation, engagement and creativity at peak levels, it becomes necessary to activate the brain's reward system and unleash the release of dopamine, which constitutes the 'wanting' part of the brain's reward system. However, maintaining elevated dopamine levels without occasional resettling or continually engaging in a 'wanting/hunting' mode can also lead to compulsive seeking behaviours and addiction tendencies, ultimately resulting in demotivation and disengagement – a consequence attributed to what neuroscience terms 'bad plasticity' or maladaptive brain adjustment of the brain reward system.

Research in neuroscience has convincingly demonstrated that consistently operating at 'peak' dopamine levels represents a significant risk factor for maladaptive addiction responses to a changing environment and therefore it is important to maintain a harmonic activation balance within the brain reward system itself and between the brain reward system and the brain threat system.

During periods of change, it's not uncommon for those involved in the change to find themselves constantly 'hunting' for the next milestone without pause for celebration and the enjoyment of the present moment. This persistent activation of the anticipatory or 'wanting' part of the brain's reward system (dopamine) can inadvertently lead to 'bad adaptation' within the brain, fostering demotivation and compulsion-seeking behaviours instead of promoting a reward-driven motivation.

When making decisions related to organizational culture design, leadership management, resilience, well-being, change management, etc., it is important to understand which brain system (threat, reward, 'wanting' or 'liking') within individuals and teams needs activation, and to what extent. Leveraging the neurobiology and associated behaviours of each system can be a powerful asset, one that's much more favourable than having these forces working against us.

The optimal state of brain stimulation

The optimal state of brain stimulation (referred to by neuroscientists as 'optimal state of arousal') lies in balancing the activity of the threat and reward systems. In this state, individuals experience a moderate level of arousal that promotes focused attention, creativity and resilience without overwhelming stress.

This delicate equilibrium is not a static state but rather a dynamic interplay influenced by individual goals, tasks at hand and environmental factors, as reviewed before. Adapting this optimal arousal level purposely is key to maximizing performance, facilitating change and overall well-being.

Different goals necessitate different levels of activation of the threat or reward systems to achieve optimal performance. When facing a challenging task or deadline, individuals may deliberately seek to heighten stimulation levels of adrenaline (threat) to enhance focus. Conversely, during periods of reflection, relaxation or brainstorming, a lower level of threat stimulation may facilitate divergent thinking and creativity. By intentionally modulating stimulation levels of the threat or reward system, individuals can align their mental state with the demands of the task at hand, optimizing performance and effectiveness.

FIGURE 2.1

The threat and reward sweet spot of the brain

The brain is wired for 2 things:

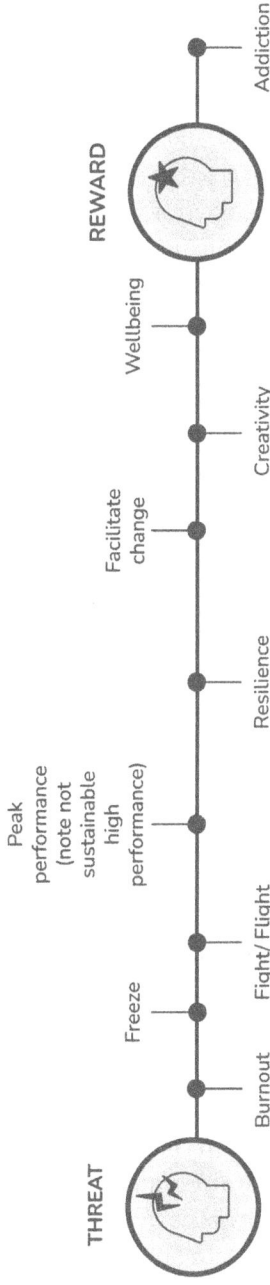

THREAT

Burnout
Freeze
Fight/Flight
Peak performance (note not sustainable high performance)
Resilience
Facilitate change
Creativity
Wellbeing

REWARD

Addiction

Behaviours:

Narrow minded
Sharp, focus
Forceful, tend to be aggressive
Anxious
Close to learn
Fixed mindset

Open minded
Excitement
Motivation
Insights
Bonding trust
Open to learn
Growth mindset

Figure 2.1 provides examples of sweet spots between threat and reward, reflecting the desired behaviours in each scenario.

For example, let's describe the case of achieving peak performance as a state of flow. A state of flow, as originally described by psychologist Mihaly Csikszentmihalyi, refers to a state of optimal experience characterized by intense focus, deep engagement and a sense of effortless control. In this state, individuals are fully immersed in an activity, time seems to distort and individuals experience a sense of effortless action and intrinsic motivation. A key component of peak performance, enabling individuals to surpass their usual limits and achieve extraordinary results, is the fact that the challenge level of a task slightly exceeds an individual's skill level. Individuals need to move slightly towards the threat system for a little while to take advantage of what adrenaline has to offer in terms of providing energy and activating the desire to confront the challenge. However, if the challenge is too high or remains so for a prolonged period of time, it can lead to hypervigilance, anxiety or frustration, making high performance unsustainable.

Likewise, a state of flow is an autotelic experience, meaning that the activity itself is inherently rewarding and enjoyable. Individuals engage in the task for its own sake, deriving satisfaction and fulfilment from the process rather than external rewards or outcomes. This intrinsic motivation fuels sustained engagement and deepens the sense of flow, helping to find 'the threat/reward sweet spot'.

Peak performance can involve elements of both the threat and reward systems in the brain, but it largely depends on the context and individual factors. In certain situations, such as facing a high-stakes challenge or responding to a sudden 'fire drill' situation where everyone is expected to stop what they're working on and respond with speed to a seemingly urgent matter, activation of the threat system can enhance alertness, focus and peak performance. This heightened state of arousal can provide individuals with the energy and motivation needed to overcome obstacles and perform at their best. For some individuals, a moderate level of stress stemming from the threat system may be necessary to mobilize resources, heighten focus and promote peak performance in challenging situations, whereas for other individuals only a little level of stress might be enough, and any more stress or threat would make the experience overwhelming.

Sustainable high performance requires finding the sweet spot where the challenge is just right to stretch one's abilities without overwhelming them. Managing high performance is about recognizing when to jump in and out of the comfort zone (controllable threat) and being able to create a safe space for individuals to do so. It is also about helping others to move towards a more rewarded state when they need to support insights, creativity and well-being.

On the other hand, in the specific context of managing change, the optimal brain state for managing and facilitating change leans towards activating the brain's reward system rather than the threat system.

As reviewed earlier in this book, change requires motivation, engagement and learning new ways of working, including learning new skills and knowledge. In this case the activation of the threat system will release a neurobiology (adrenaline, noradrenaline and cortisol) that will not be useful for the desired intention as it will trigger narrow-minded behaviours, such as stubbornness or reluctance to learn. Likewise, it can trigger a fixed mindset and therefore individuals will be working with their neurobiology against them.

Instead, change requires us to activate the neurobiology of the brain's reward system, such as dopamine, oxytocin and endorphins, which will help trigger open-minded behaviours, excitement, motivation, trust and growth mindset, and therefore will facilitate individuals to embrace change and adapt more positively to it.

Figure 2.1 illustrates the relative positioning of various psychological states and behaviours within the brain's threat and reward system. It highlights the optimal balance necessary for fostering creativity, resilience and facilitating change while avoiding burnout, anxiety and addiction.

In addition to moving towards reward, it is also important to locate the sweet spot within the reward system itself and shift between its two distinct phases: the 'wanting/hunting' phase (associated with dopamine) and the 'liking/pleasure' phase (linked to endorphins) to prevent 'bad adaptation'.

The brain reward system: the hunting and laughing sweet spot

Over the past two decades, neuroscientists have differentiated between the anticipatory and consummatory phases of the brain's reward system. The anticipatory phase, often referred to as 'wanting' or incentive salience, is connected to motivation, while the consummatory phase, known as 'liking' or 'hedonic', relates to the pleasure derived from experiencing rewards. Research has established that 'liking' and 'wanting' rewards are psychologically and neurobiologically separable.[1,2]

Furthermore, in the last few decades, researchers have provided insights into the roles of dopamine and opioids within the reward process.

Since the first dopamine hypothesis of reward was elaborated over three decades ago, with the core concept that dopamine mediates pleasure, the field has now shifted towards implicating dopamine in the anticipatory/wanting aspects of reward only, and opioids such as endorphins in the consummatory or 'liking/pleasure' phase of the brain reward system.

Recent findings concerning the link between stress and reward and the recognition of two distinct types of reward (anticipatory and consummatory) are highly significant for facilitating change. Change, whether positive or negative, often induces stress and anticipation. This can lead to unpleasant symptoms like anxiety, sadness and uneasiness, but it can also provide us with motivation and anticipation of 'wanting' something new to arrive. The outcome depends on how we perceive and balance the brain's reward system between anticipation and pleasure.

Achieving a delicate balance between dopamine and endorphins is essential for avoiding demotivation, addiction and burnout, and it is imperative for the well-being of individuals and teams. During times of change, people frequently find themselves in 'hunting' mode most of the time, resulting in an excess of dopamine and minimal endorphins and pleasure.

So, what can we do?

Balance anticipation with pleasurable activities

Leaders responsible for change, as well as individuals undergoing change, should systematically plan activities that promote the pure enjoyment of the present moment and engage in pleasurable activities to promote the release of the endorphins, before engaging in the next 'hunt', anticipation or iteration. Examples of such activities include learning sessions, positive feedback sessions, laughter, celebration, physical exercise and mindfulness. Since change often correlates with a lack of pleasure, finding activities that can stimulate (hack) the pleasure system will effectively facilitate the adaptation to change.

Applying neuroscience for managing change involves learning how to strategically and consciously map desired behaviours and beneficial neurobiological responses to different stages in the change process. At times, brief periods of threat can be beneficial, while at other times, a more rewarding state is required. Similarly, there are instances when motivation stemming from dopamine rewards is preferable, and others when pleasure and endorphins are more advantageous.

We will explore in greater depth this balance between anticipation and pleasure in Chapter 6, 'Peaks and Valleys in the Brain'.

Notes

1 KC Berridge, TE Robinson and JW Aldridge. Dissecting components of reward: 'liking', 'wanting', and learning, *Current Opinion in Pharmacology*, February 2009, 9 (1): 65–73

2 MF Barbano and M Cador. Opioids for hedonic experience and dopamine to get ready for it, *Psychopharmacology*, April 2007, 191: 497–506

03

The PEPE© Model

The PEPE© model encapsulates neuroscientific discoveries that have significantly advanced our understanding of behavioural change, adaptation and resilience. It offers a brain-based framework for approaching and managing change in a practical manner, taking into consideration how our brain resists and adapts to change.

The PEPE© model is versatile and can be applied to any type of change, whether major or minor, faced by individuals or organizations. It is specifically designed to help people in various roles who are facing or managing change as it offers practical strategies to address resistance to change and positive adaptation to change by providing a structured framework to help facilitate and navigate change at multiple levels.

As discussed in the previous chapter, titled 'The Sweet Spots of the Brain', during periods of change, the brain's threat and reward systems may become imbalanced, with a tendency to activate the threat system over the reward system. To encourage desired behaviours that align with the brain's neurobiology, it is essential to steer individuals toward a more rewarding state. The PEPE© model provides practical solutions for shifting the culture of organizations or individuals towards a more open, learning-oriented, insightful, creative and trustworthy space, thereby facilitating change.

The PEPE© model also serves as a powerful framework for designing change management processes, coaching programmes or organizational design strategies that support positive adaptation to change, encompassing aspects like engagement, resilience and well-being. It presents an opportunity to grow and thrive in an ever-changing environment. In an extended context the PEPE© model and its practical strategies have been used to help design leadership frameworks to support agility, growth and compassion. Specifically, it offers brain-based strategies to develop compassionate leadership habits and behaviours.

The PEPE© model is the result of more than 10 years of research in neuroscience and change. It was developed by Sparkling Performance founder and neuroscientist Tibisay Vera after studying the patterns of the adaptation to change and behaviour of hundreds of leaders and organizations from the human brain perspective. The recurrent observation was that our brain usually adapts to change but it does not necessarily adapt positively, and so negatively impacting individuals and organizations in the short and long term. The PEPE© model has been endorsed by the International Academy of Neuroscience and Education (ANE) and it is the backbone of the Certification in 'Neuroscience for Change' accredited by APMG International.

PEPE© model is a copyright and trademark of Sparkling Performance Ltd.

Four brain facts and principles that drive resistance to change

The PEPE© model involves four fundamental principles that drive resistance to change from the brain perspective: Pain, Energy, Peaks and Valleys, and Error Detection.

- **Pain** is the uncomfortable sensory or emotional experience that tells us something is wrong. It encompasses both sensory pain (physical sensations we feel in response to actual or potential harm, such as heat, cold, pressure or sharpness) and emotional pain (subjective feelings of distress and discomfort that can accompany sensory pain or arise independently in response to various stressors, including social interactions).

- **Energy** is the capacity for work and motion. Motion refers to the ability to produce physical movement.

- **Peaks and Valleys** refer to fluctuations in both brain chemistry and brain waves. Brain waves are patterns of electrical activity in the brain that indicate different mental states such as concentration, mind wandering, stress or sleep, and can influence human behaviour when combined with chemistry fluctuations.

- **Error Detection** is the brain's ability to signal and adapt behaviour when there's a conflict between actual responses and intended responses or expectations.

FIGURE 3.1 PEPE© model domains: four domains that drive resistance to change

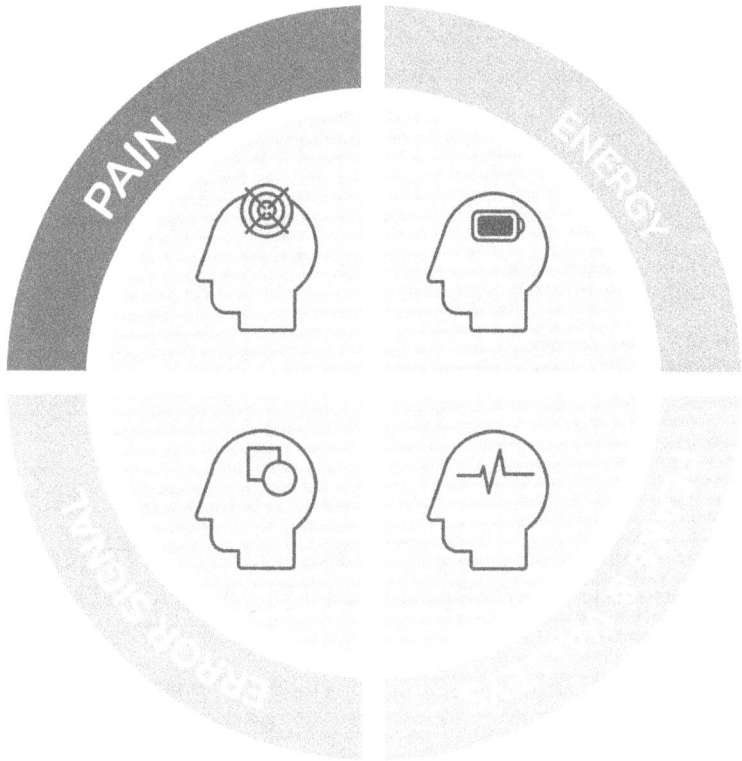

Its aim is to offer a systematically brain-friendly approach, using eight dimensions to facilitate change, promote positive adaptation and enhance resilience. Understanding and labelling these domains raises conscious awareness about otherwise unconscious processes.

The PEPE© model encompasses two dimensions each for the domains of 'pain', 'energy', 'peaks and valleys' and 'error'. It offers practical strategies aimed at fostering positive adaptation to change and overcoming resistance to change within these dimensions.

Practical application of each domain can help to manage change, improving performance and maintaining well-being during periods of change and uncertainty.

The PEPE© model can be applied at an adhoc level to address specific domains when facing change, providing practical techniques and solutions for addressing resistance associated with each of them. Alternatively, it can be systematically applied when managing change or creating leadership frameworks to ensure a holistic approach that fosters positive adaptation, including increased resilience, engagement, motivation and well-being.

FIGURE 3.2 The eight dimensions of the PEPE© model

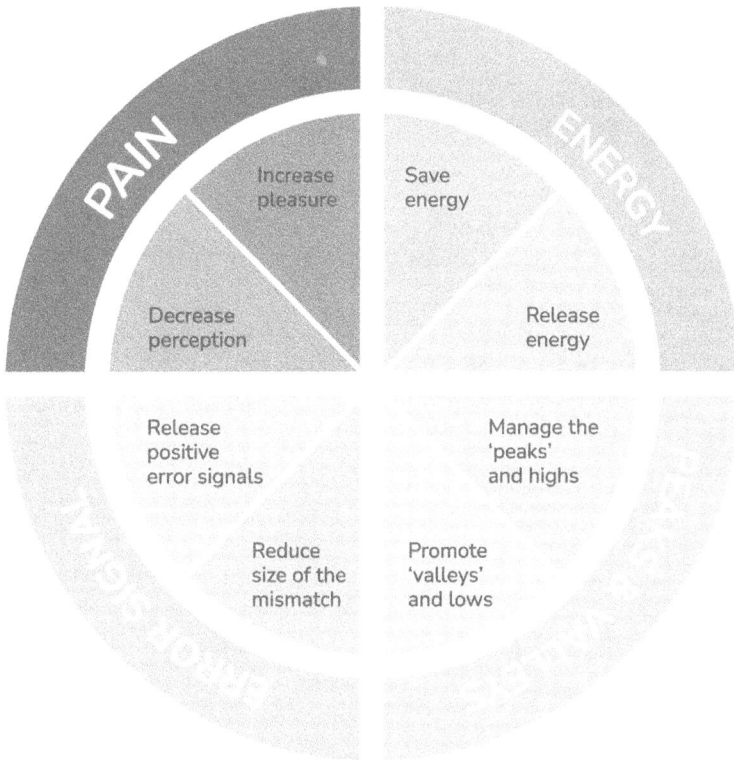

The four domains in the PEPE© model are interconnected, with direct or indirect relationships between them. They depend on each other to some extent.

These relationships will be explained in greater detail later in the book, but for now we will demonstrate the direct and indirect relationships between the domains (see Figure 3.3). Two-headed arrows denote a bi-directional relationship; the single-headed arrow denotes a one-way relationship.

Pain and energy

Shifting people away from a state of pain and towards rewards we can proactively provide the brain with a more sustainable energy to cope with change by the release of dopamine – a neurotransmitter that provides energy and motivation. At the same time, as we boost motivation, we are changing people's perception of discomfort (pain). This change in perception occurs because the brain interprets the consumption of energy as a potential threat to survival, leading it to perceive less of a threat overall.

FIGURE 3.3 The four domains of the PEPE© model are interconnected

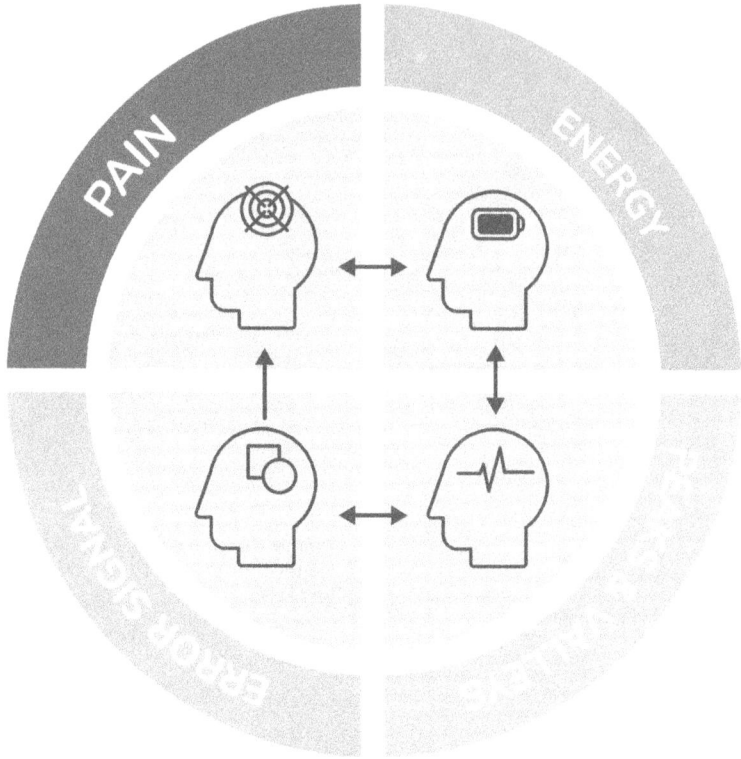

IN SUMMARY

Less pain = more reward = increase of energy.

More energy = less perception of discomfort (pain).

As we can see there is a direct relationship between pain and energy.

Energy and peaks and valleys

A direct relationship exists between the energy level individuals experience and the fluctuations in the brain's chemistry, known in the PEPE© model as 'peaks and valleys'. The more an individual operates at peak levels of work, faces challenges or experiences heightened stimulation, the greater energy they derive from their neurochemistry.

Stimulation in this context signifies a state in which your body and mind become more alert and active in response to external stimuli or internal sensations. It's akin to that sudden rush when you hear a loud noise, causing your heart rate to increase, muscles to tense and your mind to sharpen in anticipation of potential danger. Stimulation can also occur during moments of excitement or anticipation, like preparing for a rollercoaster ride or an important meeting. Your body and mind become more alert and active, preparing you to respond to the situation at hand.

Stimulation essentially serves as a natural and adaptive response from the brain, helping individuals in reacting to changing circumstances and challenges by releasing adrenaline and dopamine (both provide energy). However, excessive or prolonged stimulation can be harmful, and may lead to maladaptive responses to change, such as demotivation, stress, anxiety or other negative effects on well-being.

Therefore, it's crucial to actively promote valleys in the brain. Managing the peaks and valleys in brain activity contributes to a positive adaptation to change, including increased resilience, engagement, motivation and overall well-being.

IN SUMMARY

High level of adrenaline and dopamine (arousal) = higher energy.

Prolonged periods of peaks = reduction of energy due to bad adaptation of the brain.

Balanced levels of peaks and valleys = sustainable levels of energy.

Peaks and valleys and error

A direct relationship also exists between fluctuations in the brain's chemistry (peaks and valleys) and the error signals that the brain releases in response to conflicts between reality and expectations. The more accustomed individuals are to heightened stimulation, and the more they proactively manage the valleys to encourage positive adaptation, the more resilient they become. Consequently, when the brain does release an error signal, it will be less 'surprising' in the presence of a conflict between reality and expectations, thereby having a lesser negative impact on individuals.

When the brain releases an error signal, individuals naturally become hypervigilant or highly excited, depending on whether the error signal has positive or negative implications, increasing the level of stimulation (peak levels of the neurochemistry).

IN SUMMARY

Balanced levels of peaks and valleys = less negative impact from the error signal.

Bigger error signal = higher energy.

Error and pain

Another direct relationship exists between the error signal emitted by the brain in response to discrepancies between individuals' expectations and reality, and the discomfort (pain) perceived by the brain. The magnitude of the error signal directly correlates with the intensity of discomfort experienced by individuals.

IN SUMMARY

Bigger error signal = higher level of discomfort (pain).

The relationship between the four domains is complex, with direct relationships between some of them and indirect relationships between all of them.

04

Pain and the brain

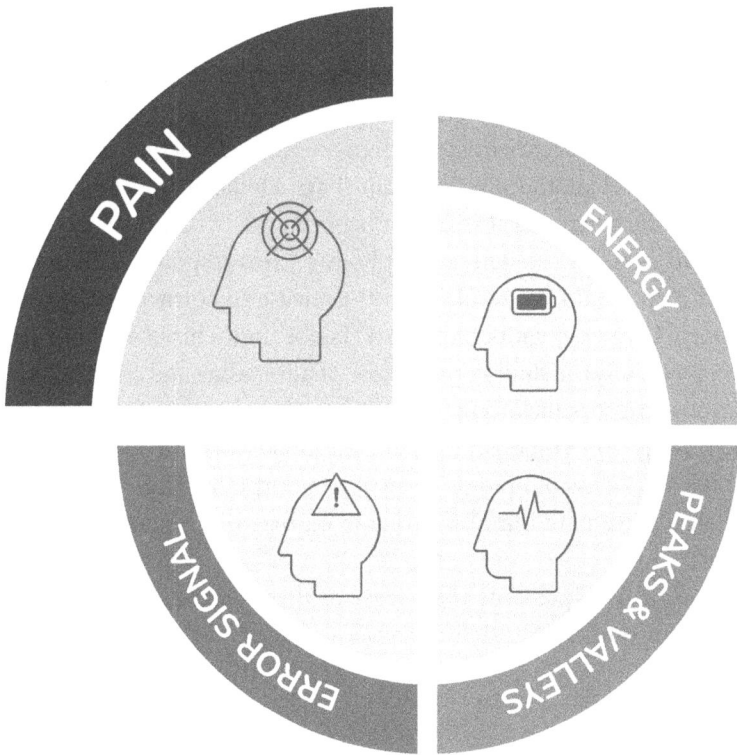

PEPE© model: Pain domain

Pain is a distressing and uncomfortable sensation encompassing sensory, emotional and social elements resulting from actual or potential damage. Pain is interpreted and processed in the brain.

The human brain boasts an exceptional sensory system, constantly detecting even the smallest of changes in the environment. Pain, in essence, serves as a sophisticated alarm system designed to detect changes significant enough to pose a potential threat to our survival. When the brain identifies such a threat, it emits an uncomfortable signal to the body, telling us we are in danger; this is what we perceive as pain.

The brain, whenever possible, resists change, as the associated signal is inherently unpleasant. Research shows that the brain does not differentiate between physical, emotional and social pain. In all these scenarios, pain can trigger a biological stress response – a release of adrenaline, noradrenaline and cortisol – prompting either confrontation with or escape from the perceived threat.

For example, neuroscientists Lieberman and Eisenberger[1] have provided evidence that social and physical pain share similar neural pathways, indicating the brain may not distinguish between the two. This evidence shows how social stressors can activate the body's stress response in the same way physical pain would do, resulting in the release of cortisol and other stress hormones. Likewise, endocrinologists Tsigos and Chrousos[2] have detailed the stress response, including the release of adrenaline and cortisol, triggered by various stressors including physical, emotional and social pain.

Interestingly, in response to pain, the hypothalamus and the pituitary gland release a class of opioids known as endorphins. These endorphins not only help relieve pain but also promote an overall sense of well-being and pleasure.

We can actively promote the release of these endorphins by engaging in the activities outlined in each dimension of the PEPE© model discussed in this book.

The hypothalamus is a small but vital structure located at the base of the brain. The hypothalamus controls and regulates essential functions, such as body temperature, sleep-wake cycle, emotions and the release of hormones from the pituitary gland to ensure the body's overall functioning and well-being.

Pain can diminish openness, creativity, high performance and overall well-being due to its disruptive effects on cognitive functioning, emotional state and physical well-being. When experiencing pain, individuals may find it difficult to focus, problem-solve or think creatively due to the heightened stress levels. Moreover, persistent pain can drain energy and motivation, hindering performance in various tasks.

When managing change, it is important to steer those impacted by the change away from pain to foster and promote high-quality conversations, trust, creativity and commitment among them. Equally vital is cultivating self-awareness regarding what behaviours tend to manifest in response to pain. Social and emotional pain can be present in many individuals without obvious self-awareness of the discomfort, yet their undesired behaviours will persist, interfering with the way we approach and accept change.

The expectations individuals have regarding the outcomes or consequences they anticipate in response to social pain within organizational settings play a crucial role in determining their experience of pain. Therefore, interventions focused on managing these expectations can effectively reduce pain.

For example, during periods of organizational change, such as restructuring or downsizing, employees may hold expectations regarding the effects on their roles, job security and relationships with colleagues. If organizational leaders fail to manage these expectations effectively, individuals may encounter uncertainty, fear and social pain, especially if they perceive the change as a threat to their sense of belonging or status within the organization. For instance, employees who feel disregarded or underappreciated during a restructuring process may experience social pain stemming from feelings of rejection or exclusion by their peers.

Demands made by change

Change will always feel uncomfortable, even if we perceive a change as positive or if the change will bring benefits. Basically, pain is the result of our internal alarm system alerting us to a shift in the status quo and the potential threat it poses due to uncertainty around the new 'state' and how 'safe' it will be for us. From the brain's perspective, there are no pre-existing connections between our neurons that can help evaluate and process the new information, which exacerbates feelings of uncertainty regarding the 'unknown' and triggers pain.

To navigate change effectively with an understanding of the brain's processes, we must first learn to manage pain. By doing so, we can reduce the discomfort and levels of perceived threat, making it easier to accept change and foster openness to the adjustment. The aim is to purposely 'trick/ hack' our brains through practical strategies that achieve the following:

1 Reduce perception of pain

2 Increase pleasure to modulate pain and increase well-being

Effectively managing pain during periods of change or transformation necessitates the incorporation of strategies that encompass both the reduction of perceived pain and the increase of pleasure. This is particularly important for those leading change and individuals responsible for guiding others away from threat, encouraging them to approach proposed solutions with an open mind. The primary responsibility of change leaders is to reduce fear and motivate individuals to view change as an opportunity rather than a threat. Ultimately, it's all about managing pain effectively.

Dimension 1: Reduce perception of pain

What do we mean?

The aim is to help ease the perception of discomfort for those individuals involved in the change, guiding them away from a state of threat and towards a more comfortable zone. This shift encourages them to view change as an opportunity rather than a threat. By moving people away from threat and into a more relaxed state, the fight-or-flight response in the brain diminishes, subsequently reducing the levels of cortisol and noradrenaline. This in turn makes individuals more open to recognizing opportunities.

Neuroscientific research has made significant progress over the last two decades, shedding light on several social factors that can significantly impact the experience of pain and discomfort. Consequently, we are now beginning to understand how to proactively influence these domains.

Fixed and growth mindset

Brain imaging technology (fMRI) shows differences between people with a growth mindset and those with a fixed mindset and how they perceive pain.

GROWTH MINDSET

Believe that talent and abilities can be developed with effort and practice.

Believe in excellence rather than success.

Focus on the effort to achieve results.

Perceive change as a challenge.

Failure is an opportunity to learn and to improve.

Result: The change situation will feel less uncomfortable (less painful). Instead, the anticipatory part of the brain reward system (dopamine) will be activated, providing motivation and excitement.

FIXED MINDSET

Believe that talents and abilities are fixed and difficult to change.

Believe in success only.

Focus on results.

Perceive change as a threat.

Failure is penalized and judged.

Result: The change situation will feel uncomfortable (painful) and fearful.

While an individual's mindset may tend to lean towards either a fixed or growth orientation, research suggests that it is not entirely static and can be influenced by various environmental factors. Conditions such as stress, threat or reward can trigger one mindset or the other at different times.

For example, under conditions of high stress or threat, individuals might unconsciously approach a challenge with a fixed mindset, becoming more rigid and resistant to change, even though under other circumstances they could adopt a growth mindset and display greater adaptability and openness to new possibilities.

Conversely, when presented with rewards or positive feedback, individuals with a fixed mindset may become more motivated to achieve, whereas those with a growth mindset may even prioritize learning and development over external validation. Therefore, it is important to recognize that an individual's mindset can be influenced by contextual factors and to create environments conducive to promoting a growth mindset, particularly in situations where learning and adaptation are essential for success.

Similarly, it is important to acknowledge that people may exhibit a fixed mindset for certain activities and a growth mindset for others. For example, a person may possess a growth mindset when dealing with technological changes but a fixed mindset when facing personal changes.

Senior leaders and line managers should strive to cultivate a culture that encourages mindset shifts and promotes processes and practices conducive to a growth mindset. This ensures that organizations are better prepared to view change as a challenge rather than a threat, especially in evolving times. For example, the focus should be on progress rather than results, embracing failure as a learning opportunity, fostering courage and risk-taking, emphasizing learning rather than natural talent, and giving opportunities to all team members and not just the 'stars'.

EXAMPLE

To encourage us to recognize the problems caused by a fixed mindset when we are involved in change, one of our colleagues runs an empathy session. The purpose of the session is to recognize when we are exhibiting a fixed mindset. She asks everyone to think of an activity that we do not enjoy, do not understand and resent doing, as this is a quick way to find where we have a fixed mindset. She then asks everyone to describe how they behave and how they feel. She asks them to work together with curiosity and to find ways to view the change more as an opportunity and less as a threat. She then reminds them that this is the approach they can take when they encounter a fixed mindset in others.

She shares her own example, which is her fixed mindset triggered by technology. She describes how frustrated she becomes when using new software. She assumes she will fail, as she knows how much she struggles to understand how things work, when other colleagues appear to find it so easy. She describes how threatened she feels, how demotivated she is and how angry she becomes.

She explains that she needs time, as she might be slower than others to understand what she has to do, and because she lacks confidence, she wants time to practise on her own. She also wants access to information so she can be as well informed as possible, training so she can learn from others and a contact person who can help her solve any issues after the training. Most importantly she reflects on small progress she has made in understanding how things with technology work, even though she is not fully there yet.

As she told us:

> This is an excellent activity for appreciating that not everyone greets change at work with delight. Not everyone thinks that change is a learning opportunity from the very beginning. They are defensive because they see it as a threat, or they are under too much stress. By empathizing, I help my Change Managers identify the support and guidance needed to encourage a more positive view of the change.

The growth mindset underpins agile principles. When we perceive change as a challenge, and failure as an opportunity to learn, we actively seek out and welcome new ideas. We are more willing to experiment and take risks because we value the experience to discover new ideas and learn new skills.

EXAMPLE

As consultants we usually get challenged on how we can balance acceptance and learning from mistakes with maintaining high quality standards, especially in industries like pharmaceuticals where errors can have serious consequences.

Here, the focus is on fostering constructive discussions about mistakes in a non-punitive manner. This creates opportunities for learning and problem-solving while also promoting accountability and responsibility. Adopting a 'learn from failure' mindset is not about actively promoting 'operational mistakes'; it is about focusing on what we can learn from them and moving individuals away from a feeling of threat. In addition, adopting a growth mindset is about creating opportunities to experiment.

A couple of months ago, we worked with an operations team within a pharmaceutical organization to help redesign the 'incident investigation report' to support a growth mindset and to avoid the 'blaming' culture. The 'incident investigation report' was originally designed to document the details surrounding the mistake, including what happened, when and where it occurred, the individuals involved, the impact or consequences of the mistake, and any corrective actions taken or recommended to prevent similar incidents in the future. It was mainly used for regulatory compliance.

The primary obstacle to fostering a growth mindset and learning from errors within this report was the significant focus placed on assigning blame to the individual responsible for the incident, rather than emphasizing the lessons to be gleaned from it. It was written in a manner that suggests punishment and judgment, even including signatures of acknowledgment of the error.

We opted to incorporate a reflective section in the report, focusing on circumstances that could have been handled differently both as a team and as an organization. This section needed to adopt a solution-based approach rather than dwelling solely on problems. It should offer solutions such as training programmes, coaching, mentoring, promoting well-being and providing access to relevant literature and resources. The aim of this new section was to encourage employees and managers to collectively reflect on their experiences, pinpoint areas for improvement and devise strategies for growth rather than resorting to performance measures.

We illustrate here three problem-based questions driven by a fixed mindset vs. three solution-based questions driven by a growth mindset:

PROBLEM BASED (LEADING TO FIXED MINDSET)

- 'Who was responsible for the incident, and what performance measures should be taken to avoid the same incident in the future?'
- 'What were the immediate failures that led to the incident, and how can we ensure accountability for these shortcomings?'
- 'How can we tighten control and supervision to prevent similar errors in the future and ensure compliance with established protocols?'

SOLUTION BASED (LEADING TO GROWTH)

- 'What systemic factors or organizational processes contributed to the incident, and how can we address them to prevent similar occurrences in the future?'
- 'In what ways can we improve communication and collaboration among team members to enhance problem-solving and decision-making processes?'

- 'How can we leverage this incident as a learning opportunity to develop new training programmes, coaching initiatives or access to resources that promote continuous improvement and growth within the organization?'

Psychological safety

Psychological safety refers to the belief that people can freely express themselves without fear of negative consequences or judgement for their words, comments or actions. It describes a shared belief within an individual or a group that the environment encourages interpersonal risk-taking. It's the confidence that the team will not shame, reject or penalize someone for speaking up, sharing ideas or making mistakes.

Psychological safety is essential for risk-taking, adopting a growth mindset and facilitating the implementation and acceptance of change. Documented processes should be established to ensure psychological safety as an integral part of the programme and systematically integrated.

To foster psychological safety for both individuals and teams, it's important to:

- feel comfortable speaking up and expressing opinions without fear of retribution or ridicule;
- trust that mistakes and failures are viewed as opportunities for growth and learning rather than grounds for blame or punishment;
- believe that your contributions are valued and that your skills and knowledge are respected by peers and managers;
- feel supported and empowered to take risks, innovate and experiment without fear of negative consequences;
- be free to express opinions or concerns, even if they differ from those of others, without fear of retaliation or exclusion from the group;
- sense that everyone in the group is collaboratively working towards a common goal, and that everyone's contributions are valued, regardless of rank or status within the organization.

Psychological safety decreases the perception of discomfort and pain, subsequently reducing resistance to change.

Senior managers and line managers play a pivotal role to ensure psychological safety measures are in place to encourage volunteers who are willing to initiate change and experiment with new ways of working within the organization. This helps reduce concerns about potential judgement by colleagues.

EXAMPLE

One of our friends must build the respect and confidence of new teams regularly, as she manages lots of projects and changes within her organization. From the earliest planning meetings, she talks about what might go wrong and encourages everyone to contribute ideas about:

- how to prevent these things from happening
- what actions to take if they do happen – to put things right and get things back on track

Her team value this approach because she is creating a safe space to speak up if things go wrong. She has acknowledged from the start that not everything will work and has asked people to work out how to fix problems, because problems are expected.

This recognition of imperfection makes it easier for people to speak up because they do not fear being criticized for a mistake. If mistakes happen, they are encouraged to tell everyone as soon as possible so that the team can move into 'recovery mode' and help each other put things right.

The growth mindset and psychological safety support other dimensions of the PEPE© model.

TABLE 4.1

Dimension	Activity	Contribution
Managing peaks	Challenge the status quo	We feel comfortable speaking up and offering a different perspective.
Managing peaks	Promote curiosity	We feel encouraged to ask questions and consider different options without the fear of being criticized.
Releasing energy	Implement a culture of risk-taking	If we take a risk and our idea does not work, we do not fear criticism or being humiliated.

Being valued and respected

Self-esteem and the feeling of being an important member of the team also reduces the feeling of pain and threat. On the other hand, if we perceive we are in front of members of the team who do not respect or value us and make us feel undermined, the perception of pain will increase. As a result, we become more closed-minded, blunt-speaking and resistant to new opportunities.

Our brain interprets being valued and respected as an increase in status. From an evolutionary perspective, higher status within a 'tribe' meant greater access to resources, enhancing opportunities for survival and reproduction. In both animal and human research, the significance of status, not just in hierarchical terms but in terms of being valued, has been demonstrated extensively.

Change can pose a threat to our status, potentially causing us to lose our expertise, skills, abilities or even our position or level of influence among others. It is important to empower people going through change and create opportunities for everyone affected by the change to feel respected from the outset of the process.

Here are some examples of how feeling valued and respected, taking into account the brain's perspective, can be achieved:

- **Being actively listened to.** When someone genuinely listens to you, it conveys the importance and value of your point. This can evoke a positive sense of being respected and boost self-confidence, which in turn reduces the perception of pain.

- **Being recognized.** Acknowledging someone's contributions and efforts can activate the brain's dopamine reward system, fostering feelings of achievement and satisfaction, thus reducing the perception of pain.

- **Being trusted.** When someone entrusts you with a task or responsibility, it instils a sense of confidence and competence. Particularly during times of change, where new skills and knowledge are required, people's self-confidence can diminish. Trust in your abilities can reduce your perception of pain.

- **Being challenged.** When given positive and manageable challenging tasks or opportunities, the brain interprets it as a boost in status, thereby reducing the perception of pain.

FIGURE 4.1 Team charter

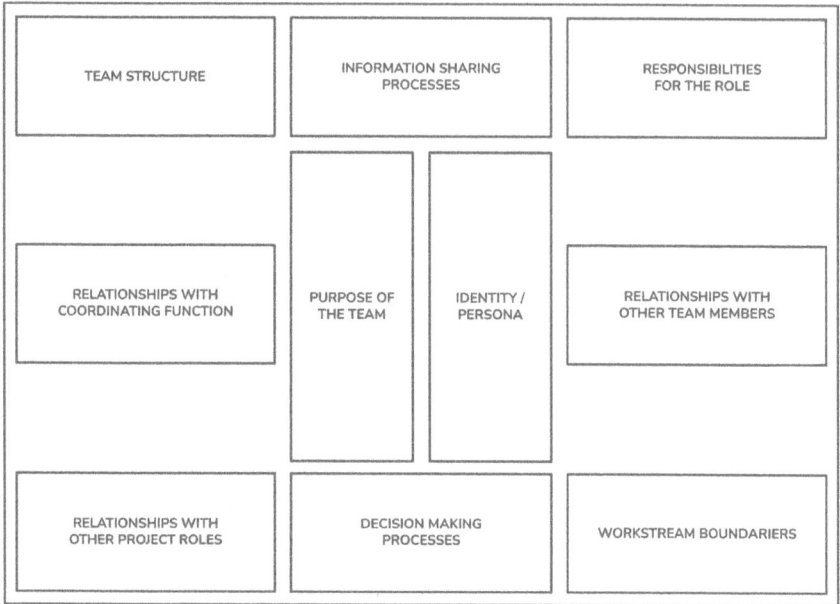

- **Being offered opportunities for growth.** Providing individuals with learning and growth prospects activates the brain's reward system, instilling a sense of progress and shifting them away from the perception of pain.
- **Actively seeking input and contribution.** Offering people opportunities for contribution to decision-making processes automatically sends signals of self-esteem to the brain. This approach helps individuals feel valued rather than undermined by new ways of working and a lack of knowledge and skills, ultimately reducing the perception of pain.

Concentrating on continuous learning can reduce the reliance on being valued solely for your existing skills and make acceptance of change more accessible. Shifting our mindset towards valuing and respecting others for their willingness to take risks, put in effort and learn is paramount.

Consider using a team charter as the mechanism to get everyone on the team talking about their contribution to the team objectives and how they want to be treated (see Figure 4.1).

Purpose of the team – why does the team exist? Why does the work need to be done by a group of people instead of someone working individually? Establish the value of the collective effort and be clear about the objectives and expected outcomes from this teamwork.

Workstream boundaries – define what is included and what work is specifically excluded based on the purpose of the team.

Identity/persona – everyone should be encouraged to set out their values and what this work means to them. Use a 'corporate identity' template to help team members define the value they bring to the team.

Corporate identity template – description of the personal characteristics for success:

- What is my purpose – why does my role exist?
- What are my values?
- What are my priorities?
- Who do I serve?
- What is the value that my role delivers for the organization?
- What do I want to achieve from my role?
- What does success look like for me in my role?
- What am I most proud of?
  o My skills
  o My experience
  o My professionalism – the quality of my work
  o My network
  o My reputation
  o My position of hierarchical authority

Responsibilities for the role – each team member should identify what they are responsible for, and the assumptions they are making for what other team members will contribute based on the purpose of the team and the workstream boundaries. Encourage team members to volunteer for work for which they have a natural talent so that, as much as possible, the team are working on things that bring them pleasure. Evaluate your responsibilities using these factors to decide who should be responsible for what:

- Speed
- Accuracy
- Ease

FIGURE 4.2

Assigning responsibilities

Accept responsibility for this work
only if others are not available to do it

Volunteer for this work

High effort	Low effort
Low speed	High speed
Likely errors/mistakes	Few errors/mistakes
Low enjoyment	High enjoyment

- Enjoyment
- Experience
- Skills and abilities

Team structure – enables team members to understand how the work is distributed across the team and how their contribution supports the work of their colleagues.

Relationships with coordinating function – this establishes the amount of power the team has for its own work, defining what it can self-direct versus the instructions it will be given by whatever organizing function exists.

Relationship with other project roles – a change involves a community of different teams, so it is important to establish the relationships that the team needs to build.

Information-sharing processes – what methods, frequency and content of information will be shared, balancing the need to know what others are doing, problems to solve and achievements to celebrate with the time needed for individual progress.

Decision-making processes – define what decisions individuals can take without referring to other members of the team and what decisions the team can take without referring to other teams or functions within the organization.

Relationships with other team members – outline the social activities that will help to build team spirit and the expectations for acceptable behaviour within the team.

A team charter also supports other dimensions within the PEPE© model (Table 4.2).

TABLE 4.2

Dimension	Activity	Contribution
Decrease pain	Control and autonomy	It is easier to take decisions and feel a sense of control over your work if you are clear about your responsibilities and how these align to the work of your colleagues in the team.
Increase pleasure	Increase sense of belonging	Having a shared purpose increases the feeling that you are part of something bigger than just your own contribution.
Increase pleasure	Common goals and objectives	The team charter encourages everyone to contribute their understanding of the purpose of the team, creating collective responsibility for these goals.
Release positive prediction signals	Manage expectations from the beginning and at every stage	Being clear about the purpose of the team, the processes for taking decisions and sharing information minimizes confusion and helps to align what we expect to happen with what actually happens.
Energy saving	Add clarity – focus on quality conversations	The act of creating the team charter is a series of quality conversations where the purpose and desired outcome of the discussion are clear from the start.

Control and autonomy

Research conducted over the past 50 years consistently highlights the profound impact of our perceived control over our environment on the level of discomfort and stress that we experience.[3] Control, in this context, refers to the extent to which we believe we can influence our surroundings and the events that affect us. When we lack control, we can feel powerless and vulnerable, leading to discomfort (pain) and resistance to change.

Autonomy, on the other hand, refers to an individual's ability to make choices about their work. In the context of change, autonomy means allowing individuals to determine their level of involvement in the change process and how they adapt to the change. Ownership signifies taking responsibility for these choices, specifically for actively participating and successfully adopting the change.

During periods of change, increasing the autonomy and fostering owner-ship of those impacted can enhance their sense of control. Ownership can be promoted by taking responsibility for these choices, specifically for actively participating and successfully adopting the change.

Autonomy empowers individuals to decide how they will engage with the change, triggering a sense of wanting and liking for the activities required to facilitate the change. When individuals choose to act themselves, they natu-rally become more invested and committed to seeing it through. Effectively, we can use autonomy to reduce the pain associated with change. People need to convince themselves that their decisions are the right ones and then exert effort to make these decisions a self-fulfilling prophecy.

Moreover, autonomy extends beyond merely deciding what change-related activities to become involved in. We also need to create an environment that supports individual decision-making regarding the change process as a whole and the degree of authority transferred to others.

To increase autonomy for those undergoing change, we should:

- encourage everyone to select the tasks and activities they wish to engage in;
- involve those responsible for the work in determining quality criteria and the process for reviewing or testing it;
- allow individuals to form their own working groups and decide who they will collaborate with;
- enable individuals to decide on the aspects of their working environment that best support their needs, including when and where they work.

Involving those delivering the tangible change and those who are impacted by the change in decision-making, providing them with a voice, cultivates a stronger sense of ownership and investment in the change. For more explanation of tangible and behavioural change, please refer to Chapter 11, 'Sponsoring Change', specifically the section on understanding the spon-sor role.

By offering them choices and involving them in the co-creation of how the change will be implemented, they gain a greater sense of control and agency. This involves granting them the freedom to determine how they will transition to the new state, engaging them from the outset and at every stage of the process. By doing so, those affected will have a greater sense of control over the change, leading to a reduction in their perception of discomfort (pain).

An influential study in 2006, led by Carlsson and colleagues,[4] validated that perception of pain increases with a lack of control and unpredictability, and decreases when individuals are in command of the situation.

It can be embarrassing if we act on incorrect assumptions about the level of control we have. By deciding on action that others expect to be consulted on we can appear arrogant and 'not a team player'. If we constantly refer decisions to others because we assume we do not have the power to decide for ourselves, we can appear insecure or indecisive and lose the respect of our colleagues.

To avoid these mistakes, hold a 'contracting conversation' within the team. Discuss and agree the level of empowerment each team member has for different decisions, creating an informal 'service contract'.

This is not easy, because the decisions involved in change involve reacting to the emotions of others. It is not as simple as setting out how much money a team member can spend before having to ask permission from the rest of the team. Change-related decisions are hard to predict because we don't know the emotions triggered by change and the impact these will have.

Instead of trying to decide on a rule for every situation in advance, discuss examples of what might happen and identify some potential solutions. These situations can then act as a guide for things that might happen.

CONTRACTING CONVERSATION THREE-STEP STRUCTURE:

Decisions that the team must make together – these are for significant events. For example, when the impact of the situation affects others outside the team, or requires more money, time or other resources to fix.

FIGURE 4.3 Boundaries of authority

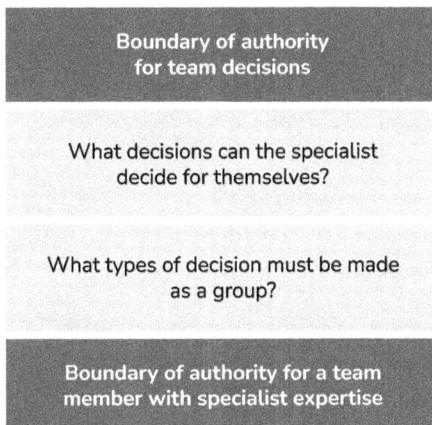

Boundary of authority
for team decisions

What decisions can the specialist
decide for themselves?

What types of decision must be made
as a group?

Boundary of authority for a team
member with specialist expertise

FIGURE 4.4 Authority for respected specialist and authority level for greater team involvement

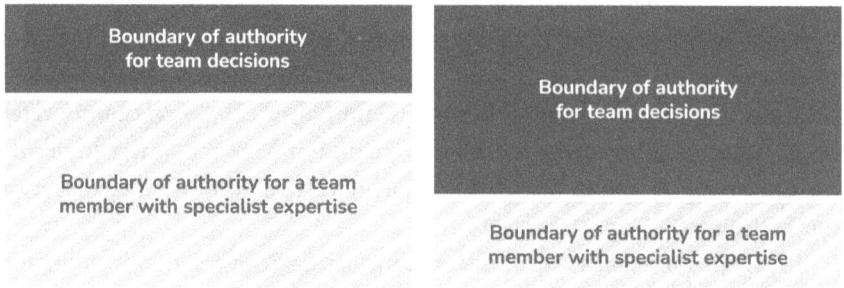

Boundary of authority for team decisions

Boundary of authority for team decisions

Boundary of authority for a team member with specialist expertise

Boundary of authority for a team member with specialist expertise

Decisions that a team member can make for themselves – they have this authority because of their expertise, experience and specialist knowledge which makes them the best person to take the decision, where no further gain is made by debating it with other team members.

Grey area – eliminate this by establishing clear boundaries of authority between the individual and the team.

EXAMPLE

Our colleague handles lots of customer queries every day. To be able to provide answers and resolve issues as quickly as possible, she needs lots of decision-making power, because asking others for a collective decision creates delays that make customers unhappy. Our colleague uses her experience to identify the most common customer issues that take up most of her time, and these remain within her power to solve. There are situations where she needs other teams to fix things, or she needs to make amendments to data or needs new features on a system and these are the decisions that she escalates to the team to decide collectively.

To demonstrate that you value the contribution of your colleagues and respect what they have to say, consider following these ground rules, which work for one-to-one meetings and group sessions:

1 Maximize the opportunity for their contribution by letting them know the agenda ahead of time, so they can form their opinions and have moments of insight.

2   Remind them that they can express any view, and that their contribution doesn't always have to be positive. Asking questions and challenging what is being said is as valuable as endorsing or adding to existing ideas.

3   In a group session, agree the order in which people will speak or decide how someone who wants to contribute will be called upon to speak.

4   Do not interrupt; let others finish what they wanted to say before adding your views.

5   Give people your full attention; do not try to answer emails or look things up on your phone when they are speaking.

6   Use encouraging body language including smiling and nodding to demonstrate you are interested in what the other person has to say.

7   Ask open questions and have some already prepared to help generate ideas. For example:

   - Using our current ways of working as the basis of your ideas, what would you change?
   - Have you seen great examples of this type of work elsewhere?
   - What do you think the advantages are of improving this area of the business?
   - Who do you think will be most or least affected by the work?
   - If you needed to explain this simply, how would you describe it to a child?
   - To explain your idea without terminology or jargon, how would you explain it to someone working 100 years ago?

EXAMPLE

We work with the CEO of a well-known company who encourages everyone to share their ideas, whatever their role or level of seniority. He often starts a session by reminding them that as the chief executive, he has many ideas about how to run the company, but he has ideas, not necessarily the right ideas, and he is really looking forward to hearing what everyone else has to say.

When he listens, he smiles and nods encouragement, and he always thanks people when they have finished speaking. He demonstrates that he has been listening to what they said by always asking a follow-up question.

It is easy to see how excited people are to have shared their ideas and been listened to, and these sessions end with high energy and lots of excited chatter.

TABLE 4.3

Dimension	Activity	Contribution
Decrease pain	Certainty and assurance	Knowing what you are responsible for, and what you can take decisions about creates the feeling of certainty, because you know what is expected of you.
Releasing energy	Implement a culture of bravery and risk-taking	By knowing the boundaries of your authority, you feel more willing to take risks within those boundaries.

A contracting conversation can have a big impact on providing control and autonomy but also positively impact other dimensions within the PEPE© model (see Table 4.3).

Certainty and assurance

Neuroscience has demonstrated a correlation between the intensity of pain, uncertainty and the number of new connections that neurons must forge to solve a problem. Simply put, when uncertainty is high, the brain must establish numerous new connections among neurons, the perception of pain is heightened, and vice versa.[5] When confronted with uncertainty or new challenges, the brain's task is to generate these new connections to process and assimilate new information effectively.

The brain forms new connections in response to uncertainty because it is continually adapting to novel situations and seeking solutions to problems. This ongoing adaptation necessitates the establishment of new associations and connections between different regions of the brain to form a coherent understanding of unfolding events.

Assurance plays a pivotal role in reducing the perception of pain, particularly during times of significant uncertainty, as it uses pre-existing strong connections to evaluate the unknown.

The aim of assurance is to provide information, or the contextual framework of information, that empowers decision-makers to make more informed choices. According to the Cambridge Dictionary, assurance is defined as the promise to cause someone to feel certain by removing doubt (not necessarily 'uncertainty' itself). Assurance significantly influences someone's state of mind by instilling confidence when facing threats or risky situations, ultimately reducing the perception of pain and facilitating change.

Those leading change initiatives should ensure the implementation of robust operational, strategic and behavioural assurance systems during periods of change and transformation. These assurance systems encompass facets such as the day-to-day management of risk, transparent communication, the robustness of a broader control framework and, most importantly, the establishment of psychological safety for all individuals involved in the change.

Psychological safety, as discussed earlier, serves as a prime example of assurance, as it dispels doubts about how individuals will be treated and creates an environment of trust and confidence.

Examples of uncertainty during change include:

- What is going to happen?
- When will we need to be involved?
- What do we have to do?
- How will we know when we have been successful?
- What do we do if something goes wrong?

We can group these uncertainties into three areas:

1 Actions we need to take when circumstances match our expectations.
2 Actions we need to take when there are unexpected, unplanned events.
3 Clear definition of what must be achieved.

ACTIONS WE NEED TO TAKE

The actions we need to take when circumstances match our expectations can be set out in a plan, defining what needs to be done, by whom and when – refer to the Change Plan for an example of this.

The actions we need to take when there are unexpected, unplanned events cannot be planned in detail, but a robust risk management process can establish rules for when to act and what action to take.

Risks are possible situations that might happen at some point in the future. They can be good things, where the change creates new opportunities or bad things, where what we wanted to happen fails and we need to fix the problem.

To increase certainty, we can collectively share our experiences of what has happened to us in the past on similar change initiatives. This defines these potential situations, making them feel known. We can then assess them, identifying how likely we think they are to happen this time.

FIGURE 4.5 Assessing probability

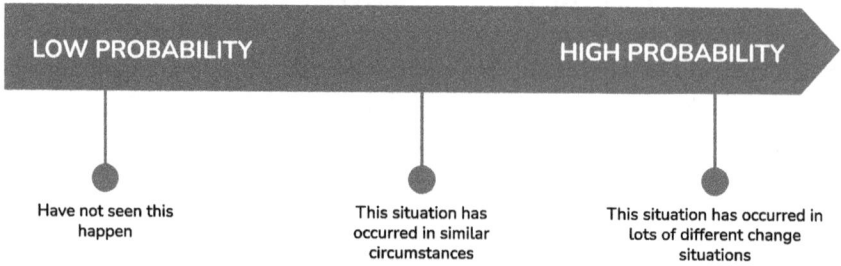

FIGURE 4.6 Assessing impact

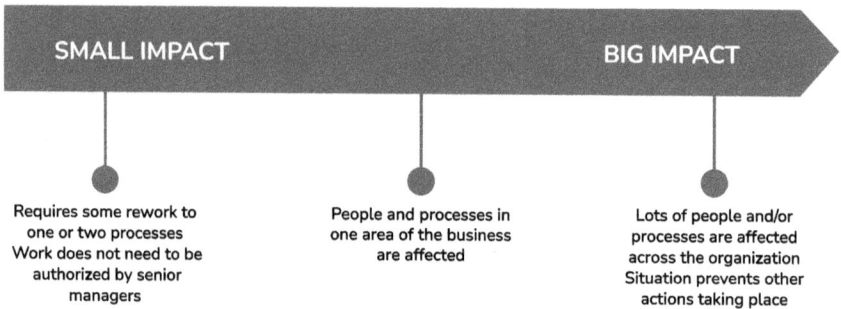

We can agree some criteria for sizing this probability. For example, a high probability would be assigned for situations that nearly everyone described happening on previous changes. Low probability are ideas people had that they have not experienced but could happen.

For each situation, ask everyone to identify the likely impact and who they think will be affected. Again, the scale of the impact can be sized. If a lot of people are affected, or the impact would stop important things happening or require lots of rework then this is a big impact. If the situation occurred but it did not make much difference to the planned activities, then the impact is small.

CLEAR DEFINITION OF WHAT MUST BE ACHIEVED
They can be minimum operating standards, definitions of capability or functionality that must exist once the change has been completed.

Step 1 Describe in general terms what the purpose of the team is, using action words like create, deliver, produce etc.

Step 2   Agree what is in and out of scope as that clarifies what is included in the objective and what can be ignored. Define the scope of your objective or goal using a simple structure. For example:

- Inputs needed to work in the new way
- Features/functionality of the new ways of working
- Outputs produced from working in the new way

Step 3   For what is in scope, describe what success and failure will look like so everyone is clear what they are aiming to achieve. Knowing in advance what failure looks like enables everyone to be clear about what they want to avoid.

Step 4   For each description of success, identify the minimum and maximum likely levels of success.

FIGURE 4.7 Defining what needs to be achieved – in and out of scope

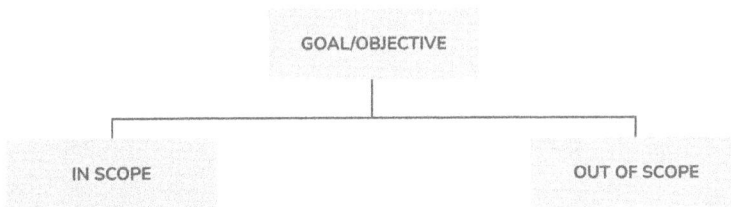

FIGURE 4.8 Defining what needs to be achieved – inputs, outputs and features and functionality

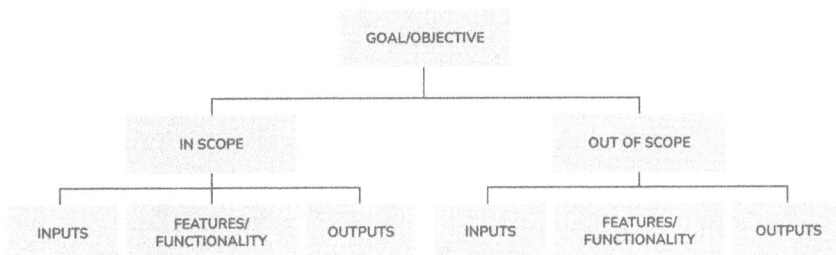

FIGURE 4.9 Defining what needs to be achieved – minimum and maximum measures of success

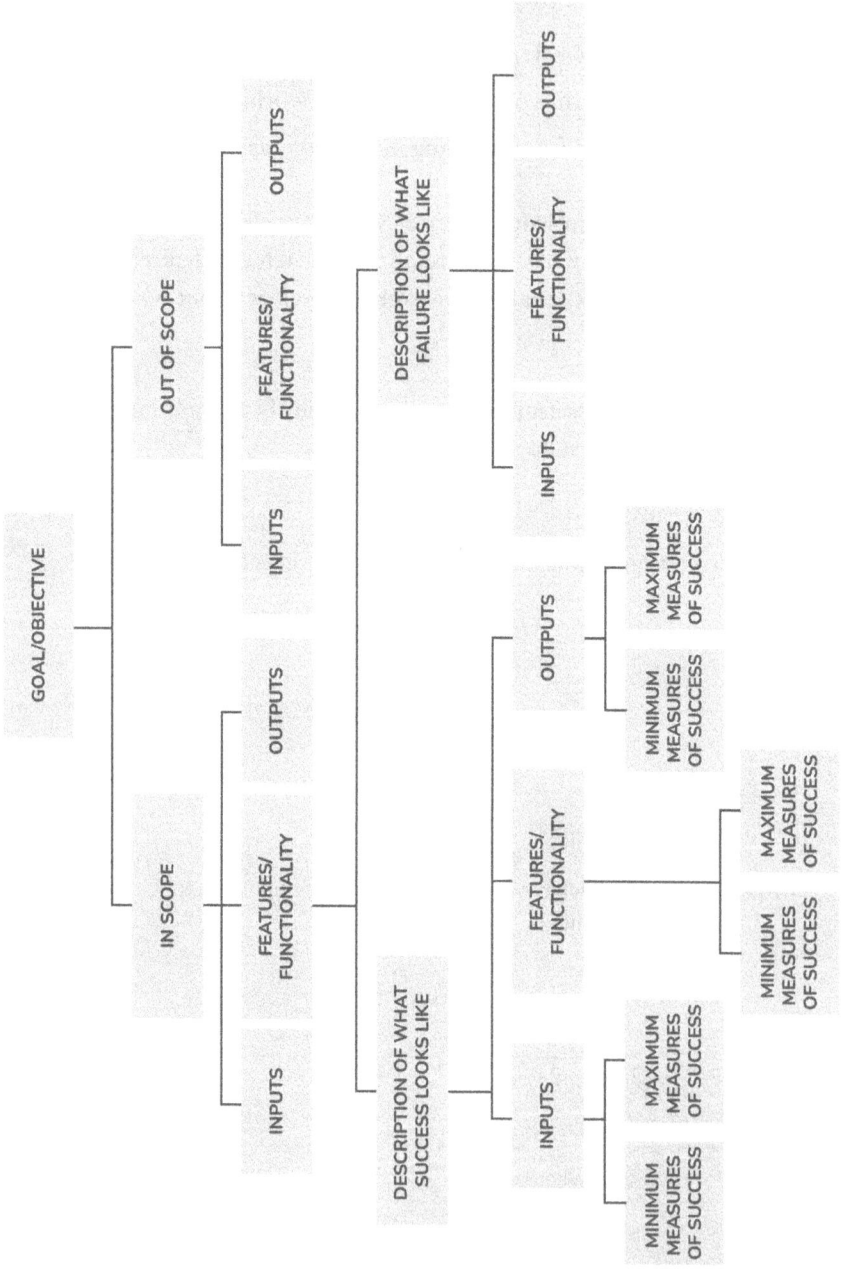

EXAMPLE

We are working with a team that wants to improve its approach to hybrid working. They are a dispersed team working in locations around the world so rarely get the chance to work face-to-face. They have decided their goal is clarity about who is responsible for what work, what progress is being made and what problems are holding them back. They have decided that they want transparency and what this means is for all their work to be recorded in one place that they can all view.

Using a description of what is in and out of scope, they have agreed that what is included in this objective is all team-related work, but they are excluding any work that they undertake as part of their personal development goals.

Inputs include project scope, stakeholder analysis and project plans. Setting out the required levels of success for these inputs helps everyone to know 'what good looks like' and to think ahead about the level of detail needed to be useful.

Features and functionality for this team means their level of knowledge about who is doing what, what the problems are, what successes they have achieved and lessons learned for future work.

Outputs are the number of completed projects and agreements on new ways of working in the future that apply the lessons learned from each of their initiatives.

These discussions on inputs, features and outputs have helped the team collectively understand their work at a deeper level than before. They have shared examples of the type of initiatives they are working on, how they individually track their progress, the issues that cause them the most problems and what types of work take the longest time.

The structured approach enabled everyone to talk about the complete cycle of their work – from inputs to outputs – which identified success criteria at every step.

Being clear about the actions we need to take and what we need to achieve, on top of providing more certainty and reassurance, also supports other dimensions within the PEPE© model (Table 4.4).

TABLE 4.4

Dimension	Activity	Contribution
Energy saving	Focus on quality conversations	By knowing what actions to take you can clearly explain these to others.
Managing peaks	Challenge the status quo	It is easier to challenge if you know what you need to achieve as a result of your challenge.
Promoting valleys	Balance anticipation and pleasure	We can promote the thrill of anticipation by being clear about what it is we need to achieve and therefore it is much easier to identify opportunities for celebration and pleasure.
Release positive signals	Manage expectations from the beginning and at every stage	By creating a clear definition of where we want to go and what needs to be achieved, we are managing expectations of people involved in the change from the very beginning.

Dimension 2: Increase pleasure during change

What do we mean?

One of the advantages of integrating neuroscience into change management is the ability to discover practical methods and procedures for naturally providing the brain with the appropriate neurochemistry. These approaches can effectively facilitate the process of change.

The intention of this dimension – increasing pleasure – is to help relieve the pain in those impacted by the change by increasing the sense of well-being and pleasure instead, what we call 'hacking' the pleasure centre of the brain.

Pain and pleasure are often managed within overlapping neural circuits in the brain. Research in neuroscience suggests that both experiences involve the activation of similar brain regions, including areas associated with reward, motivation and emotion. This shared neural circuitry allows for complex interactions between pain and pleasure perception, influencing how individuals respond to various stimuli and experiences. By enhancing the sense of well-being and pleasure through targeted interventions, such as 'hacking' the pleasure centre of the brain, it is possible to adjust the neural processing of pain and promote a more positive emotional state.

Embracing change becomes significantly easier when we have the support of favourable brain chemistry, rather than working in opposition to it. Within this framework, two key neurotransmitters assume a critical role in shaping our perception of pleasure.

Endorphins are neurotransmitters produced by the central nervous system (part of a group of neurotransmitters called opioids). They act as natural painkillers and are often referred to as 'feel-good' chemicals. The primary role of endorphins is to reduce pain and promote feelings of well-being and euphoria. They create a sense of pleasure and happiness.

Oxytocin is a hormone that acts as a neurotransmitter, also produced in the hypothalamus and released by the posterior pituitary gland, that plays a big role in modulating fear, pain and anxiety. Several research studies have also demonstrated that oxytocin helps to reduce stress and can increase the perception of pleasure and well-being.

Endorphins are known to play a crucial role in the brain's reward system, particularly during the consummatory or 'liking' phase of reward processing, where they are released 'in the moment' of pleasure, celebration or joy.[6]

On the other hand, oxytocin serves as a significant influencer in bonding, trust-building and engagement. Recent research indicates that oxytocin can foster positive attitudes towards those individuals categorized as 'in-group' members by the brain, while potentially leading to conflicts in the presence of individuals classified as 'out-group' members.

Both endorphins and oxytocin are key players in managing the experience of pain and pleasure during periods of change and transformation. The aim here is to implement practical strategies and tactics that naturally stimulate the release of these neurochemicals.

Celebrate often and bring laughter

A recent study using positron emission tomography (PET) imaging revealed that social laughter significantly increased endorphin release in regions of the brain like the thalamus, caudate nucleus and anterior insula.[7] Additionally, research from Oxford University emphasizes that endorphins produce pleasurable and calming effects, signalling safety and togetherness to the brain.

Laughter and celebration have the power to elevate our pain threshold through the release of endorphins.[8] Incorporating regular and systematic practices of celebrating small achievements can enhance the overall experience of pleasure and minimize discomfort during times of change. It encourages us to reflect on how frequently we intentionally celebrate and embrace laughter throughout the various phases of change.

Remaining in the 'liking' and 'in-the-moment pleasure' phases for longer periods before moving forward continuing in pursuit of the next achievement can significantly influence our acceptance of change. This approach takes advantage of endorphin release, which contributes to increased pleasure and reduces resistance to change.

For example, implementing small, frequent iterations of change, as suggested by the agile methodology, provides excellent opportunities for celebration after each iteration is successfully completed.

Activities that we can incorporate in our Change Plan to increase the frequency and meaningfulness of our celebrations include:

- Congratulations – having someone who is an expert in the type of achievement acknowledging the effort and the results, as their expertise is valued and will make those being congratulated feel special.

- Development opportunities – training courses, attendance at conferences, opportunities to present ideas to senior leaders, promotions, new responsibilities.

- Wellness opportunities – time for recovery via time off or mindfulness activities. Studies have shown that mindfulness meditation can stimulate the production of endorphins in the brain, contributing to feelings of well-being and pain relief. Additionally, mindfulness practices can help regulate emotions and improve mood, which may further enhance the release of endorphins.

As well as planning for celebrations during our change, we can help ourselves and our colleagues to create a personal habit of celebration. This helps to overcome toxic positivity, which is the pressure to only display positive emotions, suppressing any negative emotions, feelings, reactions or experiences, which can result from too many 'centrally managed celebrations'.

Likewise, it's crucial to tailor these celebrations to suit social preferences of individuals, including introversion and extroversion as well as neurodiversity (refer to PEPE© in action for neurodiversity). Some people may prefer private acknowledgement over public celebrations, which can be overwhelming for them; in this case instead of large gatherings, consider smaller, more intimate settings for celebrating achievements. A one-on-one congratulatory meeting or a small team gathering can be less intimidating and more meaningful for introvertive and neurodiverse individuals.

EXAMPLE

There are lots of aspects of our work that we really enjoy, but don't give ourselves a chance to savour. We're too busy thinking about all the other things we need to do. If we want to get more pleasure from our day, we should stay in the moment. We should clear away any distractions.

When we do this, we realize that what we do is interesting, often working on new things, the excitement of learning new things and working with talented people.

When we get a chance to do some interesting work, we're going to savour it. We're not going to be distracted. We're going to enjoy the moment.

Including celebrations in our Change Plan also supports other dimensions within the PEPE© model.

TABLE 4.5

Dimension	Activity	Contribution
Decrease pain	Being valued and respected	When our work is celebrated and acknowledged, we feel that our contribution is helpful, and we are a valuable asset to the team.
Managing peaks	Focus on small cycles of change	We can use our Change Plan to identify when we are expecting achievements to occur so we can prepare the celebrations.

(continued)

TABLE 4.5 (Continued)

Dimension	Activity	Contribution
Promote valleys	Balance anticipation and pleasure	By ensuring time is given to celebrating achievements, we are able to remain in the enjoyable moment long enough to promote the release of endorphins and oxytocin.
		We know that with the volume of items we have to discuss at team meetings, it is tempting to hear about an achievement and then after a brief acknowledgement of the good news, move on to the next item. We need behaviours and routines that help us stay at the point of congratulation long enough to create the positive feelings, or we waste the brain-related benefits of the achievement.

Informal meetings and gatherings

Extensive research has established that positive social interactions can stimulate the release of oxytocin, a hormone closely linked to social bonding and attachment experiences.[9] Additionally, these positive interactions have been associated with health-promoting effects.

Informal meetings and social gatherings have the remarkable ability to reduce the perception of hierarchies and status differences, bringing everyone to a common level and fostering a sense of belonging to the same 'in-group'. This in turn triggers the release of oxytocin as a natural response to being part of this inclusive 'in-group'.

During times of change and transformation, it becomes increasingly essential to encourage social gatherings among the teams delivering the change and those who will have to work differently as a result of the change. By facilitating regular, informal meetings we will actively promote the release of oxytocin, which enhances the pleasure system. This positively influences levels of discomfort, stress and overall well-being throughout the programme, reducing resistance to change.

Creating opportunities for people to meet informally, especially in a social setting, reduces the limitations of hierarchy (I cannot speak to that person as they are more senior than I am) because we can connect on a more human level by discussing aspects of our lives.

If we are to find the time for informal gatherings, we must value them and recognize their positive impact. It is hard to identify specific benefits from spending five minutes talking to a colleague about their weekend, so when we are busy, we ignore this socializing. The problem is, we are always busy and there is always a reason to get on with specific tasks and leave the informal engagement for another day.

To help my clients plan for informality (if that isn't too confusing!) I help them recognize that there are two types of productivity, each of which is valuable:

- Task productivity – this is your ability to get your work finished.
- Social productivity – this is the creation of the culture of your team by spending time together, understanding each other's motivations and priorities.

Too often we get caught up in task productivity, forgetting that effective working requires social productivity as well. After all, if you don't have relationships with your colleagues, think how much time is lost because they cannot help you solve problems or give you a different perspective or inspire new ideas.

To avoid the temptation of only focusing on task productivity, especially when we are working under tight deadlines and in a highly pressurized environment, we must make it a habit rather than waiting for the opportunity to arise. Otherwise, when we most need the impact of the endorphins arising from informal meetings, we are not going to get them.

Meeting informally in a social setting supports other dimensions of the PEPE© model (Table 4.6).

TABLE 4.6

Dimension	Activity	Contribution
Release energy	Promote a culture of bravery and risk-taking	For some, engaging socially with their colleagues is a step outside of their comfort zone and takes bravery.
Release energy	Provide opportunities for people to come up with their own insights	An insight is when we have a moment of discovery, when we find an answer or decide on a solution. We can help achieve these by including an informal follow-up session after a brain-storming meeting, so people can share their thoughts and trigger 'aha' moments.
Managing peaks	Promote curiosity	We can increase our curiosity by practising conversation and asking open questions, and informal gatherings give us a chance to do this.

EXAMPLE

In our co-working space, there is a breakfast organized on the first Monday of every month. We all know that it happens at this time, and if we are free, we attend. There is no agenda, just a chance to help ourselves to the free food and chat with anyone that we meet.

This is a very informal gathering and even though we are socially confident, it can sometimes feel a bit overwhelming to start a conversation with people we haven't met before. To overcome this, the managers of the co-working space organize a game so we can recognize things we have in common without having to introduce ourselves first. We are asked to stand up and wave if it is our birthday this month, or if we have started a new job or moved house or got a new pet, new car, new housemate or started learning a new sport or hobby. This creates lots of noise and energy in the room and gives us something to say to our neighbours without having to think of the topic for ourselves.

The value of these sessions is not something that immediately impacts our rate of work, but we know it does help with our well-being. From the session this morning, we gained a sense of calm because we could see that others were nervous returning at the start of a new year, and it wasn't just us.

We met a couple of new people so when we go to the kitchen to get a cup of tea, we have more people to smile and say hello to, which creates a feeling of connection and positivity and makes us more willing to come to the office because we know we are amongst friends.

As a team, you can define criteria that will encourage you to socialize, as you all agree when informal engagement is appropriate.

Altruistic giving and volunteering

Recent advancements in social neuroscience have unveiled that altruism is linked to a distinct pattern of brain activity, particularly activating the brain's pleasure centre. For example, a meta-analysis published in 2017 by Marsh et al.[10] analysed data from multiple studies investigating brain activity in individuals engaged in altruistic behaviour. The analysis found consistent activation of reward-related brain regions, including the ventral striatum and orbitofrontal cortex, during altruistic actions. The activation of the orbitofrontal cortex is associated with the hedonic response to pleasurable experiences, including the liking of food, social interactions and other pleasurable activities.

In this context, altruism refers to the selfless concern for the welfare of others, characterized by actions aimed at benefiting others. This can be driven by empathy, a desire to make a positive impact in the world (including within your team or organization), or a moral and ethical commitment to helping others. Altruistic behaviour can manifest in many forms, including but not limited to donating time, contributing money or providing care.

From an evolutionary perspective, acts of altruism that promote the overall well-being of the species, rather than just the individual, are crucial for the survival and perpetuation of the species. Consequently, the brain rewards such actions with a pleasurable sensation.

Within an organization, creating opportunities for individuals who genuinely believe in the collective benefit of a change to volunteer and participate in change initiatives early in the process can generate a sense of pleasure in these individuals, often referred to as change agents, but not limited to them. By involving these individuals from the outset, they become early advocates for the change and contribute to spreading enthusiasm and engagement among their peers.

To maximize the sense of pleasure and reward for those engaged in voluntary activities, it is important to offer clear and meaningful opportunities for their involvement in the change process as well as recognizing and providing feedback on the contributions of volunteers. This can bolster their sense of worth and dedication to the change initiative.

For example, implementing voluntary mentorship programmes that pair experienced change agents with newcomers can nurture a sense of purpose and fulfilment for both mentors and mentees.

A mentor is someone who can guide, advise and support you to be the best you can be in your career. They take time to understand you and the challenges you're facing and then advise you based on their understanding of the problem and their personal experience – with the aim of helping you towards your goals.

The benefits of mentoring are powerful for both mentor (as it provides opportunity for altruism) and the mentored, as it increases self-confidence, develops communication and provides exposure to new perspectives. As a result, mentoring creates a reward cycle in the brain.

It is important to make a clarification at this point about the difference between mentoring and coaching. A coach is someone who usually does not provide advice directly and instead helps others to come to their own insights. It can help also to shape and grow the mindset by asking solution-based questions.

Coaching programmes can effectively help others to come to their own insights about altruism opportunities to be involved in or other activities that can help them to increase pleasure.

In summary, voluntary activities encompass actions taken by individuals who willingly give their time and effort to support a cause or initiative without any anticipation of personal gain.

EXAMPLE

We know an organization that always starts a new change initiative with a shout-out to colleagues from across the business to share their experiences of previous similar changes. This gives those who have been involved in previous work, either for this organization or a previous employer, the chance to share their knowledge and provide advice to others. As a result of this, some people agree to act as informal mentors for the change team, offering to be a sounding board for their ideas, or to review their plans based on their previous experience.

Altruistic giving and volunteering also supports other dimensions of the PEPE© model (Table 4.6).

TABLE 4.7

Dimension	Activity	Contribution
Promote valleys	Balance anticipation and pleasure	By engaging in altruistic giving, we are helping to provide pleasure to our brain in order to balance the pressure of being 'on the go' all the time.
Releasing energy	Implement a culture of bravery and risk-taking	When there are opportunities to volunteer to participate in the change, people are more likely to stretch themselves and take risks.

Increase sense of belonging

Enhancing the sense of 'belonging' and 'engagement' from the start, among all those delivering the change and impacted by it, can be a powerful tool for facilitating change.

A sense of belonging refers to the feeling of inclusion within a group or community, being part of the 'inner-circle group', and therefore can be a powerful trigger of oxytocin. It involves emotional attachment and identification with a social group, perceiving shared experiences, goals and values with other members of that group.

A robust sense of belonging fosters positive emotions, motivation and a readiness to 'engage' and contribute to the group's success. Moreover, as a result of the release of oxytocin a high sense of belonging has been proven to have a big positive impact on well-being and the reduction of chronic stress.

Engagement relates to the degree of positive emotional involvement, enthusiasm and commitment that those affected by the change feel towards it. Engaged individuals are more likely to invest in the initiative's success and collaborate effectively to achieve the desired outcomes. Increased engagement also leads to higher oxytocin levels in the brain, promoting trust, bonding and pleasure, which facilitates the acceptance of change.

To achieve high levels of engagement, it's important to consider the perspectives and needs of all those involved, including line managers and end-users. These groups are particularly influential: if they feel excluded or not part of the 'in-group', they can become powerful blockers to change.

Promoting engagement involves creating a sense of community and shared purpose among those impacted by the change. Offer clear, meaningful opportunities for them to contribute. For example, participation in a network of 'change champions', participation in task forces to design new processes, quality standards and policies, or involvement in testing groups.

Inclusion and social connections profoundly affect how our brains perceive pain. From an evolutionary perspective, the survival and reproduction of the species was more likely when individuals stuck together. Being part of a tribe and being included within the group increased chances of survival and reproduction.

The higher the level of inclusion in a programme, the greater the likelihood of acceptance of the new state by those affected, and the lower the levels of pain and resistance among them. Feeling part of a group promotes engagement, a sense of safety and rewards, reducing resistance to change.

One of the principles of the Agile Manifesto advocates for a partnership between businesspeople and developers working together towards aligned goals. This practice is a great example of the release of oxytocin within the team, fostering increased trust and reduced tension and stress.

To create a sense of belonging and togetherness within the group, facilitate discussions of what the group is expected to achieve. Ensuring that everyone has the same understanding of their goals means that they are all working towards the same understanding of success.

Within the group, there might be lots of different views, so to help people share their perspectives and come to a shared consensus about their purpose, use the simple structure to move from a high level to more detailed understanding of the goal described in the section on certainty and assurance.

Another technique for encouraging the group to share their different perspectives and develop a consensus view of the change is to play a game where everyone selects a subject at random from a deck of cards (if playing face to face) or is sent a question to answer in the chat function of the video conferencing software you are using.

Each person is then given five minutes to think about their answer, and two minutes to share their answer. Once the two minutes is up, others can add their perspective or ask for more details, background and reasons why the person thinks the way they do.

Make sure you are capturing all the comments so that at the end of the session there is agreement on what has been discussed. If face-to-face, you can list bullet points on a flipchart, and if using video conferencing, you can record the session and get a transcript of what has been said.

Suggested questions you can use to draw out a detailed understanding of what everyone is thinking include:

1 What needs to change?
2 What impact will the change have elsewhere in the business and/or what other changes are connected to this change?
3 What skills are needed to achieve this change?
4 What parts of the change will involve the most effort and/or take the longest time?
5 What parts of the change will involve the least effort and/or be completed quickest?
6 What parts of the change will be easiest to achieve?
7 What parts of the change will be hardest to achieve?
8 Why this change is important to me?
9 Who will support this change?

10 Who will resist this change?

11 Who will benefit from this change?

12 Who will be disadvantaged by this change?

At the end of the session, everyone understands the assumptions others have been making, and some people will have changed their minds or learnt more details about the change. There is a feeling that everyone has a common view of what needs to change and what work will be needed. This creates a team atmosphere, where everyone feels they can share with and rely on others in the team.

EXAMPLE

A people manager used the card game technique for a system change. She was concerned that whilst the change appeared to only impact some of the department, everyone was going to be affected and needed to feel part of it:

We started the activity with the feeling that only a few people would have to change their ways of working, and everyone else could continue as normal. Once we started talking, assumptions were challenged, scope was questioned and by the end, there was a much clearer understanding of the change and a feeling that it was a department change, not just a single team change.

Creating a sense of belonging also supports other dimensions of the PEPE© model.

TABLE 4.8

Dimension	Activity	Contribution
Reduce pain	Psychological safety	Feeling we are part of a bigger group, with shared interests, encourages us to speak up and to take more risks, because we feel our team will support us.
Release positive signals	Create a culture of asking for and providing positive feedback	We are more likely to ask for feedback and believe what we are being told if it comes from those we have a connection with.

(continued)

TABLE 4.8 (Continued)

Dimension	Activity	Contribution
Release energy	Implement a culture of risk-taking and bravery	If we have the support of our colleagues, we feel able to try things out, knowing that others will help us fix any problems we create.
Managing peaks	Challenge the status quo	If we have the support of our colleagues, we are able to ask 'difficult' questions and challenge the prevailing wisdom of how things are currently done.
Promote valleys	Balance anticipation and pleasure	If we feel we are part of a team, we are more likely to celebrate and remain longer in the 'liking', helping to balance the pressures of the peaks.

Create common goals and objectives

Working together as a cohesive team to achieve shared goals involves a fascinating interplay of neuroscience, as it taps into fundamental mechanisms of motivation, social bonding and reward processing within the brain.

Additionally, the pursuit of common goals activates brain regions involved in social cognition and cooperation, such as the prefrontal cortex and anterior cingulate cortex. These areas are crucial for understanding others' perspectives, coordinating actions and resolving conflicts within a group setting. As individuals align their efforts towards shared objectives, these brain regions facilitate effective communication, collaboration and mutual understanding, promoting a cohesive team dynamic.

Furthermore, the establishment of common goals triggers the release of oxytocin, helping to reduce stress and increase pleasure. In this context oxytocin enhances social bonding, trust and empathy among group members, fostering a sense of belonging and unity within the team. As a result, resistance to change is significantly reduced.

See the example above for creating a shared understanding of the work and establishing a consensus for what needs to be achieved.

Notes

1   MD Lieberman and NI Eisenberger. The pains and pleasures of social life, *Current Directions in Psychological Science*, 2015, 24(1): 58–63

2   C Tsigos and GP Chrousos. Hypothalamic-pituitary-adrenal axis, neuroendocrine factors and stress, *Journal of Psychosomatic Research*, 2002, 53(4): 865–71

3   F Pagnini, K Bercovitz and E Langer. Perceived control and mindfulness: implication for clinical practise, *Journal of Psychotherapy Integration*, 2016, 26(2): 91–102

4   K Carlsson. Predictability modulates the affective and sensory discriminative neural processing of pain, *Neuroimage*, 2006, 32(4): 1804–14

5   Ibid.

6   KC Berridge. Parsing rewards, *Trends in Neuroscience*, 2003, 26(9): 507–13; D Gard, et al. Anticipatory and consummatory components of the experience of pleasure, *Journal of Research in Personality*, December 2006

7   S Manninen et al. Social laughter triggers endogenous opioid release in humans, *Journal of Neuroscience*, 2017, 37(25): 6125–31

8   RI Dunbar et al. Social laughter is correlated with an elevated pain threshold, *Proceedings in Biological Sciences*, 2012, 279(1731): 1161–67

9   K Uvnas-Moberg et al. Self-soothing behaviors with particular reference to oxytocin release induced by non-noxious sensory stimulation, *Frontiers in Psychology*, 2015, 12(5):1529

10 AA Marsh et al. Neural and cognitive characteristics of extraordinary altruists, *Proceedings of the National Academy of Sciences*, 21 October 2014: 111

05

Energy and the brain

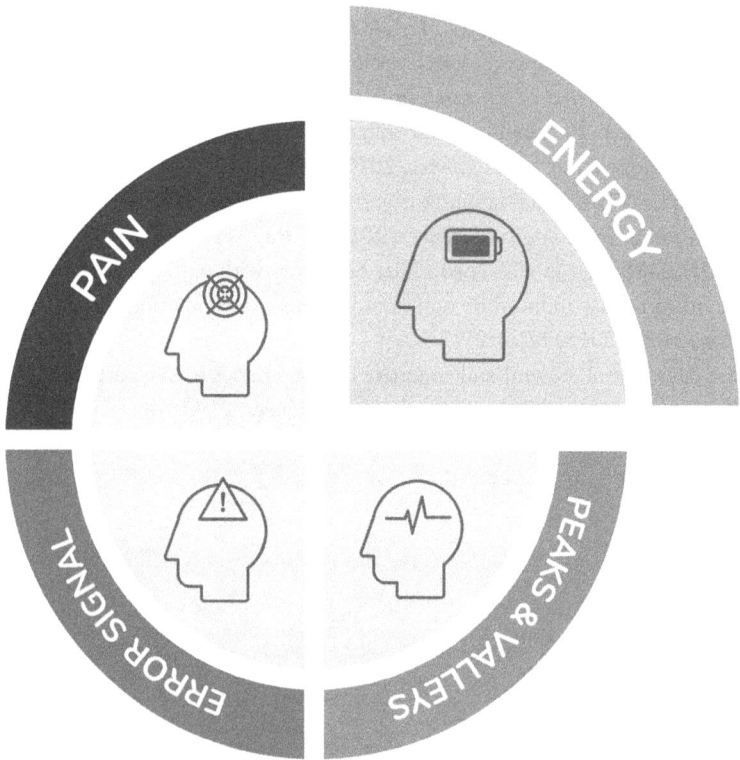

PEPE© model: Energy domain

The way our brain functions, operates and prioritizes processes is driven by the imperative of conserving energy.

The human brain, despite comprising only 2 per cent of the body's total mass, consumes approximately 20 per cent of its energy.[1] Glucose is the brain's primary source of energy. At rest, it can claim over 60 per cent of the body's circulating glucose.

Therefore, to save energy the brain automates as many processes as possible by:

a Leveraging on existing learning and data

b Relying on established habits

c Opting to delete information when possible

Brain bias is also another inherent tendency to take cognitive shortcuts to save energy while processing information. This phenomenon is deeply rooted in the brain's evolutionary history, where efficiency was crucial for survival in an environment with limited resources. To optimize energy usage, the brain has developed various cognitive mechanisms, which allow for quick decision-making and problem-solving without expending excessive mental effort.

For example, confirmation bias, a prevalent cognitive shortcut, predisposes individuals to seek information that aligns with their existing beliefs while discounting contradictory evidence. From a neuroscience standpoint, this bias reflects the brain's preference for familiar patterns and concepts, which demand less cognitive effort to process. Consequently, when confronted with change, individuals may exhibit resistance, clinging to familiar beliefs and routines to conserve mental energy and minimize cognitive dissonance.

Similarly, brain bias influences decision-making by prioritizing easily accessible information in memory. It can lead individuals to overestimate the likelihood of events based on their memorability rather than objective evidence. In the context of change, reliance on the availability shortcut may lead to resistance by exaggerating the perceived risks or challenges associated with new initiatives, thus reinforcing the status quo.

Social factors, including implicit biases and cultural norms, also contribute to resistance to change. Implicit biases, stemming from associative learning processes, can shape perceptions and behaviours towards change without conscious awareness. Cultural norms, ingrained through socialization, may discourage deviation from established practices, further reinforcing resistance to change at both individual and organizational levels.

Understanding the impact of brain bias on change and resistance to it is crucial for effective change management. By recognizing the cognitive mechanisms underlying resistance, leaders can implement strategies to mitigate its effects and foster a culture of openness and adaptability. This may involve promoting awareness of cognitive biases, providing opportunities for reflection and perspective-taking, and creating psychological safety to encourage experimentation and innovation.

It's worth noting that certain functions and regions of the brain demand more energy than others. For example, processes like hearing, learning and processing new data require more energy resources than visualization due to the necessity for faster and more precise signal transmission.

> **Signal transmission** is the process through which neurons communicate with each other in the brain. It is the way the brain sends messages to help us do things such as think, move, hear, etc. It is done by sending signals using electricity and chemicals, such as dopamine, endorphins, adrenaline

Whenever possible, the brain avoids engaging the pre-frontal cortex, responsible for cognition functions like future planning, impulse control and attention. This is because the pre-frontal cortex consumes substantial energy resources due to its precise signal transmission requirements.

Gathering information entails an energy cost for the brain, but deleting or forgetting information is seen as an energy-saving measure.

Demands made by change

The demands posed by change and uncertainty increase energy consumption. To reduce uncertainty, the brain needs to find novel information and new data to learn and adapt to change. It must also form new neuronal connections and synapses to plan, operate and learn in this new 'state'. Change necessitates future planning and adaptation, relying heavily on the pre-frontal cortex and therefore incurring high energy consumption.

The 'selfish brain theory'[2] asserts that a stress response (marked by the release of adrenaline and cortisol) supplies the brain with the necessary energy to address uncertainty. It's not surprising that individuals undergoing change or experiencing uncertainty become hypervigilant and stressed. This stress response provides the required glucose to confront change, enhancing information processing.

Novelty and excitement, characterized by the release of dopamine, also supply the brain with added energy. When the brain encounters new information sharply contrasting with existing knowledge, it perceives it as novel and releases dopamine, generating feelings of energy and excitement. However, if the disparity between the new and existing information is interpreted as a threat, the brain initiates the threat response, releasing adrenaline instead.

To effectively navigate change with a consideration for the brain's dynamics, we must learn how to manage energy levels in those facing change. Once again, the intention is to purposely 'trick/hack' our brain using practical strategies to:

a Save energy during times of change

b Release energy to support the change

Effectively managing energy during change or transformation necessitates a balanced approach that combines strategies for both saving and releasing energy.

This is particularly pertinent for change leaders responsible for ensuring that the business environment is prepared to receive the change, effectively communicating with all those involved, and persuading the organization to embrace the proposed solutions. They may encounter resistance from the pre-frontal cortex of the organization (the individuals) who are tasked with planning and reshaping the future. This can be exhausting for the brain as it is very expensive in terms of energy consumption.

Dimension 3: Save energy

What do we mean?

The aim is to guide the brain in allocating energy efficiently to essential tasks while saving energy typically spent on non-productive processes.

The brain categorizes a process as non-productive when it does not contribute to achieving a desired goal or intention. It is important to acknowledge that what may be perceived as non-productive in one context might hold value or serve a purpose in another. For example, active listening might be considered non-productive if the intention is merely to assert your point, but it becomes a productive process when the aim is to gain deeper insight or learn about a specific situation.

Saving energy can also be achieved by identifying less energy-intensive functions and activities for the brain.

Providing the right amount of information at the right time

We can save energy by delivering the necessary information to those involved precisely when they need it. However, it's essential to avoid overwhelming them with either too much information up front (cognitive overload) or too little (uncertainty). This approach minimizes the need for the brain to search for information independently, helping to save energy and reducing resistance to change.

Additionally, we can withhold detailed information while assuring those delivering the change or impacted by it when new information will become available, when decisions will be made and when they can experience aspects of the change. This 'signposting' generates a sense of certainty, reassuring those affected about what to expect without overloading them with unnecessary information.

Change leaders should emphasize the benefits of the change initially, allowing individuals impacted by the change to visualize the high-level concept before delving into the specifics. Introducing details gradually, as the programme progresses, prevents information overload.

It also prompts change leaders to reflect on questions such as, 'Are we asking those impacted by change to focus too early on too much detail? Are we overloading them with excessive new data?' We should introduce new information only when necessary and look for opportunities to reuse existing information and processes.

Change leaders play a pivotal role in managing new information and adopting an energy-efficient approach. It's prudent to venture into familiar areas that those who will have to work differently are well acquainted with and look for improvements rather than reinventing the wheel. When managing change, we should always question existing practices and identify what is genuinely new. Unnecessary new information should be promptly deleted.

We should clearly state what is not changing to prevent individuals from assuming that the change is more significant than it is. Creating a clear distinction between what is and what is not changing minimizes the distraction caused by exaggerated perceptions of change. Listing all the things that will remain the same also reduces the pain of change, reminding individuals that their current skills and experience remain relevant.

EXAMPLE

We know a successful programme manager who battles her urge to tell everyone everything because she knows that it wastes their time in two ways. They try to absorb lots of information that is not relevant, and they ask questions and start to worry about things that are not their responsibility. Over time, she has developed a technique for targeting the information she provides to her audience using this question: 'What will they do with the information?' She told us she started with the question, 'What do they need to know?' but realized this was too broad, because in her own head she could always make the argument that they needed to know something. By answering the question, 'What will they do with the information?' she is able to think through possible next steps.

- Does the information enable them to plan ahead?
- Does the information enable them to take action?
- Will this action be what the programme requires or could they do something else?
- Are they going to share the information with relevant others?
- Are these individuals the most appropriate people to share the information with?

These questions enable her to think through the good and bad impacts of providing the information and filter what she says to ensure it is relevant and that it helps get things done.

Sharing relevant information also supports other dimensions of the PEPE© model (Table 5.1).

TABLE 5.1

Dimension	Activity	Contribution
Reduce pain	Certainty and assurance	Focusing on useful information when it is relevant increases our perception that we know what we are doing, and the situation is under control.
Release positive signals	Manage expectations from the beginning and at every stage	Access to the right information at the right time minimizes the risk of misunderstandings and incorrect assumptions.

Adding clarity – focus on quality conversations

Effective communication plays a pivotal role in how much energy is spent on productive versus unproductive tasks.

Quality conversations are characterized by mutual respect, active listening, empathy and openness. They involve efficient cognitive processing, where both participants engage fully in understanding each other's perspectives rather than merely waiting for their turn to speak.

For example, if we are asking individuals to share details on how they have been impacted by the change, we should prepare questions for them to help them structure their feedback. This enables them to share the information we need, demonstrating that we respect their time.

We should actively listen, repeat key phrases and check if our interpretation of what they have said is correct. This gives them a chance to share more details or correct us if we have misunderstood. During such conversations our brain gets engaged with a wide range of cognitive processes, such as attention, memory, perception, reasoning and problem-solving.

> **Cognitive processing** refers to the mental activities involved in perceiving, interpreting, analysing and responding to incoming information.

Especially when we hear new information, our brains engage in cognitive processing to make sense of it. This involves both bottom-up processing, which involves analysing individual messages, and top-down processing, which involves using our prior knowledge and expectations to interpret and organize the information.

Cognitive processing is a complex and dynamic process that demands substantial energy from the brain.

Quality conversations, therefore, can help the brain save energy by fostering clear and concise communication. Engaging in quality conversations involves using language that is direct and succinct, avoiding unnecessary elaboration or repetition. This streamlined communication approach reduces the cognitive burden on the brain, allowing it to process information more efficiently.

Furthermore, quality conversations are characterized by active listening, which compels the brain to concentrate on the speaker's words and tone of voice. This form of active listening conserves energy by reducing the need for additional cognitive processing and the constant shift between listening and preparing a response.

This is an invitation to reflect on our approach to communication channels. Are we inviting the appropriate audience to specific meetings? Are we having too many lengthy discussions?

Leaders and managers play a crucial role in encouraging conversations that drive solutions rather than problems, and that promote learning and insights. Change leaders are responsible for elevating the quality and productivity of conversations while also acting as coaches to the business and change agents.

We should avoid long discussions and instead promote shorter, more straightforward, yet frequent conversations. To foster insightful conversations, questions should focus on forward-thinking intentions and the 'what for' rather than justification-based questions.

Have we provided those impacted by the change with enough clarity? Is there anyone else who should be engaged at a particular point in time to prevent confusion? Or are we inviting an unnecessary number of participants to meetings, wasting energy in the process?

A quality conversation seeks to minimize any misunderstandings between the participants. An example of this is using ChatGPT to simplify text, by asking this artificial intelligence engine to rewrite something so that a 10-year-old could understand it.

EXAMPLE

Michael is a successful manager in an insurance company, managing 400 claims-processing staff. He has 11 direct reports, and so does not have much time to spend with each of them. He tells us that he wants to use his limited time effectively. He believes that to have a quality conversation, thought must go into the event beforehand, ensuring there is a clear purpose and outcome:

I want us to know why we are meeting, so at least one day before we get together, I will send them my purpose for the conversation, and I want to know theirs. I also think ahead to what I think a successful outcome will be and ask them to do the same.

EXAMPLE

We know a hospital consultant who uses a structure for passing on work to others to minimize any misunderstandings or confusion about what is needed. Her argument is that if she cannot provide the information, does she really know what she wants or is she wasting someone's time?

- This is the requirement – this is what needs to happen and when it needs to happen.

- This is the recipient of this work, the customer who needs the requirement.

- These are the quality criteria for this work, the minimum it must include to be successful and the basis upon which the work will be authorized or approved.

- This is the person who will test/review the work against these criteria.

- These are the inputs you will need to complete this work and these are the suppliers.

She is very specific, but when she is planning an operation, the patients are probably pleased she has thought through what is needed!

Focusing on quality conversations also supports other dimensions of the PEPE$^©$ model:

TABLE 5.2

Dimension	Activity	Contribution
Reduce perception of pain	Being valued and respected	The amount of focus and care during a quality conversation makes the participants feel that their views and ideas are respected.
Release positive prediction signals	Manage expectations from the beginning and at every stage	Being clear about the purpose of the conversation and the desired outcome reduces mismatch between what is expected to happen and what happens.
Managing peaks	Focus on small cycles of change	Having shorter, frequent conversations where the focus is on the immediate changes to be made ensures the quality of the conversation.

Promoting visualization – reduce listening time

Research has pointed out that the brain's most energy-consuming activities appear to be related to the 'signalling' of information between neurons and the formation of synapses.[3] Synapses serve as the fundamental units of communication within the nervous system, facilitating the transmission of signals between neurons.

In this context, brain regions responsible for auditory processing seem to demand more energy compared to other sensory systems, primarily due to the very fast and precise signalling required for hearing.

Numerous studies have explored the energy expenditures associated with different communication modes. For example, research using brain imaging techniques like functional magnetic resonance imaging (fMRI) has revealed that different cognitive processes, including auditory and visual processing, activate distinct brain regions, indicating different energy requirements.[4]

This body of research encourages us to contemplate strategies aimed at reducing auditory signalling and instead promote less energy-expensive forms of communication, such as visualization. This shift can effectively save energy for those involved and reduce resistance to change.

To help you identify visual representations of your change, use these questions:

- Can you draw a linear picture of your change?
- Does one thing follow another?
- What is the starting point?
- What is the end point?
- Can you draw a proportional picture of your change?
- Is one element bigger than the other – in terms of complexity, value, resources required, importance etc?
- Can you show the elements of your change as a cascade, with one element breaking into smaller elements, which each break into smaller elements?

EXAMPLE

As part of hybrid working, many of us sit in meetings staring at a slide presentation, where we struggle to process and retain everything that we are being told. To help people absorb the right information at the right time, it is useful to use the animation feature, so that you can present one part of your diagram at a time. The benefits of this are:

- It presents the right information at the right time, giving them time to focus on one concept before moving on to the next one.
- It reduces the amount of information your audience must process at any one time.
- It explains the order or flow for your information.

Any type of diagram enables you to do this; you do not have to be a talented artist to use pictures in your presentations.

Promoting visualization supports other dimensions of the PEPE© model (Table 5.3).

TABLE 5.3

Dimension	Activity	Contribution
Reduce perception of pain	Certainty and assurance	A picture offers a different perception and can help to clarify ideas, which increases the certainty of those you are communicating with.
Saving energy	Add clarity – focus on quality conversations	Representing information visually provides a different view, which enables others to question what is being discussed and/or add their own contribution to the picture.
Managing peaks	Promote curiosity	A picture invites feedback and triggers ideas in others, which helps people question what they are being told.
Release positive signals	Bring familiarity and ensure pattern recognition	Representing information visually makes it simpler for the brain to recognize possible patterns between the different elements.

Making it local – personalize it

The principle of 'keep it local – personalize it' holds significant implications from a neuroscience perspective, particularly in terms of conserving energy resources within the brain. Providing information in a way that is relevant and personalized to an individual's experiences and interests can optimize cognitive efficiency and reduce the cognitive load on the brain.

When information is presented in a personalized and locally relevant manner, it activates brain regions associated with familiarity, relevance and personal significance. For example, when individuals encounter information that relates directly to their interests, experiences or goals, brain areas such as the medial prefrontal cortex and posterior cingulate cortex, which are involved in self-referential processing and autobiographical memory, are engaged.

Moreover, personalized information elicits stronger emotional responses, activating brain regions associated with emotion processing and motivation, such as the amygdala and ventral striatum. Emotionally salient information is more likely to capture attention and be encoded into memory, as it is perceived as personally meaningful or relevant to the individual's goals and desires.

By contrast, presenting information in a generic or non-personalized manner requires additional cognitive resources for processing and comprehension. When individuals encounter information that lacks personal relevance or significance, the brain must exert greater effort to extract meaning and integrate it with existing knowledge. This increased cognitive load can lead to mental fatigue, reduced attentional resources and diminished cognitive performance over time.

Furthermore, personalization enhances neural processing efficiency by facilitating neural synchronization and coherence within relevant brain networks. When information aligns closely with an individual's existing knowledge and beliefs, neural networks responsible for processing that information become more synchronized and coordinated, leading to more efficient information processing and retrieval.

Emphasizing the personal benefits that resonate with each individual on an emotional level, as opposed to focusing solely on strategic gains, can channel the right amount of energy in the right direction. This approach can increase motivation to actively participate in the change, as each individual perceives the change as relevant and worthy of their energy investment.

EXAMPLE

We are working on a large-scale transformation, where there are a lot of meetings and workshops. Keeping everyone informed of the outcomes will produce vast amounts of information. Instead, we apply empathy to filter the information.

We start with the responsibilities for each role. For example, in the HR function, we have HR business partners who are supporting specific teams, so they need information about how these teams will be impacted by the transformation. The Learning and Development team need information about changes to the skills needed for the transformed business. The HR Director is responsible for the staff engagement survey and wants to know how those affected by the transformation are informed and supported.

We did not decide these areas of interest unilaterally but began the transformation with a series of workshops where those impacted by the change decided their scope of involvement with the programme and their specific interests.

Personalization also supports other dimensions of the PEPE© model (Table 5.4).

TABLE 5.4

Dimension	Activity	Contribution
Saving energy	Add clarity – focus on quality conversations	When the information is specific and relevant to the person you are communicating with, it increases the clarity of your message.
Releasing energy	Provide opportunities for people to come up with their own insights	Information tailored to the needs of a specific individual feels more 'real' and helps them to imagine themselves in the changed situation. This triggers more ideas about how to work differently in the future.
Release positive prediction signals	Manage expectations from the beginning and at every stage	If the information is personalized it is more specific, which reduces the risk of a mismatch between what is expected and what happens.

Creating habits and routines

Habits and routines play a crucial role in enhancing the energy efficiency of our behaviour and preserving mental energy for more demanding tasks. When dealing with multiple changes, cultivating habits and routines becomes a powerful strategy, reducing the cognitive overload for individuals facing these changes and therefore facilitating the transition.

Recent findings in neuroscience support the idea that our brain is constantly switching (and often competing) between habits and goal-directed behaviours[5] to prevent itself from becoming overwhelmed by constant decision-making. Typically, it gives priority to habitual behaviours.

'Goal-directed behaviours' refers to actions and conduct driven by specific goals or intentions. In such behaviours, individuals consciously set a goal, make decisions and take actions to achieve that goal.

On the other hand, 'habits' are automatic, deeply ingrained behavioural patterns formed through repetition, often executed without conscious thought or decision-making.

The brain switches between these two types of behaviour as a mechanism to optimize efficiency and conserve cognitive resources. Habits are favoured by the brain because they are well established and demand less mental effort and decision-making compared to goal-directed behaviours, which involve a conscious evaluation of options and decision-making.

By relying on habits for routine actions, the brain frees up cognitive resources for other complex tasks. However, when circumstances demand adaptable responses to achieve a specific objective, the brain can transition from relying on habits to engaging in goal-directed behaviours, necessitating conscious decision-making and planning.

To create a new habit, we need to be clear about what the new behaviour is. It cannot be a vague idea; there need to be clear boundaries and a clear expectation of what success looks like.

Try to imagine yourself behaving in the new way, and ask yourself questions to make sure you have a detailed understanding of your new habit:

- When are you doing it?
- How long does it take?
- Do you do it with others?
- Do you need any equipment or materials to do it?
- Where will you get these from?
- What will you do next?

Establishing a routine requires repetition, which is easier to do if you have a plan of what you need to do. Follow the three steps in Figure 5.1 to create a new habit.

FIGURE 5.1 Establishing new routines

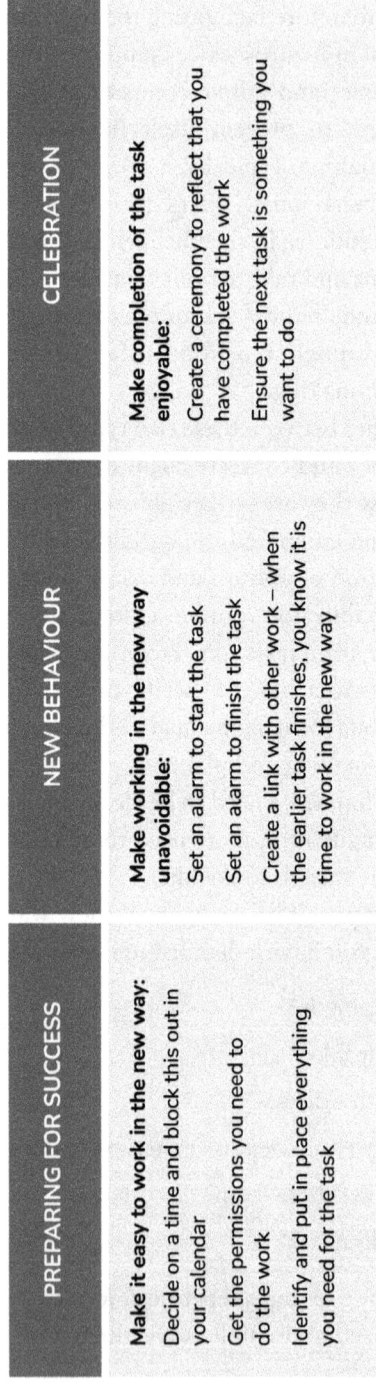

PREPARING FOR SUCCESS	NEW BEHAVIOUR	CELEBRATION
Make it easy to work in the new way:	**Make working in the new way unavoidable:**	**Make completion of the task enjoyable:**
Decide on a time and block this out in your calendar	Set an alarm to start the task	Create a ceremony to reflect that you have completed the work
Get the permissions you need to do the work	Set an alarm to finish the task	Ensure the next task is something you want to do
Identify and put in place everything you need for the task	Create a link with other work – when the earlier task finishes, you know it is time to work in the new way	

EXAMPLE

Since I started working from home during the pandemic, I often work late, and when I finish at my laptop, I continue working in the evening using my phone. To protect my mental health, I have built a new habit of finishing on time.

The first thing I had to do was decide what 'finish' means. In my job, other people need to ask me questions or get my permission before they can move on to their next tasks. My teams are based all over the world, so when it is 6 pm for me, it might only be lunchtime for them.

I have decided that 'finished' means that I stop work that requires me to be in meetings, or to concentrate and create. But after dinner, I will give myself 20 minutes to check my phone and answer any emails from team members.

The actual time I finish varies from day to day depending on what I am doing. To help me stop, each night I look ahead to the next day and work out when I am going to finish. I plan a 'wind-down period' in my schedule for 30 minutes before that time. In these 30 minutes I tidy my desk, finish any last emails and plan the finish time for the next day. To reinforce that I must not work past a specific time, I set an alarm for the end of the wind-down period.

When the wind-down period ends, I have a ritual for closing the lid on my laptop and standing up and stretching. This physical movement tells my brain the working day is over.

To encourage me to finish on time, I make sure there is something nice happening at the end of the day. This usually involves walking my four dogs with my husband, and we arrange to go somewhere fun with them, sometimes taking a picnic or stopping at a café on the way back.

Creating habits and routines also supports other dimensions of the PEPE© model.

TABLE 5.5

Dimension	Activity	Contribution
Reduce mismatch between reality and expectations	Focus on incremental and iterative change	To create a new routine, we need to break up the actions into specific tasks that we can incorporate into our current ways of working. Breaking a new behaviour into these smaller tasks enables us to build the habit incrementally.

(continued)

TABLE 5.5 (Continued)

Dimension	Activity	Contribution
Release positive prediction signals	Bring familiarity and ensure pattern recognition	By creating a routine, we are creating a pattern, and repeated use of this routine becomes familiar and makes us feel reassured we are in control of our work.
Increase pleasure	Celebrate often and bring laugher	By creating habits of celebrating often we are ensuring we are going to dedicate the time to celebrate when we need it the most (usually when we are too busy to celebrate). As it is a habit, the brain will unconsciously find opportunities to celebrate

Dimension 4: Release energy

What do we mean?

The aim is to find 'controllable' ways and processes for supplying the brain with the necessary adrenaline, dopamine and glucose to meet the increased demand for energy.

We need to stop the brain from going out of control and becoming overloaded with unwanted stress, which makes it source energy in an unsustainable way (for example, by creating the required adrenaline in negative ways including overwork, which leads to burn-out). Instead, we can implement brain-friendly practices that support the release of adrenaline in a more productive and controllable manner.

As discussed earlier, the 'selfish brain theory'[6] points out that we need a stress response (involving the release of adrenaline and cortisol) to supply the brain with the required energy for resolving uncertainty. The concept here revolves around harnessing the role of eustress (beneficial, manageable stress) to release energy, eliminating the need for the brain to distress during periods of change and transformation.

Stress response is the body's reaction to a threat or a challenge leading to the release of adrenaline, noradrenaline and cortisol, which provide energy to help confront the situation.

> **Eustress** is a term used to describe positive or beneficial stress. It refers to the type of stress that is experienced in response to exciting or challenging events that the brain perceives as manageable situations, for example a new role or promotion with increased responsibilities. Unlike negative stress, eustress can have positive effects on overall well-being.

We also seek practical strategies to stimulate gradual release of dopamine, the primary neurotransmitter associated with motivation. Research indicates that dopamine fuels the sensation of anticipation related to goal-oriented action, driving individuals to initiate and persist in their pursuit, whether the goal is positive or negative. When the brain is boosted with dopamine, individuals experience excitement and a sense of reward.

Small but frequent deadlines

To increase the release of adrenaline and dopamine, it can be beneficial to maintain higher levels of focus and attention by setting shorter deadlines and concentrating on achieving small, daily or weekly objectives, rather than attempting to tackle substantial workloads all at once.

This approach helps prevent the brain from becoming overwhelmed, fostering improved concentration and productivity while harnessing the energy provided by adrenaline and dopamine to reduce resistance to change. It can be achieved by applying the agile concepts introduced earlier in the book, including:

- delivery of early and frequent value
- an iterative approach that prioritizes delivery to agreed deadlines
- seeking out and welcoming new ideas
- experimenting, piloting and prototyping as early as possible

It is often more effective to introduce something into practice and build on it, cultivating a sense of excitement and accomplishment that fuels further efforts.

To achieve small, frequent deadlines, use an iterative planning technique:

1 Define the end goal of the change, describing the new working practices, new responsibilities, new values and priorities.

2 Break this goal into smaller, more specific outcomes and decide the order in which these outcomes will be achieved.

3 Create a visual plan that shows the time required to achieve each outcome and their order of creation.

DEFINE THE END GOAL

This iterative approach minimizes uncertainty by outlining the ultimate goals of the entire change, allowing the brain to first grasp the high-level overview and then delve into the finer details as needed.

This end goal is also called the vision, the destination or the blueprint and is an attractive, exciting description of the business capabilities achieved because of the change. It can be one or a combination of these answers:

- **What** we do – products/services
- **How** we do it – manual/automation; known/innovative
- **Who** we do it with – external suppliers/internal resources
- **Where** we do it – onshore/off shore; continents/countries; urban/rural
- **When** we do it – time of day/week/month; frequency; regularity

FIGURE 5.2 Relationship between end goal and outcomes

When you are trying to describe your end goal, ensure there is enough information to trigger the motivation to achieve it. This description needs to reflect what people prioritize, what they take pride in doing, who they are doing it for.

Ideally, the description of the end goal is created collaboratively, involving the views of all those who will have to work in new ways. Taking part in this collaborative definition can stimulate pleasure and energy for the change, whilst minimizing the pain.

Ensure that the end goal describes an ability to do, provide or operate something that did not exist before. The end goal generates benefits for your organization, but these benefits are not the end goal.

For example, your end goal might describe a situation where your organization has expanded its reach from Europe and the United States into South America. It is describing servicing a new customer base in a new location. Ultimately, delivering to these customers will bring more sales and higher revenues, but these metrics are not the end goal.

Benefits are important to articulate, but they are a way of helping you validate if the scope of your end goal will deliver the results you want. These results are not the end goal themselves.

There are activities to help establish the end goal in Chapter 11, 'Sponsoring Change', specifically the section on defining scope using the PEPE model.

In this approach, change occurs frequently, with each iteration having a short planning horizon. This design helps the brain to maintain higher levels of focus and attention compared to longer-term planning, reducing cognitive overload.

BREAK THE END GOAL INTO OUTCOMES
A successful agile plan ensures that the end goal is broken into outcomes that taken together achieve the new ways of working described by your end goal. Each outcome is an achievement that results in positive changes. These changes can be a mixture of fixes for existing problems and additional functionality, allowing your organization to do things it was not able to do before.

To break your end goal into outcomes, use these questions to stimulate discussion and ideas:

- Does the outcome fix a current problem or fix a failure? By fixing something that causes mistakes and reduces rework, you are creating more time to be spent on the change, and creating trust that you are delivering early value to the business.

FIGURE 5.3 Iterative plan

- Does the outcome add important functionality that does not exist today, but which is expected and/or demanded by internal or external customers? This is an immediate delivery of additional value for the business.

- Can the outcome be delivered quickly by limiting adoption to a small group? Consider involving a specific team, department or location. Perhaps limit delivery to a specific customer group or supplier type.

- Can delivery be accelerated by limiting the functionality that is included in the outcome? By limiting the number of features or the types of products or services that are included in the outcome you can increase the speed of delivery.

CREATE A VISUAL PLAN

The incremental nature of the plan means that each iteration adds to the change. The change can be stopped after any of these iterations. An agile approach does not assume that every iteration will be completed. If circumstances change, meaning the change is no longer valuable, or sufficient improvements have been achieved after only some of the iterations have been completed, then this is fine.

For more explanation of an agile, iterative plan please refer to Chapter 1, specifically the section headed 'Relationship with agile approaches'.

Small but frequent deadlines also support other dimensions of the PEPE© model (Table 5.6).

TABLE 5.6

Dimension	Activity	Contribution
Reducing perception of pain	Certainty and assurance	An iterative plan that sets out expected future outcomes creates a sense that the change is fully understood and the work is clearly organized.
Increasing pleasure	Celebrate often and bring laughter	Breaking the change into small deadlines provides the opportunity for frequent enjoyment of the achievement.
	Create common goals and objectives	It is easier to establish consensus on the goals to be achieved and the work involved using smaller, more specific objectives for each increment of the plan.

(continued)

TABLE 5.6 (Continued)

Dimension	Activity	Contribution
Reduce mismatch	Move from big to small	A shorter deadline brings greater focus to what work must be completed, which removes the risk of misunderstanding about what is included.
Reduce mismatch	Focus on incremental/ iterative change	When defining the small, frequent deadlines, think about how each achievement acts as the basis for the next piece of work.
Release positive signals	Bring familiarity and ensure pattern recognition	By using an iterative plan, there is a repeating pattern that the brain can follow as each increment ends in a new capability.
Managing peaks	Focus on small cycles of change	Short iterations of change provide people with an opportunity for short bursts of concentrated effort, where they are working at the peak of their ability.

This agile approach to planning supports other dimensions of the PEPE© model, so please refer to these chapters for specific activities and examples.

Implement a culture of bravery and risk-taking

Cultivating a culture of bravery and risk-taking is essential for creating an environment that encourages individuals to step beyond their comfort zones, challenge the status quo and try new things.

This environment fosters a culture that encourages change by empowering individuals to take calculated risks. This in turn triggers the release of dopamine and adrenaline in the brain. When these neurotransmitters are maintained at controlled levels, they can have a positive effect on well-being and supply the brain with the energy needed to navigate change effectively.

Implementing such a culture requires consideration from both the organizational and individual perspectives.

From an organizational perspective, leaders must create and foster a culture that values and rewards bravery and risk-taking. They should also equip employees with the necessary resources, tools, and training to enable them to take risks and innovate.

From an individual perspective, employees must be willing to step outside their comfort zones and embrace uncertainty, challenge assumptions and learn from failures. Leaders in charge of change play a crucial role in motivating and inspiring their colleagues to engage in change initiatives, fostering a sense of motivation and dopamine release in them.

By focusing on developing a culture of bravery and risk-taking, organizations can harness the power of dopamine and adrenaline to drive positive change and achieve their objectives.

Many organizations are embracing a culture of empowerment alongside a 'no-blame' ethos to support risk-taking as part of a broader initiative to encourage innovation.

Empowerment entails individuals feeling they possess the authority to make decisions and commit to their actions. To facilitate this empowerment, encourage discussion among those impacted by change to define:

1 The criteria for assuming responsibility for tasks, such as whether assignments are based on skills and experience or formal authority within the organization.

2 The mechanism for holding one another accountable for effort and the quality of work, ranging from public assessment of individual progress in a team meeting or the formal tracking of progress on behalf of a senior leader.

3 The decision-making process, whether it's the responsibility of a recognized expert or a collective team effort.

Taken together these factors create 'guard rails' within which team members can safely work, as their levels of authority and responsibility are clear to them. This encourages them to take risks as they can challenge themselves, their ideas and their ways of working without needing permission from others.

Taking a risk can involve something as simple as doing something new (novelty). A quick way to create ideas for novelty in your work is to ask yourself 'How can I do this differently?' Use these five questions to inspire ideas for making changes to your work:

- **WHAT.** What can you do differently?
- **WHEN.** Can you do things at a different time?
- **WHERE.** Can you do things in a different place?

- **WHO.** Can you do things with new people?
- **HOW.** Can you use different processes, techniques, skills, systems, short cuts?

Bravery and risk-taking mean a willingness to step outside of our comfort zone. A starting point is to be clear about what our comfort zone is and when we are challenging it. If you can answer yes to most of these questions, you are working in your comfort zone!

- Have you done this more than five times before?
- If you are working with others, have you worked with them before?
- Do you know with certainty what the results will be?
- Do you know how your work will be received by others?
- Do you know what might go wrong?
- Do you have ways to solve these problems if they happen?
- Have you developed any short cuts for doing this?
- Have you added any additions to this work, based on your experience of how to do it?
- Are you able to explain how to do this to someone else?
- Can you do this whilst holding a conversation about something else?

To step outside of your comfort zone, use these questions:

1 Will this activity stretch you to use new skills?
2 Will you need to engage with new people?
3 Are you unsure of how to get started?
4 Do you know what could go wrong?
5 Do you know how to fix things if they go wrong?
6 How will you celebrate when you have been successful?

Implementing a culture of bravery and risk-taking supports other dimensions of the PEPE© model (Table 5.7).

Provide opportunities for people to come up with their own insights

Moments of insight, often referred to as 'aha' moments, are typically associated with positive experiences, and high levels of motivation and energy.[7] In fact, research using electroencephalogram (EEG) technology has shown that

TABLE 5.7

Dimension	Activity	Contribution
Manage the peaks	Challenge the status quo	Bravery encourages us to question the current ways of working. This takes bravery because the known ways of working are comfortable and reassuring. It takes courage to consider losing that familiarity.
Manage the peaks	Promote flow	To promote flow, individuals need to perceive the challenge slightly higher than their skills. Therefore, by fostering measurable risk-taking habits, individuals would be able to get into flow more frequently.
Increase pleasure	Altruistic giving and volunteering	This is another form of challenging the status quo, because it demands a willingness to do something new, or to put ourselves in a new situation or work with new people.

during such moments of insights, gamma waves appear in the brain, facilitating the release of dopamine,[8] which increases energy and motivation, and subsequently reduces resistance to change. Insights are powerful facilitators of change.

Insights refers to a sudden realization, understanding or comprehension of something. It is a moment of clarity or a new perspective that emerges in one's mind, usually a creative cognition in which an idea suddenly emerges into awareness.

The simplest way to foster insights is to strike a balance between delivering information and offering individuals an opportunity to process it on their own. When individuals engage with information actively, they can interpret it and give it new meaning, leading to the emergence of the insight.

A defining characteristic of an insight is that it must arise within the awareness of the individual experiencing it; it cannot be provided by someone else. Otherwise, it ceases to be an insight and becomes advice, or a direct solution offered by an external source.

Insights are critical for the adoption of change as everyone who must change how they work needs these personal realizations about what they need to do differently.

Change leaders play a pivotal role in cultivating insights within their teams and among those impacted by change. They can create conditions conducive to insights by, for example, allowing for incubation time after a brainstorming session, enabling individuals to 'sleep on' an idea and generate their own insights.

Research indicates that for insights to occur, our brain should be in a positive and rewarded state rather than being in a hypervigilant mode. Therefore, it is important to establish an environment that promotes relaxation and moments of mind wandering.

Another effective strategy to stimulate insights is to pose questions that focus on solutions rather than delving into problems. Leaders in charge of change should adopt a coaching approach rather than simply providing solutions. This approach involves asking thought-provoking questions, encouraging self-reflection and empowering individuals to discover their own solution.

To encourage the flow of ideas, do not rush to judge the quality of what people are saying. Their ideas are not yet fully formed, so they might be talking things through to hear how they sound, or assessing, or getting your views so they dive deeper and add more details.

If people share their ideas with you, help them to remain creative by using these words:

1　Maybe

2　Possibly

3　Perhaps

4　Potentially

5　Tell me more

6　Can you give us more details?

7　Can we build on this?

If they want to collaborate with you, use these phrases to make suggestions to build on their initial ideas:

1　Let's + [doing word]

2　Why don't we + [doing word]

3 How about + [doing word]

4 What if we + [doing word]

5 I think we + [mood or state] + [doing word]

6 Maybe we [mood or state] + [doing word]

7 It would be great if we were able to [capability]

8 This would work if only we had [inputs]

9 How would you explain this to someone who doesn't work in our industry?

Providing opportunities for people to come up with their own insights supports other dimensions of the PEPE© model (Table 5.8).

TABLE 5.8

Dimension	Activity	Contribution
Promote valleys	Mind wandering	Provide the conditions that lead to moments of insight.
Decrease pain	Control and autonomy	Having insights and applying them involves taking control and feeling personally responsible for our outcomes.
Managing peaks	Promote flow	Insights boost dopamine and intrinsic motivation, which in turn facilitate the state of flow.

Create anticipation and promote 'hunting'

Leaders responsible for change can boost levels of dopamine to release energy and increase motivation among their teams and those impacted by change, by encouraging anticipation and striving towards goals. We can ensure this is a regular activity using an iterative plan.

For example, leaders can build anticipation by generating excitement and focusing on the benefits, highlighting positive outcomes and organizing informal gatherings or preview events where the team can gain insight into new technology and its capabilities.

Research reveals that one of the most effective methods through which our ancient brain releases a surge of dopamine is through constant pursuit and the sense of anticipation associated with envisioning the achievement.

In change, we can create anticipation by demonstrating the outcome of the change. We can create a 'day in the life of' video that shows people using new systems, equipment or materials, following new processes, working in new locations and creating new outputs.

We can host demonstrations of new systems, we can invite people to walk around a new facility, we can enable people to try a new product or service.

An experience of the change before it happens creates the excitement for making it happen because we can think through the benefits and improvements that we will enjoy.

Encourage everyone to identify the steps along the way, so they can track their progress towards achieving the change. By tracking our progress, we keep people in a state of anticipation as we ask ourselves, 'Are we there yet?' This is why we talk to children about how many sleeps there are until a holiday or we have advent calendars at Christmas that count down to the big day.

This excitement gives us the motivation to do all the things we need to do to achieve the change.

Break your goal into smaller steps so you can identify what success looks like for each step, creating a mini version of the overall anticipation by anticipating each individual success.

EXAMPLE

Getting ready to exhibit at an international conference, there is so much work to do, and it is helpful to talk to the team about the successful outcome to keep anticipation high. We want everyone to be eager for the conference day to finally arrive so they can enjoy the results of a successful showcase of their work.

To maintain focus, we can identify milestones on the journey:

- Designing the exhibition stand
- Preparing and rehearsing the demonstration
- Producing the materials to hand out at the exhibition

Each of these bigger milestones can be broken into smaller, more specific milestones:

- Producing the materials to hand out at the exhibition:
    - Produce business cards for everyone on the exhibition stand

o Produce a customer brochure

o Buy bowls and sweets

o Buy pens, bags and other giveaways

Each of these tasks has a timeline, and we can identify all the successful outcomes along the way:

- Produce a customer brochure:

  o Agree the design – fonts, logos, page layout

  o Create the draft wording

  o Amend the wording

  o Agree the final wording

  o Design diagrams to accompany the wording

  o Amend these diagrams

  o Agree the final diagrams

Each milestone can create anticipation, and these smaller milestones minimize the risk of a mismatch between expectation and reality.

Creating anticipation and promoting hunting supports other dimensions of the PEPE© model.

TABLE 5.9

Dimension	Activity	Contribution
Releasing energy	Small, frequent deadlines	Increase the amount of anticipation and hunting by ensuring there are small and achievable deadlines.
Reduce mismatch between reality and expectation	Move from big to small	It is easier to anticipate the pleasure of achievement if that achievement is clearly defined, which is easier to do if the overall objective is broken into smaller elements.
Managing peaks	Promote curiosity	Building anticipation can help to create curiosity.

Notes

1 M Watts et al. Brain energy and oxygen metabolism: emerging role in normal function and disease, *Frontiers in Molecular Neuroscience*, 2018, 11(206)

2 P Achim and P McEwen. Uncertainty and stress: why it causes disease and how it is mastered by the brain, *Progress in Neurobiology*, 2017, 156: 164–88

3 J Niven and S Laughlin. Energy limitation as a selective pressure on the evolution of sensory systems, *Journal of Experimental Biology*, 2008, 211(11): 1792–804

4 N Altieri. Learning to associate auditory and visual stimuli: behavioral and neural mechanisms, *Brain Topography*, 2015, 28(3): 479–93

5 S De Wit et al. Shifting the balance between goals and habits: Five failures in experimental habit induction, *Journal of Experimental Psychology*, General, 2018, 147(7): 1043–65

6 P Achim and P McEwen. Uncertainty and stress: why it causes disease and how it is mastered by the brain, *Progress in Neurobiology*, 2017, 156: 164–88

7 Y Oh et al. An insight-related neural reward signal, *Neuroimage*, 2020, DOI: 10.1016/j.neuroimage.2020.116757 (archived at https://perma.cc/2PBW-6N6P)

8 J Kounios and M Beeman. *The Eureka Factor: AHA moments, creative insight, and the brain*, Random House, 2015.

06

Peaks and valleys in the brain

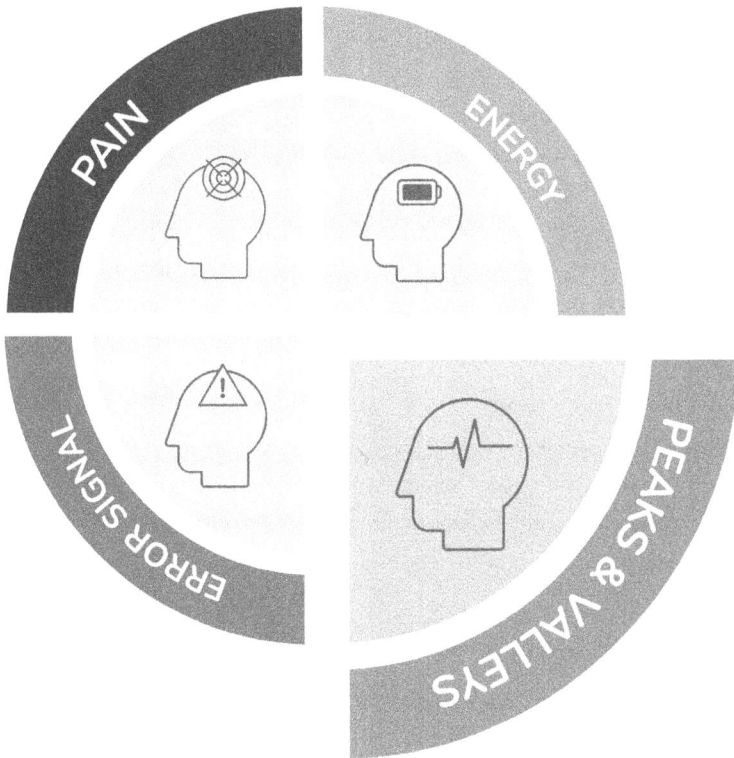

PEPE© model: Peaks and Valleys domain

Brain research has uncovered fascinating insight: our brains operate at their best when they undergo short cycles of fluctuating (high and low) levels of specific chemicals, such as cortisol, adrenaline, noradrenaline, dopamine, and endorphins, among others. These cycles enable us to adapt positively to change, becoming more resilient, and promoting overall well-being.

Likewise, research shows that fluctuations in brain waves are linked to good health, high performance, the generation of new ideas,[1] formation of memories, and heightened focus and concentration.

> **Brain waves** are patterns of electrical activity that occur in the brain and can be measured by an EEG (electroencephalogram). These patterns reflect the different states of consciousness, such as wakefulness, sleep, relaxation or deep relaxation.

Fluctuations in both brain chemistry and brain waves generally result from exposure to various mental states, experiences, actions, thoughts, emotions, behaviours, nutritional choices, and overall health.

Over the past two decades, scientists have demonstrated that there are several mechanisms and properties of the nervous system that facilitate positive adaptation to change by orchestrating alternating neurobiological (brain chemistry) and brain wave patterns, cycling between 'highs and lows' due to brain plasticity.

> **Brain plasticity**, also known as neuroplasticity, is the ability of the brain to change and adapt throughout a person's life. It is the brain's capacity to reorganize its structure, functions and connections in response to experiences, learning and environmental influences.

On the flip side, chronic or prolonged exposure to stress, excitement, pleasure or calmness, without allowing for fluctuations between 'highs and lows', challenges the systems and processes that maintain balance in the human body. This can lead to physiological and psychological harm, giving rise to what, in neuroscience terms, is called 'maladaptive plasticity'.

These changes can manifest as diminished motivation, reduced engagement, cognitive impairment, mental health issues and neurological disorders. Essentially, the brain's innate ability to adapt and change, typically a positive attribute, can become detrimental when these changes compromise brain function and well-being.

TABLE 6.1

Examples of positive brain plasticity:	Examples of maladaptive plasticity:
Learning and skills acquisition	Learned helplessness
• Memory improvement	• Declined motivation
• Resilience	• Addiction
• Adaptation to environmental changes	• Withdraw or lack of engagement
• Recovery from brain injury	• Chronic pain
• Sensory adaptations	• Chronic stress
	• Cynicism
	• Depression

Maladaptive plasticity refers to negative changes that can occur in the brain's structure and function due to various factors such as stress, trauma or prolonged exposure to some of the neurotransmitters or hormones in the brain, such as dopamine, endorphins, cortisol.

In today's context, it is more crucial than ever to foster environments that support moderate disruptions, brief periods of stress followed by intervals of calm and reflection, or peaks of anticipation and excitement followed by in-the-moment enjoyment and pleasure. This approach allows our neurobiology and brain waves to fluctuate between 'high' and 'lows', or what we call 'peaks and valleys'.

Research[2] indicates that during times of change, the emphasis tends to be on making progress and continuously moving toward new ways of operating, with little attention paid to celebrating accomplishments. In the annual global Capability for Change survey, only two out of ten change professionals state that their organizations acknowledge and celebrate achievements.

A novel theory proposed by neuroscientists, called allostasis, establishes that in unpredictable environments marked by continuous change, effective regulation requires anticipation. This means that our body's systems must predict potential challenges or changes and prepare accordingly to maintain stability and optional functioning.[3] This anticipatory capacity is developed through our prior exposure and learning mechanisms, often involving brief, controlled exposure to stress, commotion or excitement, which fosters resilience by creating a learning mechanism.

FIGURE 6.1 Effective feedback mechanisms

Effective feedback mechanisms should involve:

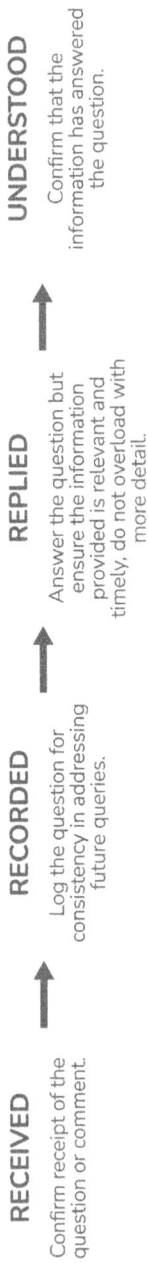

RECEIVED

Confirm receipt of the question or comment.

RECORDED

Log the question for consistency in addressing future queries.

REPLIED

Answer the question but ensure the information provided is relevant and timely, do not overload with more detail.

UNDERSTOOD

Confirm that the information has answered the question.

FIGURE 6.2 Example of healthy 'peaks and valleys' fluctuations in our neurobiology to avoid maladaptive plasticity

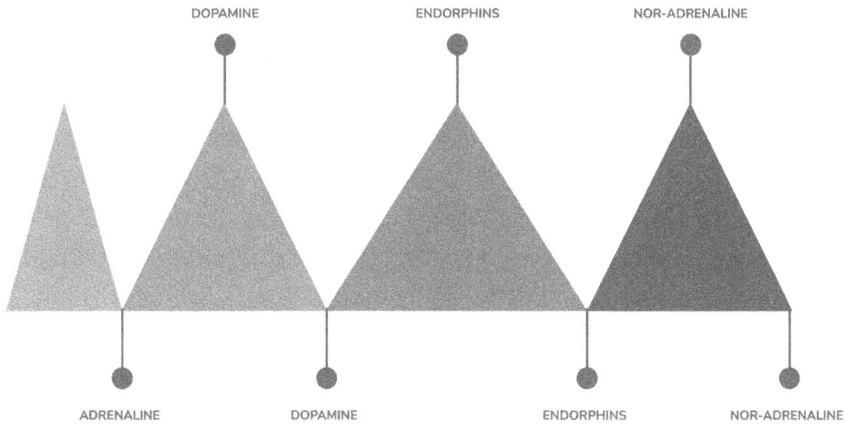

DOPAMINE   ENDORPHINS   NOR-ADRENALINE

ADRENALINE   DOPAMINE   ENDORPHINS   NOR-ADRENALINE

Allostasis challenges the conventional regulatory model of 'homeostasis', which seeks perpetual constancy. Instead, it highlights the need for efficient mechanisms that can anticipate and correct errors via feedback, rather than merely restoring original values.

This principle extends to organizational and individual change, recognizing that in today's rapidly evolving business environment, the traditional pursuit of constancy and maintaining the status quo is no longer tenable. To adapt to changing circumstances, organizations must develop efficient mechanisms that enable them to anticipate and swiftly implement corrective measures through feedback, rather than aiming to revert to the prior state.

For example, suppose a company aims to implement a new customer relationship management (CRM) system. To successfully introduce this change, the organization should anticipate potential errors and establish feedback mechanisms that will enable them to correct these errors quickly.

To anticipate potential errors, the organization can invest in employee training programmes to ensure that all staff members are proficient in using the new system.

To facilitate swift corrections, the organization can establish a feedback system that allows employees to report issues and suggest improvements (Figure 6.1).

By incorporating the principles of allostasis, organizations can proactively manage change and adapt to the challenges of a dynamic business environment. One way we can apply these principles in facilitating change and reducing resistance to change is by intentionally allowing our neurobiology (brain chemistry) and brain waves to fluctuate between 'peaks' and 'valleys' according to our needs during the change process (see Figure 6.2).

Demands made by change

In today's fast-paced modern life and the continuous and constant change that organizations must contend with, the way our brain chemistry and waves fluctuate faces unprecedented challenges.

Consider the perpetual 'hunt' for new operating models, products, systems and organizational structures, which results in an unending quest for dopamine-driven peaks. This constant pursuit reduces the satisfaction derived from achievements and demands ever-increasing dopamine levels, fostering addictive behaviours, demotivation, disengagement and resistance. Prolonged exposure to elevated dopamine levels from the brain's 'wanting' and anticipatory reward system (as discussed earlier in Chapter 2, 'The Sweet Spots of the Brain') disrupts the functioning of the brain's reward system, limiting the range of small pleasures and celebrations, and ultimately stopping the release of endorphins, which arise from the 'liking' and pleasure portion of the brain's reward system. Hence it becomes crucial to proactively manage the 'peaks and valleys' of the brain's reward system.

Similarly, perpetual change challenges the brain's threat system by perpetuating a state of continuous hypervigilance. This impedes the system's ability to complete the threat cycle and rest, reset and resume normal functioning. Consequently, the brain remains under a constant barrage of noradrenaline, adrenaline and cortisol, making individuals overly reactive and resistant to subsequent changes. Thus it becomes imperative to manage the 'peaks and valleys' of the brain's threat system.

To effectively manage change with the brain in mind, leaders must embrace and implement processes and best practices that foster commotion and calmness, 'hunting' and celebration, while ensuring these elements co-exist harmoniously.

In summary, to adapt positively to change and fortify resilience, it is essential to recreate the natural 'highs and lows' of the neurobiology and brain waves, allowing us to anticipate and predict the inevitability of 'errors'. However, this must be achieved without succumbing to 'burnout' and the potential adverse effects on our bodies and brains.

Once again, the intention is to purposely 'trick/hack' our brain with practical strategies to:

a Manage the peaks

b Promote the valleys

Especially during periods of change and uncertainty, where the risk of remaining in a constant state of 'hunting' and stress is high, it is more vital than ever to ensure that fluctuations in the brain activity occur.

Dimension 5: Manage the peaks

What do we mean?

The aim is to identify 'controllable' opportunities for high levels of stimulation (in neuroscience this is called high levels of brain arousal) to promote motivation and resilience. This involves adopting processes and techniques that are sustainable, striking a balance between anticipation and celebration.

Focus on small cycles of change

Working in short, focused periods on small cycles of changes (sprints) allows those delivering the change and those impacted by it to rapidly elevate neurobiology levels (adrenaline, noradrenaline, dopamine, oxytocin) and enhance focus and engagement. After each sprint, the team reflects and celebrates its small achievements, which naturally lowers the levels of the brain activity relatively quickly.

To prevent the brain from becoming overwhelmed by frequent, almost constant small changes, it's vital within an agile culture to allocate time effectively in the 'valleys'. This includes moments for mind wandering, quality relaxation, short periods of 'ideas' incubation' or discovering new ways for the brain to reset before diving into the next sprint (refer to the 'Promote the valleys' section later in this chapter for more details and examples).

By working for a short period of time, we accelerate the pace of our work. We instinctively know that we do not have time to waste. This increases our focus on what we have to do and our commitment to getting it done. It avoids the negative impact of delay discounting, which is when the brain de-prioritizes an issue because it is so far in the future it doesn't feel real to us.

By outlining the expected outcomes over the life of the change we signpost to the brain what will happen next, which generates a sense of certainty without compromising the benefit of some moderate levels of adrenaline. We also reduce the level of unwanted stress because we do not give the brain lots of detail about things that will happen in the future, reducing the risk of overload as the brain does not have to hold onto information that is not immediately useful for it.

The smaller the scale of the work, the less the brain becomes overwhelmed by the things it needs to remember. This leads to higher levels of concentration and therefore higher levels of productivity. This is important in a world of continual interruptions, as with a shorter time period we are more likely to get something finished before we have to give our attention to another piece of work.

These small cycles increase the frequency of achievement and the associated celebration of those achievements.

However, one thing that these incremental plans do badly is allow for a re-set before we move on to the next cycle of work. We need to build time into these plans to stay in celebration longer, so that the emotional imprint of the positive feelings of achievement is greater. We also need to build in time to review how we worked, allowing our brain time for mind wandering and incubation of ideas, otherwise any outcome from our retrospectives will not be built into how we approach how we work in the next round.

Challenge the status quo

We can purposely raise moderate levels of adrenaline and noradrenaline to enhance focus and attention by fostering an organizational culture that encourages individuals and teams to challenge the status quo and create 'good trouble'. However, mechanisms must be in place to allow individuals to switch in and out, reset and celebrate as needed.

To create environments where challenging the status quo can occur safely, it's crucial to:

a Ensure psychological safety (no fear of individuals being penalized or judged for making mistakes)

b Empower individuals to make decisions

These measures will naturally enable individuals to fluctuate between 'peaks' and 'valleys' as they will feel more autonomy and control over the perceived 'threats' and 'rewards.' This approach promotes resilience and increases the sense of reward and pleasure.

To be able to challenge something, we need our own ideas. Review the techniques in the 'Promote curiosity' section for suggestions on how we can strengthen our idea-generating capability. To create the conditions for having our own ideas, also review the sections on mind wandering and incubation periods in the 'Promoting the valleys' section.

We need to feel safe to raise our ideas so review the section on creating psychological safety in Chapter 4.

Challenging the status quo means not settling for the first solution but continuing to question until more options emerge.

EXAMPLE

We know one high-performing team who have a simple process for making decisions. Whatever the question, they view it from three perspectives:

FIGURE 6.3 Three factors to challenge the status quo

1.
KEEP THINGS AS THEY ARE -
THE DO NOTHING OPTION

2.
KEEP DOING IT BUT DO
IT DIFFERENTLY

3.
CHANGE HOW MUCH IS DONE
- DO MORE OR LESS OF IT

EXAMPLE

Another team challenges any discussion with the question 'What if this goes wrong?' This is because when someone proposes a course of action, they usually describe the 'happy path', assuming that everything happens as expected. To counter this, they ask for a more pessimistic assessment.

If we challenge the status quo we are more likely to avoid confirmation bias (looking for information that supports our beliefs rather than for evidence suggesting we are wrong) and stereotyping people (making broad judgments, such as that women or minorities don't make good leaders).

Challenging the status quo supports other dimensions of the PEPE© model.

TABLE 6.2

Dimension	Activity	Contribution
Reduce perception of pain	Being valued and respected	When we challenge the status quo, we can feel an increase in the amount of respect others have for us as they listen to our opinions.

(continued)

TABLE 6.2 (Continued)

Dimension	Activity	Contribution
Reduce perception of pain	Psychological safety	For individuals to feel comfortable challenging the status quo it is vital to create psychological safety, so they do not feel pressure of being judged or penalized for mistakes or doing things differently.
Reduce perception of pain	Growth and fixed mindset	We need to support a growth mindset and allow individuals to feel comfortable with failure as opportunities for learning in order to challenge the status quo.
Releasing energy	Implement a culture of bravery and risk-taking	We gain a burst of dopamine when we use our courage to challenge pre-existing behaviours and values.

Promote flow

Flow is a cognitive state characterized by complete immersion in an activity, marked by intense focus, creative engagement and the distortion of time and space. It was initially conceptualized by psychologist Mihaly Csikszentmihalyi in the 1970s. Recent neuroscience research has revealed that during a flow state, all neurobiology markers reach peak levels, facilitating peak performance. The remarkable aspect of flow is that once an individual exits this state, the neurobiology markers quickly return to normal or even lower levels.

Implementing practices, processes and activities that foster flow is a great way to keep brain chemistry fluctuating and facilitate engagement with change.

Key conditions to promote flow include working within a ratio of 60 per cent challenge vs. 40 per cent skills. Individuals and teams need to perceive the challenge as slightly exceeding their skill level to achieve peak performance and full engagement. They should feel confident that they possess the necessary skills to participate effectively.

This invites leaders and managers to consider this ratio when designing the new state and ensure that those affected by change and their teams align closely with this ratio from the outset of the change. It is vital to ensure that the challenge posed by the new change remains within this ratio. The organization

FIGURE 6.4 Achieving a state of flow

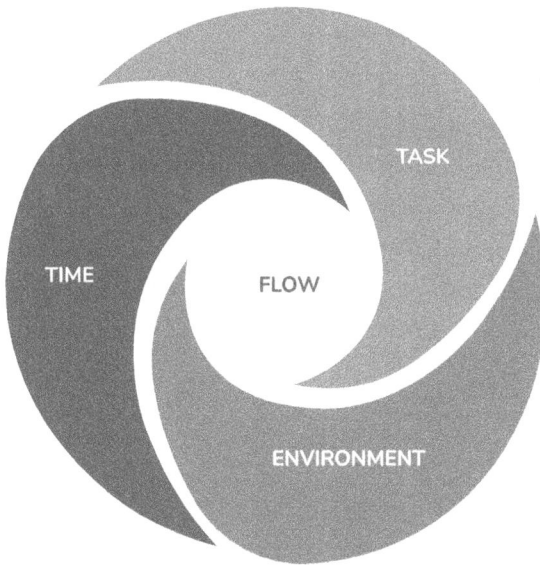

must maintain a balance between skills and task allocation, adhering to the 60:40 challenge/skill ratio rule.

Another crucial condition for promoting flow is minimizing physical and emotional distractions during each sprint as much as possible.

We can do a lot to influence our ability to achieve a state of flow, by addressing the factors shown in Figure 6.4.

TASK

To lose yourself in a task, you need something that achieves the right mix of skills and personal effort.

- Skills – you need something that stretches your ability, but if you pick something that you do not have the skills to do, you will feel anxious and your negative inner voice doubting your ability will prevent you from losing yourself in the task.
- Personal effort – effort can be mental or physical. It is easy to imagine physical effort, as we can visualize lifting a heavy weight. If it is too heavy you cannot lift it, so you cannot do the work so you cannot lose yourself in a state of flow. If the weight is too light, it requires no effort at all. You are not being stretched, so you do not need to concentrate, so you cannot

FIGURE 6.5 Identifying tasks that create a state of flow

Task

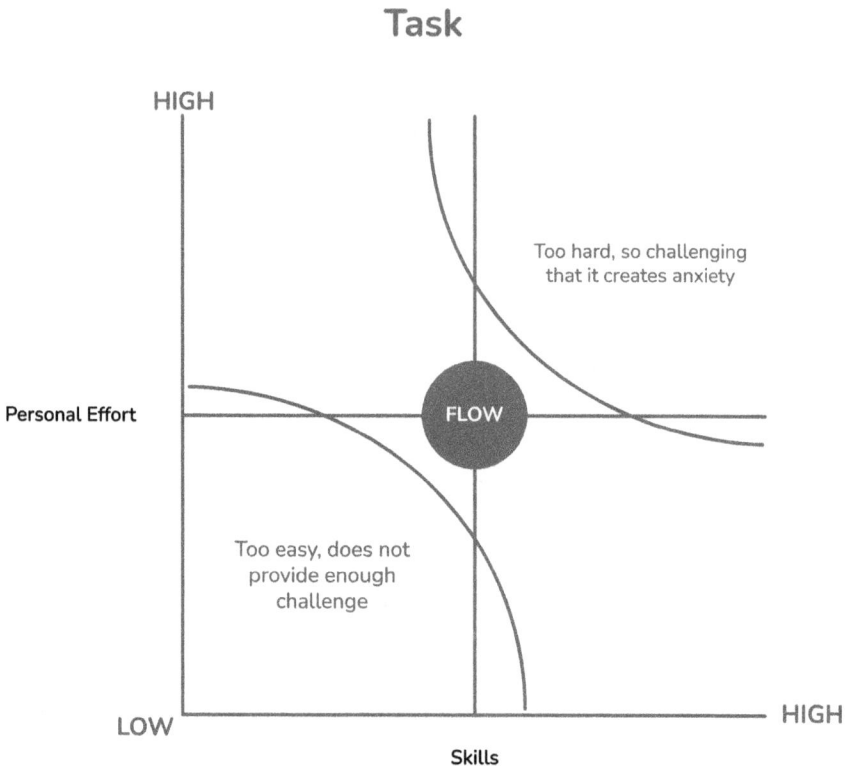

lose yourself in the task. It is the same for mental effort. Think about something that requires some 'push' from you. Perhaps something you are not confident about, so you have to apply effort to quieten your 'imposter syndrome'. Perhaps it is something that goes against how you like to work. For example, high levels of concentration, when you are used to working in short bursts, enjoying doing many things at once.

You will not achieve flow with a task that is very easy; you need something that requires effort and uses your skills. It must provide some stretch, so that you gain a feeling of accomplishment as you work.

You need to know you are making progress so identify success points that you need to achieve. If you are writing a document, this could be word count; if you are preparing a presentation, this could be number of slides. For an event, it could be the number of responses from those you are inviting.

TIME

Make the time available, ensuring that the time you set aside is enough to lose yourself in the task, without having to keep checking your watch.

Select the time of day when you are at your most focused and most creative.

ENVIRONMENT

You need to be able to focus in the present moment, so you need to remove all distractions. At work you need to remove yourself from messages; emails and instant messages will capture your attention and bring you out of your task focus.

EXAMPLE

Writing this book is the right task for me to achieve a state of flow because it stretches my skills and requires personal effort.

To write this book, I have applied these three factors to give myself the greatest chance of achieving a state of flow, which enables me to complete the task and enjoy the work. Writing a book is a tremendous effort, which needs to be fitted into an already busy schedule. This means giving up personal time to make room for the extra work, which impacts time for me and time I would normally spend with my family.

I am aware that when I am in a state of flow my productivity is higher, and I enjoy myself more. But I need to prepare the tasks I am doing otherwise the work feels too difficult and I find reasons not to get started. I make sure I am clear which section of the book I am going to concentrate on. I prepare my research papers so I can easily review them. I make a list of the points I want to make, so that I can track my progress as I complete each paragraph and design each diagram.

I create the time for writing at the time of the day when I am most productive, which for me is the early mornings. It doesn't matter whether it is a workday or a weekend, I think better at sunrise, I have more creative thoughts, I connect the dots more (insights) and I write faster.

To create the right environment, I need to remove all distractions – people and technology. I turn off my emails, put my phone out of sight and go into my office before anyone else arrives who will interrupt me.

Promoting flow supports other dimensions of the PEPE© model.

TABLE 6.3

Dimension	Activity	Contribution
Reducing the perception of pain	Growth and fixed mindset	One of the conditions to go into flow is having no concern with the outcomes as they are in any cases opportunities for growth.
Increase pleasure	Celebrate often and bring laughter	Flow will lead to achievements, often new ideas as well as increased productivity and achievements from this productivity which are to be celebrated and enjoyed.
Releasing energy	Provide opportunities for people to come up with their own insights	Being lost in our work creates a state of concentration which enables the brain to connect pieces of information, leading to 'aha' moments.

Promote curiosity

Research demonstrates that learning and curiosity release dopamine, which drives peaks of motivation and excitement within individuals. Curiosity is a fundamental driver of engagement with change.

Leaders and managers should inspire curiosity within their teams by being curious themselves, asking and responding to open-ended questions, practising and encouraging active listening, and providing resources for self-learning.

Triggers for curiosity are humility, modesty, humbleness.

EXAMPLE

We work with the CEO of a global transport company. When he is explaining a situation, he will often describe his solutions or actions that he thinks he should take, but he always reminds everyone that he has ideas, but he might not have the right ideas, so please ask questions, challenge his assumptions, add, subtract and build upon what he has said.

To encourage us to know more about things, use these practical ideas:

- List what you don't know and look it up – general search tools like Google, or use ChatGPT to get fuller answers.

- Have a list of open questions to ask – when you are reading and when you are listening to others.

- Observe closely, increase what you notice – how long, who is involved, what are their inputs, what are they producing etc.

- Make it easy to find information – identify trusted sources of information and regularly review their output.

- In brainstorming sessions with others, provide information with only a loose connection to the work to generate discussion and ideas

---

EXAMPLE

We have a client who regularly provides open training sessions on subjects tangential to but not directly supportive of their work.

For example, although few of the staff are involved with pricing work for clients, every year at the company away day there is a 'Where does the money go?' session to explain all the costs involved in delivering a service to a client.

This enables the group to discover information about suppliers, costs and profit margins that they are not exposed to as part of their jobs. It triggers questions and ideas and leads to innovation in service design and delivery, sales material and process efficiencies.

EXAMPLE

We know a talented people leader who inspires her team to be curious. She ensures that whenever anyone asks a why question she congratulates them for asking. Before she answers, she always asks why they want to know, as that demonstrates she is also curious.

Even if she does not have the time to answer them in that moment, she agrees a time when she will, and she offers to share the answer with the rest of the team. She explains that if one person has asked the question there might be a couple more thinking the same thing.

Promoting curiosity supports other dimensions of the PEPE© model.

TABLE 6.4

Dimension	Activity	Contribution
Reducing the perception of pain	Growth mindset	Curiosity is one of the building blocks of a growth mindset, because it creates the questioning attitude that leads to openness to change and flexibility.
Reducing the perception of pain	Being valued and respected	We can use our curiosity to develop feelings of self-worth, as we recognize how seeking out new knowledge increases our skills and abilities, which increases our value to our organization.
Increase pleasure	Common goals and objectives	We are more likely to agree the common objectives if we are willing to be curious in our discussions with others. We will seek out greater understanding of their reasons for their objectives, which will help us find common ground between our views and theirs.
Reduce mismatch between reality and expectations	Provide the right amount of training at the right time	Adults learn best when they need to know something. Using our curiosity, we identify a need for more information, which makes us open to training.

Dimension 6: Promote the valleys

What do we mean?

The aim is to establish 'controllable' methods and processes that allow the brain to experience periods of lower levels of stimulation (arousal) in their neurobiology activity and brain wave activity.

Descending into valleys from the brain's perspective is crucial for preventing burnout and promoting the activation of the brain's 'liking' and 'at the moment' reward system, which ultimately facilitates the positive adaptation to change in individuals. By intentionally creating habits and engaging in activities that induce relaxation and lower levels of arousal, individuals can effectively regulate their brain's activity to reset.

This intentional regulation is closely tied to the brain's default mode network (DMN), which is a network of the brain regions that are active during restful states (not focused on the external environment) and involved in internal thought processes, self-reflection and imagination. Activation of the DMN is associated with introspection, creativity and problem-solving, making it essential for cognitive and emotional well-being.

Furthermore, the activation of the parasympathetic nervous system, often associated with rest and relaxation, plays a pivotal role in facilitating these valleys within the brain. The parasympathetic system promotes a state of rest and recovery by counterbalancing the stress response of the sympathetic nervous system (refer to Chapter 1 for more details). This activation leads to the release of neurotransmitters such as acetylcholine, which is known to induce feelings of relaxation, contentment and learning. By engaging the parasympathetic system and releasing acetylcholine, individuals can be more open to learn and to adapt positively to change.

When we need to enter the valley, encourage people to do a self-check for when they need to reset. Questions can include:

- Are you noticing you are making more mistakes than usual?
- Are you finding that regular tasks take longer?
- Are you finding yourself getting annoyed at things that do not usually bother you?
- Are you quick to defend yourself if someone questions work you have done?
- Are you suspicious of the motives of others?
- Are you less willing to share your ideas and your work with others?
- Are you unwilling to collaborate with others?
- Are you forgetting small pieces of information you would normally remember?
- Do you feel a sense of anxiety the night before work or when you wake up in the morning?
- Are you having difficulty sleeping?

An example of self-checking to know if you need a break is to ask yourself how you are feeling on a scale of 1–10 and ask if you feel more or less confident than you felt yesterday.

FIGURE 6.6 Example of scale for assessing feelings

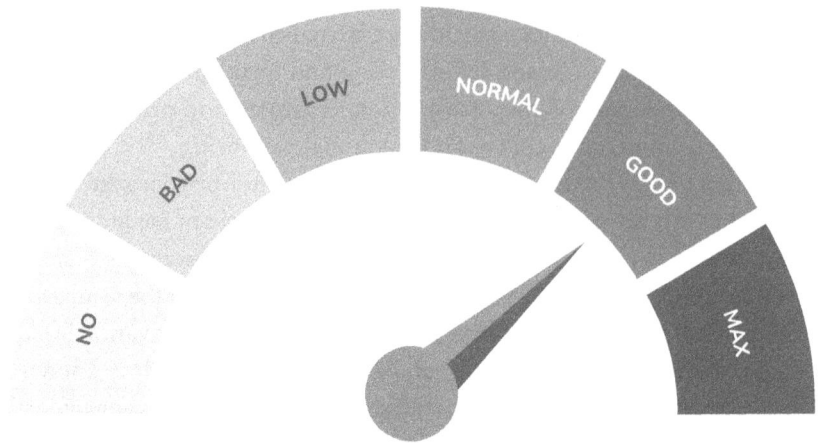

Mind wandering matters

Mind wandering is a major activity in the brain that spontaneously occurs when individuals are not engaged in cognitively demanding tasks.[4] It involves uncontrolled, spontaneous thoughts unrelated to the current task or environment. Mind wandering activates the brain's default network, a network of regions active when the mind is at rest and not focused on the external environment.

While mind wandering may not always be welcome – sometimes leading to rumination, distraction or procrastination – it is a powerful tool for generating new ideas, consolidating memories and allowing the brain to rest from intense cognitive states and high cerebral activity.

EXAMPLE

In one organization, innovation and continuous improvement are core values so they encourage idea generation by everyone. They encourage their version of mind wandering, called 'creative review'. They encourage team leaders to hold team meeting sessions each month for staff to focus on creativity and play with new ideas in a safe environment.

They have set a criterion for this time to be effective, which is that it must be intentional, otherwise, whilst individuals might take the time to think and be creative, it might not produce useful results.

Intentional means they ask individuals to book this type of session especially if they have had a relevant experience:

1 If they have recently undertaken some training, they should book a creative review so that they can consolidate their learning by reviewing what they learnt and how they have applied this learning to their work.

2 If they have a problem that needs a solution, they should book a creative review to focus solely on the solution for the problem rather than the problem itself.

Cultivating a habit of intentionally allocating time for mind wandering can coexist with periods of focused attention. Although we cannot direct our brain to wander in specific ways, we can create conditions conducive to a more positive and creative mental state during rest periods.

For instance, taking breaks from tasks to engage in relaxing activities that do not require intense focus, like going for a walk, can reduce mental fatigue, restore focus and enhance creative thinking through mind wandering.

Another approach involves designating 'quiet spaces' within the workplace where employees can go to take breaks or engage in quiet, non-stimulating activities such as reading or meditation.

Promoting mind wandering can also involve encouraging diverse perspectives within teams, fostering idea sharing and focusing on brainstorming solutions rather than dwelling solely on problems.

Leaders and managers play a crucial role in creating this space within change activities to promote 'valleys' and fluctuations in different states of mind, ultimately reducing resistance to change.

Particularly when there is a risk of being overloaded due to a continuous stream of sprints, leaders and managers should systematically allocate time between sprints for semi-directed mind wandering and design team activities that support it.

EXAMPLE

We know an organization that has started to encourage mind wandering as part of their cultural shift to becoming a more innovative company. They have re-labelled mind wandering time from being viewed as unproductive (especially by some senior managers) to productive time by calling it Innovation Time. They encourage staff to book this into their schedules and to get away from their desks to do this.

EXAMPLE

As consultants we were involved in a project to create relaxation spaces with the brain in mind to intentionally promote habits of mind wandering within individuals in the organization. In a joint effort between HR, facilities and senior leaders of the operations and sales teams, specific areas in the office were designated where employees could go to relax and unwind. In fact, the programme was announced and communicated as a priority for all the sales and operations teams (including senior leaders) to create habits of spending time in these designated areas. These spaces were equipped with comfortable seating, calming deco and some amenities like relaxing gadgets and soft music to promote relaxation and encourage mind wandering.

Mind wandering supports other dimensions of the PEPE© model (Table 6.5).

TABLE 6.5

Dimension	Activity	Contribution
Releasing energy	Provide opportunities for people to come up with their own insights	The conditions for mind wandering enable our brains to connect information in new ways, leading to 'aha' moments.
Save energy	Make it local – personalize it	One of the aspects of allowing our minds to wander is that our brains will inevitably 'localize' our thoughts – asking 'What is in it for me ?' and enabling us to find personal meaning and value from the change.
Save energy	Build habits and routines purposely	It is fundamental to create habits for mind wandering so we can ensure it happens at an unconscious level and therefore has more opportunity to happen during times of high pressure and stress where typically we 'do not have time' for mind wandering.

Allow incubation periods

Traditional theories of creativity have emphasized the significance of incubation time. When individuals encounter problems they can't immediately solve, setting them aside for a period – the incubation period – often leads to fresh insight that helps resolve them.

From a neuroscience perspective, incubation periods entail shifting from beta waves (associated with attention and focus) to alpha, theta and delta waves (associated with relaxation, unfocused thoughts, daydreaming and deep sleep). The shift reinforces the concept of creativity and is also linked to well-being, adaptation, healing and facilitating change.

While mind wandering, as explained in the point above, can be considered a relatively short incubation period when brain waves move into a slower rhythm (alpha), 'allowing incubation periods to occur' refers to more extended periods like sleep, power naps, meditation, reflection days or learning workshops.

The intention is to proactively provide the brain with slow rhythm patterns, allowing it to consolidate information, heal and unconsciously facilitate adaptation by creating new connections in the brain.

Sponsors should ensure that the Change Plan includes tasks that actively and systematically promote incubation periods. These periods help individuals impacted by change to explore new approaches and adapt by enabling the unconscious mind to establish new connections related to the new state.

The challenge of applying activities to create a valley is making the time to do them. We make the time for important tasks, so we need to ensure that time to reflect and reset is one of them, hence the importance of creating habits rather than consciously thinking about it.

Many time management techniques prioritize urgent and important tasks. We can define a valley as important because of the benefits it creates for our brain. It is harder to label something as urgent if it does not have a deadline. In these situations, we can define urgency by the amount of time since it last happened. Creating a valley becomes increasingly urgent the longer we leave it.

EXAMPLE

I know that if I haven't had time for what I call 'a good think' every four to five weeks I get increasingly panicky. My job is to share knowledge and help others develop their capability. This means knowing lots of information and having lots of ideas. Every few weeks I like to spend a Saturday morning reviewing articles, reading books, and listening to webinars and podcasts. This provides sources for new ideas and sometimes will produce insights for new products and services for my clients.

Applying the agile concepts of incremental working helps ensure there are planned times to reflect and celebrate our achievements.

Often, these formally timed retrospectives are too infrequent for our brains to enjoy the positive chemicals that come from personal reflection. We need to create a habit that includes some of these activities every day.

EXAMPLE

I have named this activity 'valley time' and to include it in my day I have had to alter my morning routine. To ensure I have an hour every day where I can think rather than do, I come into the office an hour earlier than I need to. I also protect the times that I go to yoga, as this is my time to unwind.

I have created a ritual at the start and the end of the day where I identify:

- *A situation that has been successfully resolved, recognizing the release of anxiety.* This week I have decided to change one of my suppliers, who has been sub-standard for most of the year. This is time to recognize how much time I will save not having to chase them and not having to listen to their excuses.

- *A decision that has been taken so the options no longer need to be agonized over.* I have decided when to hold a course, so now my team can advertise the dates.

- *Something I am pleased to have achieved so I can congratulate myself.* Yesterday this was the creation of an agenda for a demonstration that has been in development for several weeks.

- *An event I am looking forward to.* It doesn't have to be big, just something that will make me smile. This morning it was remembering that my colleague is coming to my house so we can work together today.

To identify times when you can build in reflect and reset, review:

- Each day – can you find 30 minutes to an hour that you can block out and keep free from distractions?

- Each week – are you creating these times at least several times a week, even if you cannot manage it every day?

Allowing incubation periods supports other dimensions of the PEPE© model.

TABLE 6.6

Dimension	Activity	Contribution
Releasing energy	Provide opportunities for people to come up with their own insights	Incubation requires the right environment, so build time in your Change Plan for individuals to reflect on information and experiences.
Save energy	Provide the right amount of information at the right time	To get the most from incubation of information, we need to ensure we are not asking the brain to process too high a volume of information.
Save energy	Make it local – personalize it	Make sure the information that is being incubated is relevant, specific to their role in the change.
Save energy	Build habits and routines purposely	Building habits of incubation time is paramount during times of change, high pressure and complexity otherwise the brain will give priority to the immediate need or fire drill rather than allow time to reflect.

Promote mindfulness

Mindfulness is a mental state characterized by a complete presence in the current moment, accompanied by awareness of our thoughts, sensations and feelings without judgements.

Over the past decade, extensive research has investigated brain activity during mindfulness practice, revealing that it changes both brain function and physical structure. For example, mindfulness has been associated with increased grey matter in the hippocampus, a region of the limbic system linked to memory consolidation and emotional regulation.[5] Practising mindfulness helps adaptability to change, reduces hypervigilance and enhances the experience of reward and pleasure. Additionally, it increases self-reflection time, a valuable tool during periods of change and transformation.

The anterior singular cortex, an area in the brain connected to self-control and perception of pain, has also been proven to change with the practice of mindfulness.

To stop over-thinking we should engage at least three senses at the same time:

1 See

2 Hear

3 Touch

4 Smell

5 Taste

EXAMPLE

Since learning this aspect of neuroscience, I have a plant on my desk, so that when I want to change what I am thinking about, and let my mind think about anything it wants, I take a few minutes to touch the leaves, smell the earth and look at the plant.

In my home office, my dog sits with me and I cuddle her and play games with her, so I touch, see, smell and hear her, engaging four senses. It is a regular habit because she regularly demands my attention.

EXAMPLE

I purposely created a habit of drinking sparkling water when I feel under pressure, stress or I need a quick time to reset. Drinking sparkling water in a mindful way allows me to focus on the bubbles coming out of the bottle (sight), on the noise the bubbles make (sound) and the feeling of the bubbles going through my throat while I am drinking it (touch). By focusing on the three senses at the same time it allows my mind to remain 'at the present moment' and to stop overthinking.

Promote mindfulness supports other dimensions of the PEPE© model.

TABLE 6.7

Dimension	Activity	Contribution
Releasing energy	Provide opportunities for people to come up with their own insights	Mind wandering occurs when we are not under pressure to perform. Balance time for achievement alongside time for reflection.

(continued)

TABLE 6.7 (Continued)

Dimension	Activity	Contribution
Promote valleys	Mind wandering matters	Mindfulness encourages the conditions for mind wandering.
Reduce pain	Growth and fixed mindset	Mindfulness helps to reduce stress and anxiety, a big driver of adopting a fixed mindset. In order to promote a growth mindset, we need to keep levels of stress lower.

Balance anticipation and pleasure

As outlined in Chapter 1, scientists have established[6] that the brain has two distinct reward systems driven by different neurotransmitters. One system is dopamine-driven and activated during the 'wanting' or 'hunting' mode associated with working toward objectives or experiencing the thrill of achievement. This produces feelings of motivation and excitement.

The other system, driven by endorphins, is the 'liking' or 'pleasure' part of the brain's reward system, also known as the 'in-the-moment' reward. Rather than being driven by any sense of wanting, it is purely about enjoying the present moment.

To prevent demotivation, addiction and burnout, it is essential to find a balance between these two systems – what we refer to as a balance between 'peaks' and 'valleys' of dopamine and endorphins. This balance can be achieved by dedicating time to celebrate after each iteration and spending longer periods 'in the moment' as reviewed in the 'Increase pleasure' section in Chapter 4.

Particularly during periods of change, it is especially important to systematically plan activities that encourage pure enjoyment of the present moment before engaging in the next 'hunt' or iteration. This allows neurobiology stimulation to fluctuate into the valleys and assists in coping with change and reducing resistance.

It is an invitation to managers to incorporate time in their change plans for activities that enable teams to remain in the 'liking' or 'pleasure' state to balance the brain's reward system.

EXAMPLE

I am lucky that after delivering a training course, many of my attendees get in touch and write thoughtful thank you messages, describing how much they enjoyed the training, how much they have learned and the difference it is making to their confidence.

I have developed a habit of printing these messages and putting them in a 'compliments scrapbook', which gives me a reminder of all the good things that people say about my work.

I do not look at this book often, but just knowing it exists helps me stay in the 'pleasure' zone before I rush off to deliver another course.

Increased pleasure means increased sense of belonging. The bonus of having this compliments scrapbook is that by looking through all the thank yous it reminds me to get in touch with people I haven't spoken to in a while. Connecting with my network in this way gives me a bonding feeling, which makes me feel good.

Balancing anticipation and pleasure supports other dimensions of the PEPE© model.

TABLE 6.8

Dimension	Activity	Contribution
Releasing energy	Create anticipation and promote hunting	Establish clear outcomes that stimulate anticipation.
Save energy	Build habits and routines purposely	Creating habits of remaining longer in the 'flavouring' and 'enjoyment' helps to balance the pressure of being on the 'go' all the time.
Increase pleasure	Celebrate often and bring laughter	Find more opportunities to celebrate achievements.
Increase pleasure	Increase sense of belonging	Balancing the time we spend working towards achievement of objectives and time for celebration and reflection helps to increase the sense of belonging in teams and give them more time to reflect together.

Notes

1   D Scheinost et al. Fluctuations in global brain activity are associated with changes in whole-brain connectivity of functional networks, *IEEE Transactions in Bio-Medical Engineering*, 2016, 63(12): 2540–49

2   Capability for Change Survey 2023, https://capabilityforchange.com/survey/ (archived at https://perma.cc/U4MD-JKHV)

3   P Sterling. Allostasis: A model of predictive regulation, *Physiology & Behavior*, 2012, 106(1): 5–15

4   M Bar (2022) *Mindwandering: How your constant mental drift can improve your mood and boost your creativity*, Hachette Go

5   BK Hölzel et al. Mindfulness practice leads to increases in regional brain gray matter density, *Psychiatry Research*, 2011, 191(1): 36–43

6   K Berridge and M Kringelbach. Pleasure systems in the brain, *Neuron*, 2015, 86(3): 646–64

07

Error detection

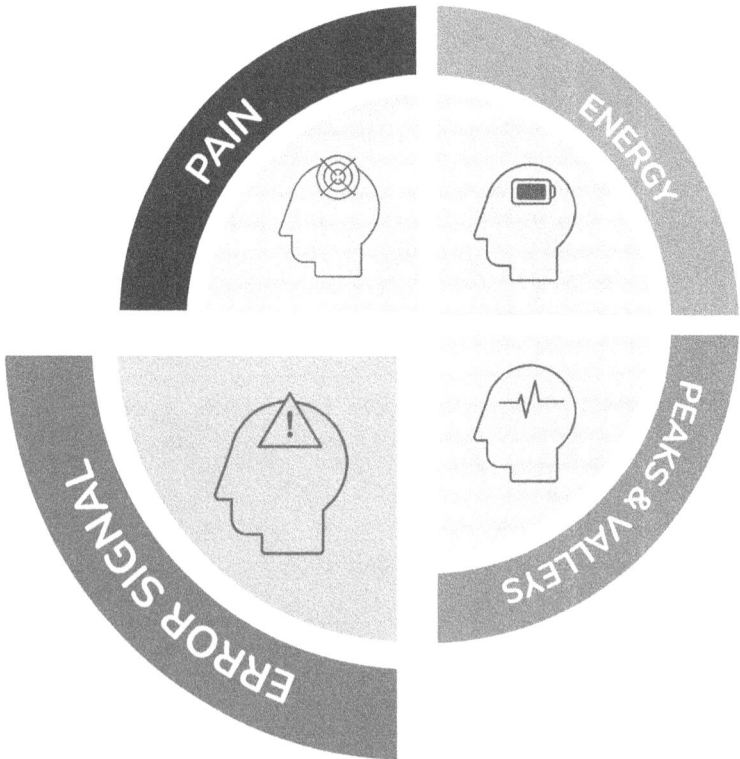

PEPE© model: Error domain

The human brain is a remarkable 'anticipation machine'. Its primary function revolves around continuously using past experiences and current information to make predictions about the future. This unique ability assists in planning, preparation and decision-making, ultimately helping us avoid future adversities. This predictive capacity is a significant evolutionary gift, supporting the survival and continuity of the species.

Recent theories suggest that the neocortex, the largest part of the cerebral cortex, may primarily serve as a predictor of 'future states'.[1] In an ever-changing world, these predictions require constant updates and fine-tuning based on new, sometimes conflicting information, resulting in prediction error signals.

A prediction error signal is essentially the disparity between the expected outcome and the outcome result, the mismatch between expectation and reality. This discrepancy can either be positive or adverse, leading to a corresponding release of a positive or negative signal in the brain. These prediction error signals are fundamental to the learning process: a positive signal encourages openness and motivation towards change (reward signal), while an adverse signal fosters resistance and demotivation (threat signal).

Numerous structures and neurons in the brain encode these error signals, including dopaminergic neurons, noradrenaline neurons, striatum, basal ganglia and amygdala among others.[2]

Demands made by change and uncertainty

Change disrupts an individual's ability to predict the future using past experiences, as this ability is closely linked to the certainty of future events.

When the status quo is interrupted, the amygdala becomes activated and the brain becomes hypervigilant regarding potential threats. Depending on past experiences or available information about the future state, the brain will release either a positive or adverse signal, leading the individual to feel motivated or demotivated about the change. The brain has a natural bias toward maintaining the status quo (safety), relying on past experiences to make predictions about the future (from an evolutionary perspective it protects the survival and reproduction of the human species from an unknown territory).

Any type of change, whether behavioural, environmental, procedural or biological, generates a prediction error signal (positive or adverse) unless reality perfectly aligns with the expectations. This error signal serves to update the prediction system, preparing the individual for similar changes in the future.

Here's how the brain responds to different scenarios:

a If expectations are completely met and satisfactory, there will be no prediction error signal (no activation of dopaminergic neurons in the limbic system).

b If the reward exceeds expectations or the reward is entirely perceived as positive unexpected, it triggers a strong positive signal, leading to increased dopamine release and strong motivation.

c If the reward falls short of expectations, the negative signal inhibits neuronal activity, suppressing dopamine release and causing adverse error signal, resulting in demotivation and resistance to change.

When managing change with the brain in mind, it is important to set realistic expectations among those facing changes to ensure a positive signal is released. Leaders must strive to exceed or at least meet expectations with reality to prevent adverse prediction error signals in the brains of those facing changes, which can lead to stronger resistance to change in the future.

Organizations should also foster a positive change culture that systematically supports a culture of positive prediction errors, where reality consistently meets or surpasses expectations. This approach keeps individuals motivated and receptive to new changes. Failure to do so may lead individuals and the 'consolidated brain' of the organization to develop a negative memory of change, resulting in negative error signals whenever the status quo is disrupted, making the organization increasingly resistant to change over time.

Some individuals might learn from the 'error' and positively adapt to the observed reality. However, in other individuals (especially when individuals approach the challenge with a fixed mindset), experiencing frequent negative mismatch between reality and expectations may create cynicism as a defence mechanism against the discomfort of acknowledging a mismatch. Over time, the brain becomes more skilled at processing information through a cynical lens, solidifying the individual's pessimistic outlook, which could cause an 'emotionally contagious' cynicism within the team or organization.

Putting prediction error into practice

The objective is to effectively manage expectations among those impacted, including the size of those expectations. This approach serves two key purposes:

a Reduce the size of the mismatch between reality and expectations (to reduce the prediction error).

b Release positive prediction signals.

Leaders overseeing change play a pivotal role in this process by reinforcing messages in communication, setting realistic yet challenging targets and engaging end-users from the outset and throughout all the phases of the lifecycle so there are no negative, unexpected surprises. Managers can also cultivate familiarity and promote a culture of change, enhancing pattern recognition within the organization, ultimately promoting a culture of positive prediction errors that boosts dopamine levels and motivation within the team, rather than adverse errors.

Dimension 7: Reduce the size of the mismatch between reality and expectation

What do we mean?

The intention is to minimize the impact of the negative prediction error signal, which could be generated if the anticipated expectations do not

FIGURE 7.1 Examples of positive and negative mismatches

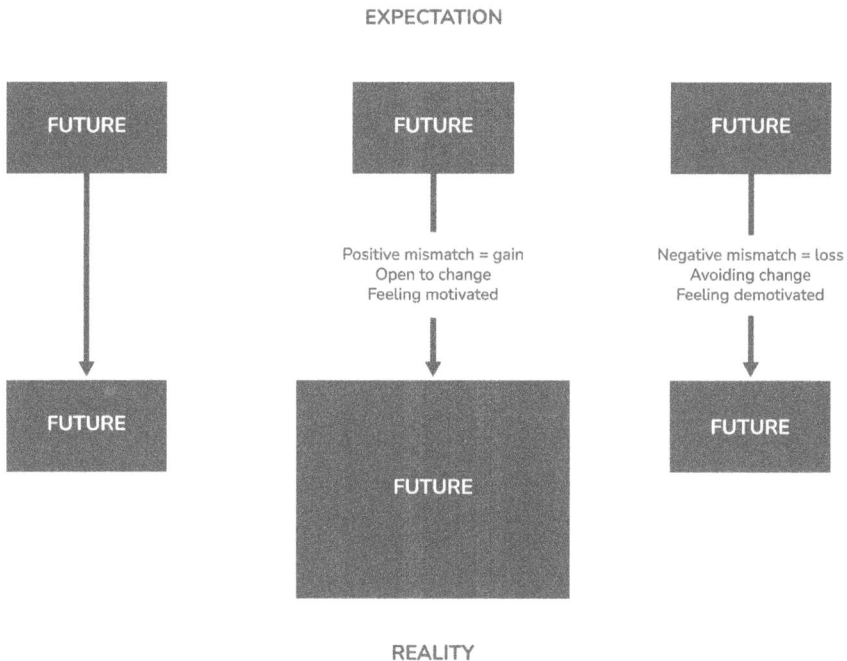

materialize, making dopamine levels fall well below baseline, which in consequence can create a sense of let-down, demotivation and pain.

The higher the size of the gap between expectations and reality, the higher the plunge in dopamine if they are not achieved. On top of managing expectations in those involved to reduce the gap between reality and expectations, it is important to reduce the size of the magnitude in the exposure itself by making expectations smaller and more frequent. We know that even if we do our best in managing expectations, there are possibilities for a negative mismatch to occur. A negative error signal will cause pain and we want to decrease the amount of pain.

Move from big to small

As humans, we tend to place importance on the scale of things: our brains are biased towards big and important, thinking bigger means better. However, when it comes to programmes, team sizes, timelines and predictions, larger scales often translate to greater margins of error, making it more challenging to adapt to and manage change effectively.

Our aim should be to keep the error signal size as small as possible. In our actions, decisions and processes, we should strive to minimize the potential for errors or mistakes. Despite our natural inclination to equate bigger with better, particularly in the context of programmes and projects, embracing efficiency, accuracy and agility means reducing the likelihood of errors associated with larger scales.

In Dimension 4: 'Release energy' in Chapter 5, when we described small but frequent deadlines, we described how to break the end goal into smaller, more specific outcomes.

One of the difficulties of taking a thin slice through the overall outcome of the change and doing a small piece of work is the fear of being criticized:

- Overcoming the fear of leaving things out when we do a small piece of work first:
  o Key customers are not involved initially
  o Not all products and services are included
  o Functions, teams, locations are excluded initially
  o Not all processes are changed, not full coverage of how we work
  o We pilot with only one supplier, putting them in a privileged position

Any one of these can be an uncomfortable conversation – a blocker to keeping things small because to exclusion, we take the default position and include it!

- Have ready-made phrases for the justification for leaving things out:
  - Quicker confirmation that the change works – don't waste others' time, don't create more rework than necessary if it doesn't work
  - Get certainty of the results with the minimum disruption to business as usual
  - Fewer resources needed to achieve the results so less pressure on business as usual
  - Smaller scale of work, easier to measure the results

Focus on incremental/iterative change

This approach involves making gradual, small-scale adjustments over time rather than implementing sweeping large-scale changes all at once. By adopting an incremental approach to change, we inherently reduce the size of the error signal in the brain when reality deviates from expectations. This method can help to manage any negative signals that may arise during change due to discrepancies between expectations and reality.

Incremental change minimizes the gap between expectations and reality, reducing its impact on the threat system, which means people will be less over-whelmed and therefore less resistant to change. Additionally, it allows for the measurement of error signals received by those involved throughout the change process. Encouraging them to express their views and align their expectations with reality throughout the change can significantly help in reducing error signals.

The goal here is to identify opportunities to shrink the error signal by either aligning expectations with reality or ensuring the brain releases a positive signal due to the realization or surpassing of expectations. Employing feedback, particularly through an iterative and incremental approach to delivering change, contributes to this goal. It fosters a strong sense of reward and motivation among those impacted and plays a crucial role in alleviating resistance to change.

Provide training at the right time

Training represents a valuable opportunity to prepare those impacted by the change for new ways of working and shifts them into a more rewarded state by providing assurance regarding their ability and competence to function within the new operational model. It effectively narrows the gap between expectations and reality by imparting the necessary skills, capabilities and confidence for the new way of working.

Training also equips those affected with the ability to anticipate errors and manage expectations. Typically, training is the final milestone before a change goes live, and it often focuses solely on technical skills and abilities. However, managing change with a focus on the brain necessitates anticipating the needs of each individual involved from the outset and making adjustments at various stages of the change journey, rather than solely at the end.

For example, at the beginning of a change process, training may be focused on imparting more 'soft' skills to prepare individuals for the impending transformation, gradually transitioning to more 'technical' skills training based on evolving needs.

Providing training earlier in the process reduces the potential for major error signals to emerge and helps individuals better prepare for the impending change. In essence, when delivered in a timely manner, training becomes a powerful tool for reducing resistance to change, as it goes beyond just providing the required skills and abilities, encompassing the broader spectrum of behavioural and cognitive adjustments needed to thrive in the new environment.

What support does someone need to step out of their comfort zone? Increasingly, organizations are making coaching and learning available on demand to support people at their point of need.

To put these ideas into practice, we can apply a set of principles that reflect how we learn as adults and how we learn in the workplace:

Context – unless we have a reason for learning, adults do not learn. We are too busy and have too many distractions to make time for the joy of learning something new. Within the context of change, we have to make it clear how the learning will create the ability to do something that the learner cannot currently do.

Autonomy – as adults, we do not like to be told what to do, we like to decide for ourselves. This means that choice has to be a fundamental part of the approach to learning – even if there cannot be choice about what is being learnt, there can be choice about how or when the learner undertakes training.

Relevance – we learn best at the point when we need to know something. This means that the learning has to be available when the person encounters a new situation or is facing a problem that they need to solve.

Content – connected to our reason for learning, we are seeking a solution, not just content that explains what we need to do, but also content that explains how to do something.

Dimension 8: Release positive prediction signals

What do we mean?

The intention is to purposely find opportunities that can trigger positive prediction signals to the brain in order to raise dopamine levels from baseline when we need to increase extra motivation, engagement or to reduce resistance to change. An important caveat with strategies that boost dopamine is that they should be intermittent and always making sure they follow the rule of the 'peaks and valleys' to allow the dopaminergic system to reset, otherwise releasing constant and high levels of dopamine all the time can change our brain (due to plasticity) and therefore change the required base line to feel excited and motivated.

Bring familiarity and ensure pattern recognition

Pattern recognition is the remarkable ability of the human brain not only to find patterns but also to logically figure out their implications for future events. Continually seeking patterns in the environment is a cognitive strategy that saves energy in the learning process and sharpens our predictive capabilities.

This innate ability contributes to the assurance of human survival over time by minimizing the likelihood of errors that could threaten our existence and increasing the chances of being rewarded.

Various cognitive and neurobiological studies provide compelling evidence that the brain employs several mechanisms that help 'humans' figure out, in a logical way, what happens next. Some examples of these mechanisms are 'chunking' and 'pattern recognition'.

Chunking is a cognitive process where the brain groups small bits of information into more meaningful and manageable chunks. This makes it easier for the brain to remember, process and absorb new information. For example, if you're trying to memorize a phone number, it's easier to remember it as three chunks (e.g. 555-123-4567) rather than 10 individual digits.

An example of applying this concept to a real-life scenario is when you're given driving directions in an unfamiliar city. Instead of trying to remember each individual turn, you can chunk them together by recognizing patterns in the directions. For instance, you might remember the sequence as 'left-right-left-right' instead of each individual turn. This makes it easier for your brain to remember and follow the directions.

On the other hand, pattern recognition refers to the ability to detect and identify recurring patterns within information or data. This process involves the extraction of features or characteristics that are common among different stimuli or events, and the classification of these stimuli or events based on these features.

In the context of organizational change, pattern recognition can be a useful tool for identifying common themes or trends that emerge from feedback or data collected during the change process. For example, if multiple teams report similar challenges or concerns, this could indicate a recurring pattern or issue that needs to be addressed. By recognizing this pattern and taking action to address it, leaders can improve the success of the change initiative and reduce resistance.

EXAMPLE

We shared this part of the book with a finance manager whose department has been transitioning to a new system over the previous 15 months. He explained that whilst he was not aware he had been asking his team to look for patterns, it was an agenda on the team meetings to share feedback about the new system. To encourage positive feelings, everyone is encouraged to come to the meeting listing three things that they are happy about and one thing that is causing them concern.

As people share their experiences, the information is captured on a virtual whiteboard (they meet virtually). This positive feedback is organized under three headings:

- What system functionality is working well and/or the team are confident about how to use.
- What processes and features are making a positive difference, including fewer mistakes, faster processing, simpler flow of work.
- What steps are now feeling 'normal'.

An outcome of this part of the team meeting is to agree what processes can be documented and confirmed officially as 'this is how we work'.

For the things causing concern, the feedback is grouped into headings:

- Unexpected errors, system not performing as it should or how it needs to.
- More complicated processes, more manual intervention than expected or tolerated.
- Parts of the system that are causing confusion, that the team are still not sure how to use.

The outcome from this part of the meeting is to nominate a couple of team members for each category to act as a 'task force' to resolve the issues via more training, more development work from the IT project team or more process design work with the business analysts.

Similarly, by recognizing positive patterns, such as high levels of engagement or collaboration, leaders can reinforce these behaviours and encourage further adoption.

Another example of pattern recognition could be when an organization is trying to identify areas for improvement in their business processes. By analysing data and identifying patterns of inefficiency or waste, they can make targeted changes to improve their operations and increase productivity. For instance, they may notice a pattern of delays in their supply chain and implement changes to streamline the process, reducing the time and resources required for each step. This can lead to cost savings and improved customer satisfaction.

From a personal change perspective, an example of pattern recognition would be if someone wants to start a new habit of exercising regularly. At first, it may be difficult for them to remember to exercise every day, but as they repeat the behaviour, their brain begins to recognize patterns in their routine. They may notice that exercising in the morning before work is easier to stick to than waiting until the end of the day. They may also start to notice that on days when they exercise, they feel more energized and productive throughout the day. By recognizing these patterns, their brain can start to reinforce the habit of regular exercise, making it easier to maintain in the long term.

The techniques of chunking and pattern recognition are powerful tools when facilitating change and coping with change resistance because they help the brain to release positive signals. Many scientists argue that one of the major functions of emotions such as fear, anger, pleasure and love is to reinforce patterns of particular significance to support survival and reproduction.[3]

For example, recalling the vivid details and emotions associated with a predator attack serves as a survival mechanism, increasing the probability of avoiding similar threats in the future. Similarly, remembering exhaustive and frustrating experiences of consecutive change implementations with no desired results can lead individuals to avoid further changes. These memories of past adversities reinforce patterns of resistance to change.

Conversely, memories of pleasurable change experiences create positive patterns, encouraging individuals to embrace and work towards a new status quo in the future. Such positive memories promote a willingness to adapt and contribute to the success of change initiatives.

Especially during times of change, when the future state is uncertain, the human brain tends to rely on patterns and sequences for decision-making. It prefers the predictability they offer, as this reduces the chance of errors and fosters a sense of security. During periods of change, emotions are heightened to reinforce and memorize these patterns.

Leaders responsible for change play a pivotal role in how change is 'presented' and 'sold' to end-users. By introducing elements of familiarity in the new state, they can reduce the fear of error detection. For example, is there anything that will remain the same for end-users? Are there any patterns in the way the new software would process new data that could help to reduce error messages? Is there any pattern in the way we enter information in the new accounting system that mirrors the old one? What emotions should we be eliciting?

EXAMPLE

As change is continuous our friend has developed a technique for coping with all the differences she experiences at work. She has built the habit of reassuring herself that things are not as uncertain as they appear, by identifying all the things in her life that are still the same. Whenever she adopts a new process, has to use a new system or work on a different assignment, she starts by 'isolating' the change, making sure it is surrounded by everything that has not changed.

In her words, 'This is the quickest way to make me realize that the change is relatively small so it feels less intimidating.'

Her technique is to review her day and remind herself of what has not changed:

- I still have the same smoothie for breakfast.
- I am still working from my kitchen table two days a week; driving to the office three days a week.
- I am still responsible for digital marketing campaigns, dealing with LinkedIn and Google advertising.
- I am still working for the same clients.
- My clients still have the same needs.

She finds these reminders soothing, as she reminds herself that all the things that make her successful and enable her to enjoy her job remain unchanged.

Bringing familiarity and pattern recognition supports other dimensions of the PEPE© model.

TABLE 7.1

Dimension	Activity	Contribution
Energy saving	Create habits and routines	Habits build familiarity because they are an established routine.
Reduce perception of pain	Certainty and assurance	Familiarity creates certainty as the brain knows what is going to happen next.
Reduce perception of pain	Growth and fixed mindset	Creating patterns of learning from failure helps the brain to feel more familiar and comfortable with errors and failure, which in turn encourages the adoption of a growth mindset.

Manage expectations from the beginning and at every stage

As reviewed earlier, a prediction error signal is the difference between the expected outcome and the outcome received or the disparity between expectation and reality.

When managing change, it is important to understand the expectations held by different individuals or groups at every stage, from design to implementation. Not everyone will share the same expectations.

Our expectations are formed from multiple inputs:

- Our past experiences – what went well and badly in previous attempts at similar work.

- Our skills and talents – what we assume to be easy or difficult based on what we are able to do.

- Our current situation – feeling tired and stressed means we are more pessimistic and expect things to go wrong; feeling energized and motivated means we are more optimistic and assume things will be easy and will work first time.

It is helpful to bring all those working on a task together to understand the different perspectives. Using an example of a change to software purchasing procedures, some of those affected expect a 5 per cent saving in costs, others expect better integration between systems, and some expect a reduction in bespoke development.

Reducing the mismatch between expectations and reality should be managed proactively and should be part of the change management activities.

Outlining, documenting and becoming aware of the expectations of all those impacted by the change allows you to take action to minimize error signals associated with unmet expectations from the early stages and therefore reduce the error signals of the change.

Our expectations are often captured at the start of a task in documents including the Change Plan and the Team Charter. Although we might say these are 'living documents' and are updated regularly, very often they are not. When we are busy getting things done, we do not step back and consider what we expect to happen, because our focus is on making progress.

Incorporating interim reviews of our expectations is a good idea, because when we are part-way through the work, if we realize that our results are not going to match our expectations we can:

- step in with activities to improve the chances of achieving the results we expect;

- accept that what we expected to happen is not the best outcome, and we can adopt new expectations based on the results to date.

To build a habit of interim reviews, whenever you return to a piece of work, ask yourself these questions:

- What does a good outcome look like?

- What problems do I expect to encounter?
- What techniques am I going to use?
- What information do I need to get this work finished?
- Do I have access to this information?
- How long do I expect to spend on this work?
- Who do I think will be helpful to me in getting this work done?
- Who do I think is going to cause problems for me?

Any of these questions can highlight a discrepancy between what we assume will happen and what is actually happening, allowing us to re-set our expectations. At this point our brain will suffer some stress, as it recognizes the mismatch, but this will be less stressful than a more significant mismatch at the end of the work when we have no chance to do things differently.

Managing expectations from the beginning at every stage supports other dimensions of the PEPE© model.

TABLE 7.2

Dimension	Activity	Contribution
Reduce perception of pain	Certainty and assurance	When the brain is certain about what will happen next, it has formed an expectation, so we need to understand what these assumptions are so that they can be managed.
Manage the peaks	Focus on small cycles of change	Focusing on smaller cycles of change and smaller tasks makes it easier to achieve expectations, therefore having more opportunities to release positive signals.
Increase pleasure	Common goals and objectives	Managing expectations from the beginning can facilitate creation of common goals and objectives within the team.

Create small habits of providing unexpected rewards

Introducing positive perceived unexpected rewards can trigger positive signals in the brain, reinforcing desirable behaviours. These signals are generated when individuals receive rewards that they were not expecting, triggering the release of dopamine associated with pleasure and positive reinforcement. This release of dopamine creates a positive signal, which reinforces the behaviour that led to the reward.

This can be a powerful tool for creating positive change because we are more likely to repeat behaviours that have been associated with positive outcomes. By creating small habits of providing unexpected rewards, those affected by change are more likely to feel motivated and engaged in the change process, which can lead to greater success in achieving desired outcomes.

Creating small habits of providing unexpected rewards for those affected by the change means regularly surprising them with positive experiences that exceed their expectations.

This approach cultivates engagement, motivation and loyalty among those impacted, creating positive associations with the change initiative.

For example, if you are managing a team working on a new project, you might provide unexpected rewards such as a surprise catered lunch or a small bonus for meeting certain milestones. These small gestures can help to boost morale and keep team members motivated and engaged. Creating small habits of providing unexpected rewards can also be effective with customers or clients. For instance, a company might surprise its customers with a discount or a small gift to show appreciation for their business. This can cultivate customer loyalty and increase the likelihood of repeat business.

EXAMPLE

A friend decided to surprise her team with an awards ceremony at their next face-to-face team meeting. She got the idea from watching the Oscars on TV:

> I made a list of everyone in the team and thought about all the great things they had been doing. Some had been supporting new team members, others had stuck with a problem until it was solved, others had innovative ideas. I decided I didn't have the money to buy gifts, so I created a nice-looking certificate and printed them on card. At the meeting I wanted it to feel like a celebration, so I ordered food and arranged drinks.
>
> I started the meeting with a thank you for everyone, and then presented every team member with their certificate. There were two who had to video call because they could not get to the office so just like the Oscars, I asked a colleague to come and collect their certificate for them.

We took lots of pictures and created a picture board for the office wall as a permanent reminder of our celebration.

Although this is so popular it has become an annual event, I will never forget the surprise and enjoyment this first event created.

Overall, by creating small habits of providing unexpected rewards, individuals are more likely to have a positive view of the change process, leading to higher levels of engagement and motivation and ultimately reducing resistance to change – a valuable tool when dealing with complex, ongoing change.

EXAMPLE

A colleague shares her experience of unexpected rewards:

The impact of rewards was one of the first things I learnt in neuroscience, and I find it so helpful in encouraging my team to adopt new ways of working. My personal criteria for my rewards are:

- Small – I have learnt that something too big can be counterproductive, because it sets an expectation for future rewards, and big rewards apply to big impacts, which are less specific. This means the connection to the desired behaviour can get lost.

- Genuine – the main way I reward people is via praise and encouragement, so I share specific actions and their impact, highlighting why they are helpful.

- In the moment – it is not always possible to immediately share praise with someone, so to ensure I do not forget, I immediately write myself a short email, or if I am somewhere private, I record a short voicenote or video clip and send it to the person.

- Cost effective – I do not have a budget for rewards, so in addition to praise, I keep small chocolate bars in my office to hand out to people in team meetings, or I send a chocolate bar in the post to my remote team members.

For me, rewards have a positive impact on how I feel. I know I am sharing happiness with others, and searching for ways to encourage others means I am always hunting for good news, which is a nice way to spend my time.

Whilst the delivery of the reward needs to be unexpected to be effective, those sponsoring and leading the change need to agree what rewards to use. Rewards available for participating in a change initiative need to be budgeted for and must be in line with the organization's overall rewards strategy, to avoid disincentivizing individuals who are not involved in the change.

Create a culture of asking for and providing positive feedback

Creating a culture of asking for and providing positive feedback within an organization not only promotes professional growth and development but also has profound effects on the brain's neurochemistry.

Positive feedback triggers a cascade of neurochemical responses in the brain, primarily involving the release of dopamine. When individuals receive praise or recognition for their work, dopamine levels increase in brain regions such as the ventral striatum and nucleus accumbens, leading to feelings of reward, motivation and satisfaction.

Moreover, positive feedback not only boosts individual morale but also enhances social bonding and cooperation within teams. When someone receives positive feedback, it not only rewards their individual efforts but also strengthens interpersonal connections and trust among team members. This is due in part to the release of oxytocin, which is associated with social affiliation, empathy and trust. When individuals feel appreciated and valued by their colleagues, oxytocin levels rise, fostering a sense of belonging and unity within the team.

Likewise, providing positive feedback also has profound effects on the brain's neurochemistry, both for the giver and the receiver. When individuals offer praise or recognition to others, they experience a 'helper's high', characterized by the release of endorphins. Endorphins are natural opioids produced by the brain that promote feelings of well-being and reduce stress and pain. Thus, when someone provides positive feedback, their brain releases endorphins, leading to a sense of satisfaction and fulfilment.

Furthermore, the act of giving positive feedback activates brain regions associated with empathy and perspective-taking, such as the prefrontal cortex and anterior cingulate cortex. These areas enable individuals to understand others' perspectives, recognize their contributions and express genuine appreciation effectively. As a result, providing positive feedback not only benefits the recipient but also strengthens social bonds and enhances interpersonal relationships within the team.

From a neuroscience perspective, creating a culture of asking for and providing positive feedback is essential for optimizing brain function and promoting overall well-being in the workplace. By understanding how positive feedback influences the brain's neurochemistry, organizations can cultivate environments that foster collaboration, motivation and mutual support among employees.

Providing positive feedback to yourself can also be a powerful tool in reducing resistance to change. When you acknowledge and celebrate small wins and successes, this activates the brain's reward centres, releasing positive signals. This practice fosters positive association with the change, making it easier to overcome resistance.

During times of change, employees may experience uncertainty and anxiety about their role and the future of the company. This can lead to resistance to change and negatively impact the success of the change initiative due to negative error signals. One way to combat this resistance is to provide positive feedback to employees throughout the change process.

Recognizing individuals for their contributions and accomplishments with positive feedback can activate the brain's reward system, reinforcing positive attitudes toward the change initiative. Positive feedback allows individuals to reflect on their strengths and experience internal celebrations, easing the hypervigilant brain's transition from a threat to a reward state:

- Masterful communication requires planning.
- Positivity comes from a coaching perspective.
- It takes effort to identify the behaviour that you want to address – their reaction in a meeting, how they talked to a customer, colleague or supplier, how they handled a problem, how they did their work.
- How you felt, and what impact it had.
- It must have positive intent so ask yourself what you want to happen as a result of this feedback.
- Enable this person to recognize the boundaries of their authority – they can take action without escalating to you next time.
- Explain your thinking behind your solution so the feedback becomes a teachable moment.

- Clarify quality criteria so they will know why their work is sub-standard.

- Thank them for asking for help, spotting the problem early, having the courage to speak up and having the courage to question something.

- Reduce the pain of feedback by showing respect through the effort you have put in and the thoughtful process of giving autonomy on the actions they take.

EXAMPLE

To be able to give positive feedback, we have built the habit of noticing when things have gone better than expected. Finding these positive examples gives us something to thank others for, and to let them know we are grateful for their effort.

Things that go better than expected often happen because someone has put in the hard work ahead of time. If a piece of work is quicker, simpler or has fewer errors than expected, can we thank the person who initiated the work or provided the inputs for it?

Other examples of things that might be more positive than expected include:

- Calling to apologize to a customer for poor service, expecting them to be very angry but instead having a calm conversation identifying improvements that will prevent the problem in the future.

- Being able to find the information I was searching for (because the file structure on a shared drive had been set up in an intuitive, easy-to-follow way).

- Something I thought would take a long time being resolved quickly because those I was working with were feeling positive and were prepared to compromise.

Creating a culture of asking for and providing positive feedback supports other dimensions of the PEPE© model.

TABLE 7.3

Dimension	Activity	Contribution
Increase pleasure	Celebrate often and bring laughter	Positive feedback is something that can be celebrated, which creates dopamine and feelings of pleasure.
Release energy	Implement a culture of bravery and risk-taking	Positive feedback can have a powerful impact in fostering individuals to take moderate risk and go out of their comfort zone.
Increase pleasure	Being valued and respected	Positive feedback has a big impact in individuals to feel valued for their contributions.

Notes

1 EM Hanneke den Ouden et al. How prediction errors shape perception, attention and motivation, *Frontiers in Psychology*, 10 December 2012
2 W Schultz and A Dickinson. Neuronal coding of prediction errors, *Annual Review of Neuroscience*, 2000, 23: 473–500
3 M Mattson. Superior pattern processing is the essence of the evolved human brain, *Frontiers in Neuroscience*, 8: 265

PART TWO

The PEPE© model in action

08

Creating active resilience: bouncing forward

Resilience, in its essence, represents the ability to endure and recover from adversity. While traditional resilience focuses on bouncing back from challenges, the concept of active resilience introduces a forward-looking perspective, emphasizing not just recovery but thriving in the face of adversity.

The concept of resilience has its origin in metallurgy, originally referring to the ability of a material to absorb energy and then return to its original shape or form after being subjected to stress or deformation. In the context of materials science and engineering, resilience is a measure of a material's elasticity and its capacity to withstand impact or deformation without permanent damage.

The metallurgical sense of resilience influenced the broader use of the term to describe the ability of individuals, communities and systems to recover from adversity and bounce back from challenging situations.

On the other hand, active resilience goes beyond mere survival; it involves a proactive approach to challenges, embracing them as opportunities for growth and transformation. It's about bouncing forward, using setbacks and eustress (good and controlled stress) as stepping-stones towards greater personal and collective well-being.

At a biological level the ground-breaking work of neuroscientists Peter Sterling and Bruce McEwen,[1] among other neuroscientists, has revolutionized our understanding of stress and resilience. Their research has highlighted the adaptive nature of the stress response and the importance of considering the long-term consequences of physiological adaptations to stressors: the novel theory known as allostasis.

Allostasis refers to the body's ability to achieve stability through physiological changes in response to stress and adversity. It does challenge the conventional regulatory model of 'homeostasis', which seeks perpetual constancy. Homeostasis establishes that when environments are relatively stable and predictable, thriving would be achieved by trying to restore the original values.

However, when environments are unpredictable, uncertain and facing constant changes, efficient regulation requires anticipation as an optimal predictive fluctuation can only be obtained by previous exposure and learning mechanisms, rather than merely restoring original values. For example, exposure to brief/moderated high levels of stress or learning from errors and failures arising as a result of the 'error predictive system' (refer to Chapter 7) can help with the learning experience and required anticipation to regulate more unpredictable environments, according to new allostasis research.

Conversely, the cumulative toll of these adaptations and anticipation is known as 'allostatic load', which can have significant physical and mental health implications. Allostatic load is the price the body pays for prolonged exposure to stressors which can lead to wear and tear on the body, contributing to various physical and mental health issues such as cardiovascular problems, metabolic dysregulation, chronic stress and compromised well-being.

Allostasis provides a foundation for building resilience whereas allostatic load highlights the fact that being resilient does not necessarily protect individuals from the impact of prolonged stress and constant change.

Active resilience, therefore, encompasses not only bouncing forward but also emphasizes proactive self-care to mitigate the potential negative consequences of being resilient on well-being.

The PEPE© model offers practical solutions to build active resilience by incorporating the concept of allostasis and allostatic load. It provides the 'what to' and the 'how to' adopt efficient practices to support anticipation, learning and correction of errors as well as to re-set and minimize the impact of the constant adaptation on well-being.

In particular the 'Peaks and Valleys' domain of PEPE© offers the pillars of building active resilience. We can build active resilience by creating habits and processes at individual and organizational levels, applying the concept of managing sustainable 'peaks' and promoting 'valleys'. Likewise, adopting some habits and best practices from the 'Error' and 'Pain' domains can also help build active resilience by proactively 'hacking' the error system of the brain.

Building habits that promote active resilience during times of change

Leverage the power of allostasis

- Focus on small cycles of change (PEPE© dimension: Manage the peaks)
  - Iterative approach
  - Incremental
  - Continuous improvement
- Challenge the status quo (PEPE© dimension: Manage the peaks)
  - Regularly go out of your comfort zone
  - Invite all perspectives
  - Listen without judgement
  - Focus on possibility (yes and…) rather than probability (yes but…)
- Approach with curiosity (PEPE© dimension: Manage the peaks)
  - Choose to learn something new every day
  - Ask/promote expanding questions
  - Experiment
- Create a positive error culture (PEPE© dimension: Release positive prediction signals)
  - View failures as opportunities
  - Share mistakes openly
  - Share learnings

Minimize allostatic load

- Allow time for positive reflections
  - Allocate at least two days between each cycle of change
  - Ask for positive feedback
  - Provide positive feedback
  - Promote gratitude
- Celebrate often (PEPE© dimension: Increase pleasure)
  - Bring laughter
  - Stay longer in the pleasure before engaging in a new 'hunt'

- Allocate time for mind wandering (PEPE© dimension: Promote the valleys)
  - Create a physical environment that promotes positive distractions
  - Allow daydreaming
- Allow incubation periods (PEPE© dimension: Promote the valleys)
  - Do not rush decisions
  - Take some time and space before making conclusions
- Create personal 'peaks and valleys'
  - Set personal goals
  - Celebrate achievements
  - Incorporate enjoyable activities in daily routine
  - Practise mindfulness activities
  - Physical exercise
  - Be part of 'something' – sense of belonging
  - Incorporate gratitude in your daily routine

Note

1 P Sterling. Allostasis: A model of predictive regulation, *Physiology and Behavior*, 2012, 106(1): 5–15; Bruce Mc Ewen. Stress, adaptation and disease: allostasis and allostatic load, *Annals of the New York Academy of Scientists*, 1998, 840: 33–44

09

Overcoming cynicism

Cynicism in modern times has been defined as a general lack of trust or scepticism towards the motives of others. While it has long been a prevalent attitude in society and often considered the result of life experiences, cultural influences or mere attitude (even back to the 4th century BC and the Cynic school of philosophy), recent studies in neuroscience suggest that cynicism has its roots in the complexity of how the human brain works.

Recent research in neuroscience has offered insights into the neurological basis of cynicism. For example, the amygdala, a key player in the brain's emotional processing, reacts strongly to potential threats and fears. Individuals with a heightened amygdala response may be more prone to cynicism, perceiving the world and/or organization as a hostile and untrustworthy place. This heightened emotional sensitivity could lead to a quicker and more intense perception of threats, contributing to a general sense of lack of trust.

Likewise, neuroplasticity (the brain's ability to change and adapt throughout a person's life) plays a crucial role in shaping our thought patterns. The repeated engagement in cynical thinking can reinforce neural pathways associated with negativity, creating a self-perpetuating cycle. Over time, the brain becomes more adept at processing information through a cynical lens, solidifying the individual's pessimistic outlook.

Cynicism is not solely an individual phenomenon but is also influenced by social dynamics. Mirror neurons play a big role in the generation of collective cynicism, empathy and social understanding. In the context of cynicism, an overactive mirror neuron system may lead individuals to transfer their own distrustful attitudes onto others, fostering a collective atmosphere of scepticism.

Mirror neurons are a type of neuron found in the brains of primates, including humans. These neurons respond to actions that we observe in others. The interesting part is that mirror neurons fire in the same way when we actually recreate that action ourselves. In other words, mirror neurons 'mirror' the actions of others. They play an important role in imitation, learning, empathy and social interaction among other complex behaviours of human interactions.

Cynicism is a pervasive attitude of scepticism and lack of trust that can quickly 'infect' teams and organizations through a phenomenon called 'emotional contagion' by overtaking employees' thoughts and emotions, resulting in overwhelming negativity, irritability and increased vulnerability to burnout. In the last 30 years, research in organizational cynicism has demonstrated that when a team or organization 'gets infected', people shift from doing their best to doing the very minimum required, costing organizations millions due to lack of engagement and poor performance.

Moreover, cynicism can also have implications for well-being and its impact on individuals' mental, emotional and physical health. Constant negative emotions can contribute to stress, anxiety and overall dissatisfaction, impacting overall well-being and affecting how individuals perceive and engage in relationships, which can lead to cardiovascular problems and weakened immune function.

Cynicism often arises from a sense of helplessness and lack of autonomy, as well as from a mismatch between expectations and reality; in the case of cynicism within organizations it can also be a mismatch between what leaders say and what actually happens.

Psychologists Steven Maier and Martin Seligman[1] have undertaken a number of experiments demonstrating the impact of 'learned helplessness'. Learned helplessness happens when individuals, after experiencing repeated negative events beyond their control, begin to believe they have no influence over their circumstances. This sense of helplessness becomes deep-rooted in the brain and lays the groundwork for the development of cynicism.

In the event of a mismatch between expectations and reality, the brain produces an error signal at neural level, and it will use this error signal to update its internal models and improve its predictions in the future to support learning, what is called in neuroscience a 'prediction error signal'. Some individuals might learn from the 'error' and adapt to the observed reality. However, other individuals (especially when they approach the challenge with a fixed mindset) experiencing this negative mismatch between reality and expectations may intensify their cynicism as a defence mechanism against the discomfort of acknowledging a mismatch. Over time, the brain becomes more skilled at processing information through a cynical lens, solidifying the individual's pessimistic outlook, which could cause an 'emotionally contagious' cynicism within the team or organization.

Constant change and the increased speed at which changes are taking place have worsened the collective contagious atmosphere of scepticism and disbelief in the 21st century as there are more probabilities of mismatch between expectations and reality and more opportunities for individuals to feel they have no influence over their changing environment. Hence it is more important than ever for leaders to manage change with the brain in mind in order to reduce cynicism.

The PEPE$^©$ model offers practical solutions to overcome cynicism by providing strategies to minimize the impact of the 'negative error' signal and the mismatch between expectations and reality in individuals and organizations. Likewise, it provides the 'what to' and 'how to' adopt brain-friendly habits to avoid the phenomenon of 'learned helplessness' during times of change.

We can proactively build habits at the individual and organizational levels to promote a sense of control and autonomy as well as to release positive prediction error signals instead of negative ones and to reduce the size of the negative signals.

Building habits to overcome cynicism during times of change

Minimize the impact of the mismatch of expectation vs. reality

- Move from big to small (PEPE$^©$ dimension: Reduce the size of the mismatch between reality and expectation)
  - Break down tasks and objectives into manageable steps
  - Create smaller teams
  - Define smaller functional and cross-functional units
  - Prioritize tasks, focus on impactful tasks first
- Focus on incremental/iterative change (PEPE$^©$ dimension: Reduce the size of the mismatch between reality and expectation)
  - Focus on small cycles of changes

o Adjust cycles based on feedback and changing circumstances

o Continuous improvement

- Collaborative decision-making (PEPE© dimension: Reduce the size of the mismatch between reality and expectation)

  o Inclusive decision-making process. Include diverse perspectives

  o Leverage collaborative tools

  o Promote cross-functional collaboration

  o Regular brainstorming sessions

- Manage expectations from the very beginning and at every stage (PEPE© dimension: Release positive signals)

  o Regular check-in points

  o Set realistic goals

  o Communicate clearly and transparently

  o Encourage questions and feedback

  o Evaluate capacity before making commitments

  o Regular surveys

- Create a culture of asking for and providing positive feedback (PEPE© dimension: Release positive signals)

  o Express gratitude regularly

  o Make positive recognition a regular practice

  o Connect positive feedback to individuals or team goals

Counteract 'learned helplessness' and foster a more empowered mindset

o Provide control and autonomy (PEPE© dimension: Reduce perception of pain)

o Encourage self-initiates

o Involve those doing the work in deciding the quality criteria and how the work will be reviewed or tested

o Focus on development; provide training and skills development

o Delegate responsibilities

o Encourage feedback and suggestions

- Promote a growth mindset (PEPE© dimension: Reduce pain)
  o Value progress – celebrate progress
  o Embrace failure and learn from failure
  o Avoid judgement
  o Encourage new learning
- Value and respect others (PEPE© dimension: Reduce pain)
  o Active listening
  o Acknowledge contributions and effort
  o Actively seek out input and contribution
  o Cultivate empathy
- Celebrate often and bring laughter (PEPE© dimension: Increase pleasure during change)
  o Celebrate small victories
  o Set aside time each day for reflection
  o Celebrate often; integrate celebration practices as part of the workflow
  o Track progress; keep a journal or use a digital tool to log your achievements, both big and small

Note

1 SF Maier and ME Seligman. Learned helplessness at fifty: Insights from neuroscience, *Psychology Review*, July 2016, 123 (4): 349–67

10

Leading compassionately for impact during times of change

Researchers define compassion as an emotional response to the pain and struggles of others that involves an authentic desire to help. It does differ from sympathy, empathy, love or sadness, as on top of sensing and understanding others' feelings, it goes beyond by also taking responsive action. Some scientists have referred to compassion as empathy plus action.[1]

Several studies have shown that compassion matters not only in meaningful ways but also can be measured in terms of less burnout, not only for the receiver of compassion, but also for the giver. In fact, research in psychology and neuroscience has demonstrated that compassion activates the parasympathetic system in both the giver and the receiver, helping to maintain health, immunity and well-being at optimum levels during times of disruption and when we change the status quo.

From an evolutionary perspective, individuals will favour enduring relationships with more agreeable, compassionate individuals because this emotional trait predicts increased cooperative, trustworthy behaviour and mutually beneficial exchanges among individuals not bound by family relations. Compassionate individuals show altruistic and caring behaviour, which ultimately has an impact on the perpetuation of the species and on themselves.

In the context of career progression and leadership, a study from the University of California – Berkeley Haas School of Business[2] has shown that leaders who act in selfish, aggressive and manipulative ways were less likely to move up the ranks and to a position of power in comparison with those who were generous and compassionate. Likewise, a major and influential study[3] carried out by the University of Montreal and involving circa 3,000 participants who were followed over 30 years (from kindergarten to professional life), showed that those showing the most kindness to other individuals in kindergarten had significantly higher annual earnings compared to those who were aggressive or selfish, independently of IQ and family background.

Every day there is more research demonstrating the benefits of leading with compassion and the importance of fostering compassion as part of the organizational culture. Numerous studies show that when compassion is part of an organizational culture, job satisfaction, loyalty, trust, well-being and team performance are boosted.

For decades compassionate leadership was considered a 'soft skill' and was the domain of social workers or coaches, not corporate executives. However, the recent COVID-19 pandemic and the increasing amount of constant change at all levels in individuals and organizations have prompted executives at the highest levels to consider how leading with compassion can be fundamental for managing teams and organizations. We now have CEOs of leading organizations around the world publicly saying that leading with compassion is not just nice to have but is a business outcome game changer and a crucial quality to lead people moving forward.

Organizations are concerned with retention, engagement and the welcoming experience of Generation Z, who have challenged societal norms and are growing up valuing purpose, appreciation, inclusion, diversity and empathy more than ever before. Moreover, organizations are facing the challenge of increasing numbers of employees who have reported that stress is impacting productivity and are considering quitting their jobs as a result of chronic stress.

A recent report carried out by Mental Health UK in January 2024 reported that one in five workers in the UK needed to take time off work in the past year due to poor mental health caused by pressure from changes or stress, and 93 per cent identified they have experienced symptoms of burnout during the past year.[4] Another report conducted by Deloitte in June 2023 reported that 60 per cent of employees, 64 per cent of managers and 75 per cent of the C suite are seriously considering quitting for a job that would better support their well-being. On the other hand, 76 per cent of managers say 'organizational obstacles prevent them from doing more to support their team members' well-being'.[5] Those two reports are just a fraction of similar statistics and reports coming from all over the world.

Leaders, CEOs and several business cases have now demonstrated that leading compassionately and proactively helping to move employees from pain and threat into a more comfortable and rewarded state have delivered unexpected positive results, both in individuals' well-being and business performance.

Compassionate leadership is about helping others to move out of pain by taking action. It is about using influence to help build a context where people feel safe, understood and included, as well as providing them with tools and space to increase their energy in a sustainable way rather than sourcing the energy from a brain stress response. It involves a deep understanding of the human experience, empathy for the challenges faced by individuals, and a commitment to fostering a positive and supportive work environment.

It means working with humility and caring by consistently creating environments and setting expectations that empower individuals to thrive, perform at their best and continuously develop their capabilities. This approach goes beyond immediate goals but rather focuses on sustaining performance by fostering a culture of empowerment and well-being.

During times of change and transformation (as reviewed in this book) individuals often experience higher levels of pain, stress and uncertainty. Compassionate leadership becomes a guiding force in alleviating the pain, enhancing well-being and creating an environment that encourages positive adaptation and growth.

Research in neuroscience and especially the PEPE© model offers practical solutions and strategies to help create a compassionate leadership framework by providing the 'what to' and 'how to' brain-friendly habits to adopt at individual and organizational level.

Integrating the four domains of PEPE© into a leadership framework will give leaders the tools to lead with compassion, facilitate change and move towards sustainable high performance, well-being and growth with the brain in mind.

Integrating the PEPE© model into a leadership framework for leading compassionately

Pain

The main intention of leading with compassion is moving people away from pain and threat. PEPE© offers a range of strategies to help reduce the perception of pain and provide pleasure. At the core of compassion, for example, lie:

- 'Being valued and respected' by deeply listening to another's point of view, paying full attention to what has been said, engaging with non-verbal cues, being fully present, providing space for reflection and empowering others to have a voice and to share their opinions.

- 'Altruistic giving and volunteering' by acting for the benefit of others, motivated by a sense of empathy and a desire to make a positive difference in the individual and the team. Leaders should notice challenges and suffering at work (both their own and others'), be curious and ask questions about challenges and difficulties to direct efforts to help and alleviate suffering. For example, leaders should start every conversation with the simple question: 'How are you?'

- 'Increase sense of belonging' by finding common ground, being inclusive, creating a sense of community and shared purpose. A sense of belonging will help the brain to release oxytocin, which in turn will increase trust and well-being and decrease levels of chronic stress.

Energy

A powerful and compassionate approach to mitigate threats in others, shifting them towards a more rewarding state, involves assisting them to save energy or harness sustainable energy release. This not only helps alleviate feelings of overwhelm but also addresses the problem of uncontrollable stress as a source of energy for the brain. Both of the dimensions' strategies in the PEPE© model can help leaders to lead more compassionately, especially:

- 'Add clarity – focus on quality conversation' by providing transparency, lifting people up and focusing on solutions rather than problems.

- 'Provide opportunities for people to come up with their own insights' by allowing time to reflect, asking solution-based questions and creating environments that help move people away from problem-solving. Insights empower individuals and are powerful motivators to initiate change and sustainable high performance.

Peaks and valleys

Recognizing emotional fluctuations, different mental states and creating environments and habits that promote the 'valleys' and sustainable 'peaks' as provided by the PEPE© model are necessary skills and tools that leaders need to develop in order to promote well-being, active resilience and sustainable high performance in individuals and teams. Focus on:

- 'Promote flow' by managing a ratio of about 60 per cent challenge to 40 per cent skills. As discussed in Chapter 6, individuals and teams need to perceive the challenge as slightly higher than their skills in order to perform at their peak and fully engage in an activity, but they need to feel confident that they have the skills required to jump in.

- 'Promote curiosity' by being curious themselves, asking open questions, asking about difficulties, challenges and learnings. Also encouraging others to learn, experiment and ask questions.

- 'Promote the valleys' by encouraging others and themselves to take time for their own well-being and promoting activities and environments that help the brain to reset, such as building time and space for mind wandering, reflection, relaxation, mindfulness, exercise or other activities. Leaders need to become aware and take care of their levels of stress to avoid burnout in themselves and to also avoid projecting it into their teams; mirror neurons can activate the same emotions in others.

Error

Compassionate leaders should proactively reduce the size of a possible negative error signal arising from a mismatch between reality and expectation, as those negative error signals can cause pain (in others and themselves). Likewise, they should provide positive signals to their own and others' brains by building habits and strategies provided by the 'error' domain of the PEPE© model. Leaders should especially focus on:

- 'Move from big to small' by breaking down tasks and objectives, creating smaller teams and acting with humility. Even if sounds counterintuitive, one of our biggest barriers as leaders to being compassionate is the innate need to increase our status and project ourselves as bigger than others. Therefore, showing humility is not a natural attitude in every leader, but it is a key enabler of compassion for both the leaders and team members.

- 'Create a culture of asking for and providing positive feedback' by showing appreciation, acknowledging their contributions and expressing gratitude openly and consistently. Whenever you appreciate something someone has done, make it a point to share your positive thoughts with that person. Likewise, ask others what they have done well and how their contributions have impacted the change. Whenever we ask for or provide positive feedback, the brain will release a positive prediction error signal, which will release dopamine and therefore promote learning, motivation and excitement.

By embracing compassion as a core leadership principle and leveraging the neuroscience-based strategies of the PEPE© model, individuals and organizations can navigate change with positive impact and sustainable success to thrive during times of change and transformation.

Notes

1 S Trzeciak, A Mazzarelly and E Seppala. Leading with compassion has research backed benefits, *Harvard Business Review*, 27 February 2023
2 C Anderson et al. People with disagreeable personalities (selfish, combative, and manipulative) do not have an advantage in pursuing power at work, *Proceedings of the National Academy of Sciences*, 2020, 117(37): 202005088
3 F Vergunst et al. Association between childhood behaviors and adult employment earnings in Canada, *JAMA Psychiatry*, 2019, 76(10): 1044–51
4 Mental Health UK. The Burnout Report 2024, https://mentalhealth-uk.org/burnout/ (archived at https://perma.cc/6UKF-7C9U)
5 J Fisher et al. As workforce well-being dips, leaders ask: What will it take to move the needle? Deloitte, 20 June 2023, https://www2.deloitte.com/uk/en/insights/topics/talent/workplace-well-being-research.html (archived at https://perma.cc/2AEW-DBN2)

11

Sponsoring change

If you are not a sponsor, you might question if it is worth reading this chapter, but the answer is Yes! The techniques in this chapter are tailored for those with responsibility for the scope of the change, and the resources to make the change happen, but not exclusively so. Many of the techniques described below can be used to generate positivity and participation, whatever your role.

Understanding the sponsor role

As a sponsor you have a short-term tactical objective of successfully implementing your change and a longer-term strategic objective of contributing to your organization's capability for change:

- Tactical objective: successful implementation of your change is an achievement that combines a shift to new ways of working with the realization of benefits from this shift.
- Strategic objective: this capability for change is the ability of your organization to maintain its ability to deliver 'business as normal' whilst simultaneously reimagining what this normal is.

In this chapter, we will describe each of these objectives in detail and provide practical ideas for how to achieve them, using the PEPE$^{©}$ model.

Successful implementation of your change

Achieving the adoption of new ways of working is complex, involving two elements:

1 Tangible change: the creation (or amendment) of systems, data models, processes, policies and organization structures. This is not an exhaustive list, because you are sponsoring changes to any of the structural elements needed to run the business. You will have to oversee the project teams responsible, to ensure their work is developed on time, to the required quality and does not exceed the agreed budget.

2 Behavioural change: using the tangible changes as the basis of new ways of working, you are sponsoring the adoption of new behaviours, new values and priorities that define what, how, when, where and with whom work is done. Included in this are changes to the culture, which might be limited to the working environment in your part of the organization or might affect the cultural norms for the whole organization.

There are two elements that require your leadership:

- Activities needed to implement and adopt change – in the form of multiple, interdependent workstreams that reflect tangible and behavioural change
- Resources delivering and affected by the change – a broad range of individuals and groups, each with their own responsibilities, skills and perspectives

FIGURE 11.1 Workstreams for change

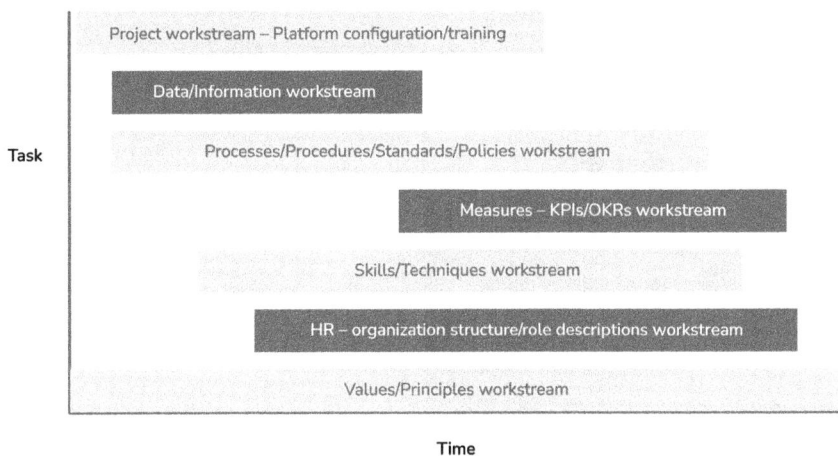

FIGURE 11.2 Impact of sponsor attitude to managing the change

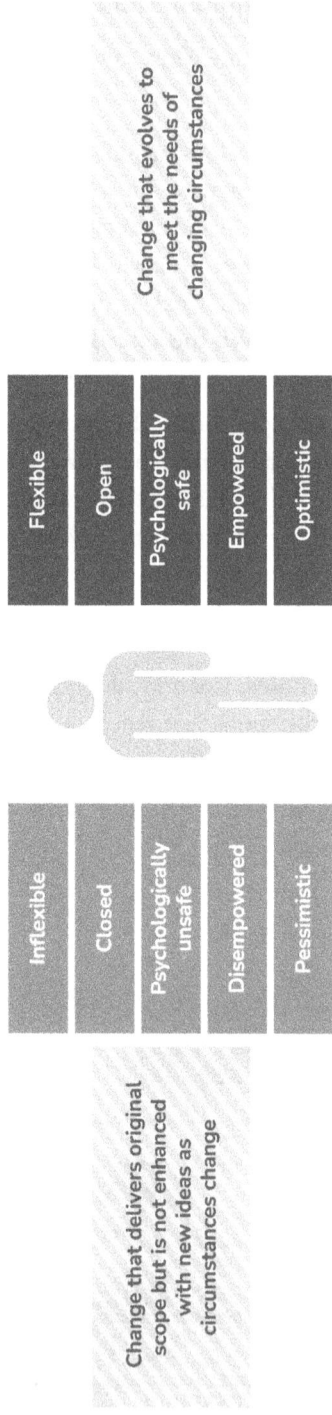

Change that delivers original scope but is not enhanced with new ideas as circumstances change

| Inflexible |
| Closed |
| Psychologically unsafe |
| Disempowered |
| Pessimistic |

| Flexible |
| Open |
| Psychologically safe |
| Empowered |
| Optimistic |

Change that evolves to meet the needs of changing circumstances

Activities needed to implement and adopt change

These workstreams are best illustrated using a simple example of a change to replace an existing finance system:

- Tangible workstreams to define the system requirements, manage the procurement process, configure the new system and ensure it is ready for use by the agreed launch date, for the agreed budget and meeting the required quality standards.

- Behavioural workstreams to create a new approach to work that makes use of the functionality of the new system, definition of and training in new roles, agreement of new measures of success and a cultural shift that embraces greater automation.

A complicating factor for any change is that whilst the work needed to achieve the tangible change can be defined in a project plan, with defined dates for the achievement of key milestones, this is not the case for behavioural change. The activities needed to motivate and persuade everyone to work differently are hard to predict and will depend on individual emotional reactions to the change.

As a sponsor, you can have a significant impact on these emotional reactions. Your attitude to the change will help to shape the atmosphere within which your teams operate.

By embodying the approach on the left of Figure 11.2 you may still achieve change, but it is in its original form. Elements of the change have not been reimagined as circumstances have changed, so there is a shift to new ways of working but they are not as effective as they could be.

The approach on the right of Figure 11.2 ensures you continue to question what needs to change and how to make these changes happen. This is responsive, actively managed change that keeps or outpaces other changes that are happening.

The flexibility, openness and optimism of the growth mindset and the provision of psychological safety described in Chapter 4 on reducing the perception of pain encourages the change to evolve. Those affected can shape the change using their expertise, so feel an increased sense of ownership. It is this ownership that gives the change energy, leading to motivation and momentum.

Equally, an atmosphere that is closed to this engagement will be slower to adopt the changes. More time is needed to manage the adoption of the change. There is a requirement for staff to comply with the new ways of working, but without their energy and motivation, the work will lack a natural momentum.

Resources delivering and affected by change

As a sponsor, you are leading a cross-functional, temporary community to achieve the change. In the finance example above, the range of workstreams demonstrates the breadth of the roles involved. The community includes groups focused on tangible and behavioural change, with subgroups, each with different motivations. For this reason, although you are leading this pool of resources, we have referred to your engagement with teams (plural) because these resources are a composite of multiple teams and groups:

1 The 'tangible change' group are all those with specialist skills to deliver tangible changes. They are motivated to deliver their outputs and to design new ways of working.

2 The 'behavioural change' group are those affected by the change, comprising multiple teams.

Those implementing and adopting the new ways of working are motivated to deliver services to their colleagues and customers. They are experts in the current ways of working, and will have to unlearn what they do now, to adopt new values, new behaviours and new tasks.

FIGURE 11.3 Identifying the community involved in the change

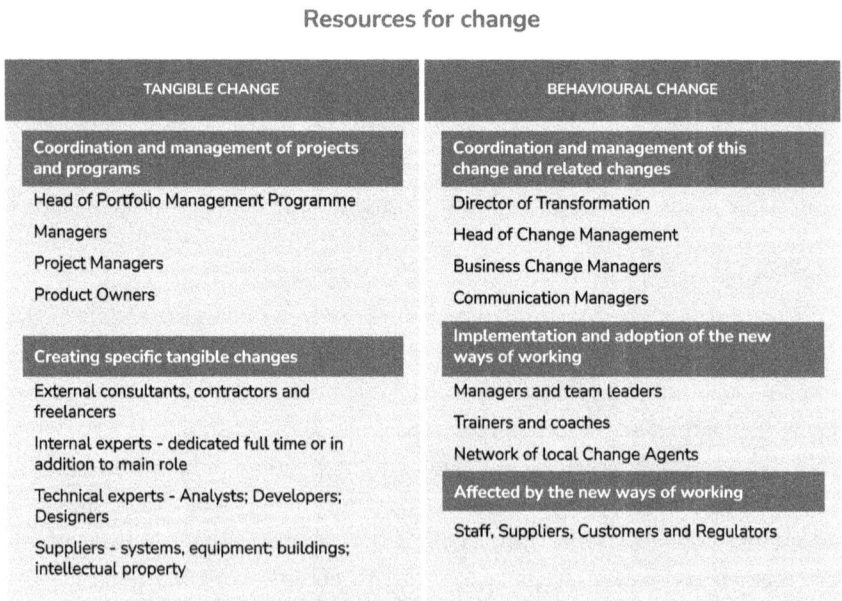

Resources for change

TANGIBLE CHANGE	BEHAVIOURAL CHANGE
Coordination and management of projects and programs	**Coordination and management of this change and related changes**
Head of Portfolio Management Programme	Director of Transformation
Managers	Head of Change Management
Project Managers	Business Change Managers
Product Owners	Communication Managers
Creating specific tangible changes	**Implementation and adoption of the new ways of working**
External consultants, contractors and freelancers	Managers and team leaders
Internal experts - dedicated full time or in addition to main role	Trainers and coaches
Technical experts - Analysts; Developers; Designers	Network of local Change Agents
Suppliers - systems, equipment; buildings; intellectual property	**Affected by the new ways of working**
	Staff, Suppliers, Customers and Regulators

FIGURE 11.4 Identifying those with additional information affecting the change

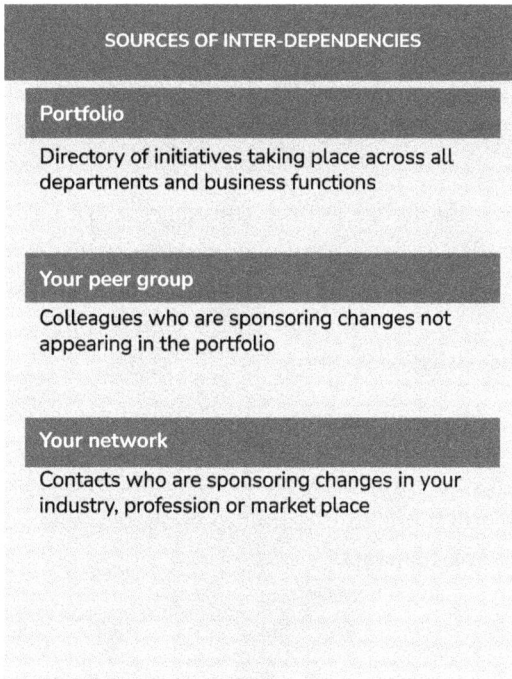

SOURCES OF INTER-DEPENDENCIES

Portfolio

Directory of initiatives taking place across all departments and business functions

Your peer group

Colleagues who are sponsoring changes not appearing in the portfolio

Your network

Contacts who are sponsoring changes in your industry, profession or market place

Those affected include customers and suppliers, potentially surprised by the change and having to adjust how they interact with your organization. Failure to include them sufficiently can have a negative effect on their view of your organization.

You will be called upon to mediate between these different roles, their different needs and priorities. This is made more complicated by the limits of your power. Only some of these resources will directly report to you. You will need to build alliances with other parts of the business affected by your change, as well as manage expert resources, often from external supplier organizations. Other areas of your business and your network will be a source of ideas and may impact the scope of your change so you will need a strategy for engaging with them.

Areas of responsibility

Instead of listing specific responsibilities for sponsorship, this chapter explains your role using three broad categories of activity:

1 Scope

2 Participation

3 Information

Each category has co-dependent relationships with the other two, meaning that when you address one aspect, you must consider how it impacts the others. For example:

- Scope – this is a description of all the elements that will change, creating impact and benefits for individuals and groups inside and outside of your organization.

- Participation – the initial impact and benefits establish who needs to participate in the change. The number of participants increases as more is understood about the scope of the change. As more participants are identified, they will add to the scope of the change by discovering specific impacts to their ways of working.

- Information – those affected need to be informed of the scope, impact and benefits as this motivates them to participate. Their involvement leads to the discovery of more details about the scope, impact and benefits, which creates more information to be shared, leading to the identification of more participants

FIGURE 11.5 Three core sponsorship activities

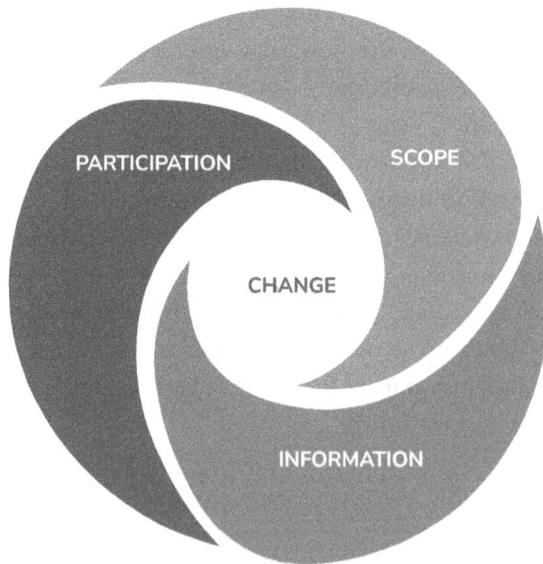

SCOPE

It is your responsibility to confirm the scope of the change, and to continually review and where necessary re-define this scope in response to changing circumstances.

To do this, you need to facilitate the identification and agreement of what needs to change. Bring together those involved in the tangible and behavioural changes, reassuring them of their value, respecting their contribution and motivating them to share their insights.

This includes being clear about what the change includes and what is excluded, cross-checking this scope against other initiatives planned and taking place at the same time, and remaining open to new ideas as circumstances change.

PARTICIPATION

Participation applies to you as well as all those affected by the change:

- Your involvement demonstrates your participation and commitment to change.
- The involvement of those affected enables them to feel a sense of ownership and interest in achieving the change and builds their motivation for making the change happen.

Your participation gives you additional information to share, beyond the messages about what should happen or why it needs to happen. You will be able to tell stories about your own experiences, what has worked well for you, what you are struggling to adapt to and the short-cuts you have created as you have built new habits and routines.

To help others participate in the change you need to create an environment that encourages them to take responsibility for making changes to their ways of working. This includes solving problems that they cannot solve for themselves, the most common of which is insufficient time for change alongside existing workload.

INFORMATION

You have a responsibility for providing information, but this is balanced by your responsibility to listen to the views and experiences of others; therefore, establishing a structure and a culture that supports two-way communication is key to your role.

FIGURE 11.6 Sponsorship activities mapped to workstreams

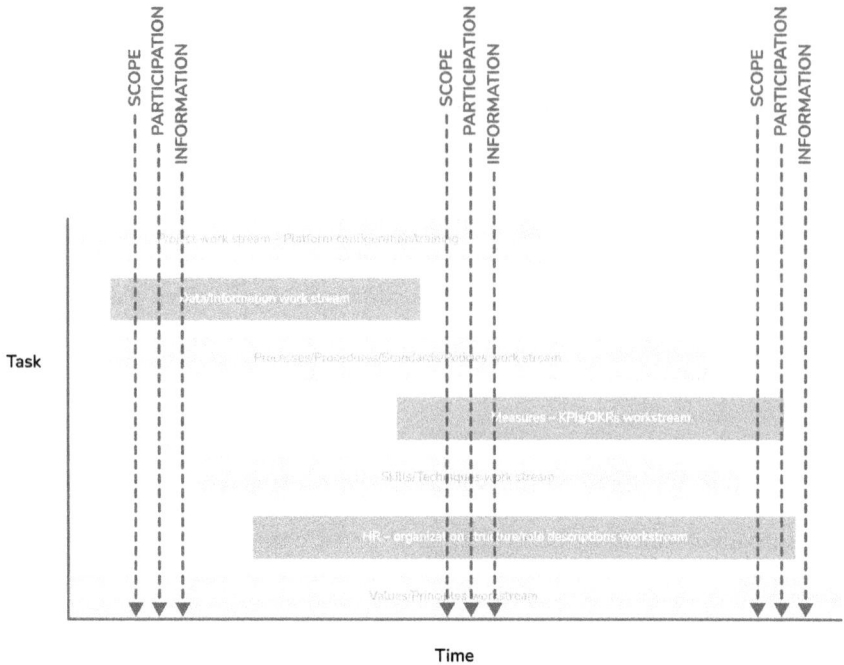

You need to ensure those affected by the change have enough of the 'right' information to feel informed and enthused. As we will demonstrate using the PEPE© model, the 'right' information means that it is local and personalized to the audience, that it is delivered at the right time and covers an immediate/short-term time frame to prevent the brain processing information that is too far in the future to be relevant.

Your information provision is not only via what you say, but also how you behave. Your willingness to participate in the change, by role-modelling the changes you are making to how you work, is important. It sends a powerful message that you are part of the change, removing the feeling that you are telling people to change whilst your work remains unaffected.

SCALE OF YOUR WORK

Earlier in this chapter we identified the tangible and behavioural workstreams needed to implement and adopt change. You will have to fulfil your responsibilities for scope, participation and information for each of these workstreams. Figure 11.6 highlights the ongoing, unrelenting nature of the sponsor role and is a reminder of how much time and energy you will need to set aside to complete your actions.

Using the PEPE© model for sponsorship

The PEPE© model provides you with a wealth of brain-smart activities to generate the cooperative, supportive environment that enables all those involved in the change to make their best contribution. We have selected activities from each domain of the PEPE© model that we believe will provide the most help in achieving this.

Each element of PEPE© is described with a suggested technique and an example of how that technique is applied to a common change situation.

Defining scope using the PEPE© model

The activities described below apply when you first introduce the scope of your change, and for each further announcement of your change.

In deciding what action to take, be mindful that the change you are sponsoring is not the only change your teams are experiencing. Reactions to the scope of your change can be exacerbated by the pressure of other changes.

TABLE 11.1

Dimension	Activity	Technique	Example
Reduce perception of pain	Growth mindset	• Environment assessment • Open questions	• Horizon scanning • What am I missing? technique
Reduce perception of pain	Certainty and assurance	• Context map	• Context map for a new app
Increase pleasure	Common goals and objectives	• Inputs/Outputs diagram	• Questions to create an Inputs/Outputs diagram
Reduce mismatch between reality and expectations	From big to small	• Iterative plan/ breakdown technique	• Breakdown of scope to become a premium supplier
Energy saving	Promote visualization Reduce listening time	• Visuals to match your personal style	• Using YouTube

REDUCE THE PERCEPTION OF PAIN – GROWTH MINDSET

As a sponsor, you are an important role model. Your actions can significantly affect the working atmosphere. Demonstrate the growth mindset to encourage the perspective that the scope of the change is not fixed and that you remain open to new information.

Recognize that the change description you provide in your initial presentations is not fixed. Explain that you value the contribution of ideas. Suggestions for additions and amendments to the change are vital to ensure the relevance and usefulness of the change you are sponsoring, for two reasons:

1 When the initial scope of the change is applied to real-world situations, there will be differences in expectations. When the expected change is compared to the detailed procedures, policies, quality standards and success measures currently in use across the business, there will be unexpected differences. In some cases, these will make the change more workable, and in others, changes will be needed to how the change is implemented or exactly what the change is.

2 The situation that triggered the original idea for the change is itself changing. The original assumptions may prove to be wrong, or new ideas may overtake this one.

Demonstrating that you are constantly listening, evaluating and redefining the change in response to actual rather than assumed events is key to ensuring the workability of the change and the motivation of those involved in making the change happen. The quickest way for those affected to lose faith in the change is when situations flex but the scope of the change does not. People feel they are trapped working on something that is less useful, less relevant and less helpful than was originally expected.

Technique – Environment assessment Build in regular reviews of your change and the wider environment by carrying out an Environment Assessment. This is also known as horizon scanning and is a technique to help you identify other changes that impact the scope of the change you are sponsoring.

Use this Environment Assessment table (Table 11.2) as a source of ideas:

• Complete column 1 with the broadest possible view of your environment.

- Use column 2 to capture potential and actual changes, trends and possible new directions.

- Describe how you think your original change might be affected in column 3.

As with many sponsor responsibilities, you are not the only source of information. Use this table to facilitate discussions with others, to generate the broadest range of information. Your focus is on asking questions, not supplying the answers.

Example – Horizon scanning   A talented programme director shared their experiences in this area:

> I am a big believer in the importance of horizon scanning, because when I define the scope of any change, I recognize that I am taking a decision about what to include at a moment in time. Tomorrow, next week, next month, the situations we face and what our competitors are doing will be different.

TABLE 11.2 Horizon scanning template

	Changes, updates, ideas	Impact on your scope
Your organization:		
Strategic direction		
Key players,		
Impact of other initiatives		
Your market:		
Your customers		
Your suppliers		
Partnerships/alliances		
Your competitors		
Your regulators		
Industry trends		
Global view:		
Economies your organization operates in – financial and political trends		
Social trends		
Technological trends		

Every five or six weeks, I ask myself:

- What do I think will be possible that isn't possible now? An important source of information is my peer group, as we are all involved in creating new outputs and outcomes, and hearing from a colleague how their department has solved an issue or adopted something new can make the scope of my change more or less useful.

- What are our customers asking for, what trends have they mentioned recently, what objectives have they shared? I want to avoid a myopic view, driven only by internal pressures and opportunities. We exist to serve our customers so we must continually consider their needs, as these are not static.

- What has changed significantly over the last few weeks on the world stage and does any of this affect my work?

- If I assume our change will be successful, what is the next logical step and should we be including this expanded scope in our change now rather than waiting for later?

- What pressure points are we experiencing now and can they be solved by altering our scope?

- What has captured our imagination recently, where is our energy pointing and does this impact the scope of my change?

    Sometimes I take action as a result of my answers, but other times I just find it reassuring to have given things a little more thought, away from the daily pressure to deliver.

Technique – Open questions   Another technique is to role-model your willingness to flex your scope by demonstrating curiosity and asking open questions. Unlike closed questions, which are answered with yes or no, open questions invite longer responses. These responses lead into other areas which can deepen the conversation, leading to new information and insights.

Make it clear you are interested in hearing different views and that you do not expect to hear the 'right' answer because you want to learn new perspectives, not confirm your existing view.

Example – What am I missing?   My friend is great at asking 'What am I missing?' whenever he presents to those who have to change how they work. By asking this simple question he:

- Recognizes that he does not know everything, and is showing humility to an audience who have detailed knowledge of their processes and transactions

- Demonstrates that there is more to add. The word 'missing' captures that not everything has been included yet

REDUCE THE PERCEPTION OF PAIN – CERTAINTY AND ASSURANCE

As a sponsor, you understand the strategic contribution that the change makes to your organization. Add to the understanding of change by sharing this perspective, especially with those focused on how the change will affect how they work now. This can identify more reasons for making the change happen:

- More benefits – for other teams inside the organization and for customers outside of the organization. This wider perspective can trigger positive feelings from an altruistic viewpoint, where those affected by change appreciate how their work can benefit others.

- More people involved – making the point that the change affects more than one team, so failure to change negatively impacts others in your organiza-tion. This wider perspective enables those affected by the change to feel less disadvantaged, as they know they are not the only ones to suffer the impact of the change. Knowing that others are involved in the change creates 'social proof' as one group can see that others have adopted the change and are coping. This provides reassurance that it is safe to change.

Technique – Context Map   Use a Context Map to describe the wider context of your change. A context map lists the business functions involved in the change on the left of the diagram, and for each function, describe how the change contributes to the strategic objectives of your organization.

The Context Map demonstrates how the change affects more than one area of focus. In Figure 11.7 we have shown the impact on IT, Customer Services, Finance and HR but equally we could have shown wider objectives including efficiency, innovation or agility. Setting out the initial and subse-quent contributions to strategic objectives gives the team directly responsible for the change a broader understanding of how their change impacts and supports other parts of the organization.

Example – Context Map for a new app   Figure 11.8 shows the Context Map from a colleague who was sponsoring the creation of a new app. The purpose of the app is to increase the responsiveness of customer service, enabling customers to use the app to ask questions and have them immedi-ately answered by a chatbot using AI. This frees up time for customer services teams to provide more support to customers with more complex questions.

FIGURE 11.7 Context Map template

IT strategy	Initial contribution to strategic objective	Additional contribution to strategic objective	Additional contribution to strategic objective
Customer services strategy	Initial contribution to strategic objective	Additional contribution to strategic objective	Additional contribution to strategic objective
Finance strategy	Initial contribution to strategic objective	Additional contribution to strategic objective	Additional contribution to strategic objective
HR strategy	Initial contribution to strategic objective	Additional contribution to strategic objective	Additional contribution to strategic objective

INCREASE PLEASURE – COMMON GOALS AND OBJECTIVES

Creating the feeling that everyone is contributing to the same goal involves bringing in everyone who is involved, and enabling them to see where they fit. A simple way to achieve this for any change is to describe the change as an end-to-end process, so that all those involved can clearly see the complete chain of events from start to finish, and their contribution.

At every meeting, establish this wider context to ensure that whoever you are with understands they are part of a community affected by the change and that their objective is the successful completion of the end-to-end flow of the transaction, and not just their business function within that flow.

Without this common objective, there is the risk that changes made in one part of the process will trigger unexpected changes for others, leading to delays, but also to conflict as others feel that one group is forcing their changes on the others.

Use your authority to broker compromises. For example, take action where there are disagreements about who is responsible for the work, or the order in which work must be done, or where one team is positively impacted by the change but other teams are negatively impacted.

Your intervention will lead to more debate about the workability of the change. Maintain a growth mindset and be prepared to add and remove elements from the scope of your change as more becomes known about the impact of your change.

FIGURE 11.8   Context Map example

IT strategy	Benefit from AI innovations	Using real-time data	Using AI to learn more about our customers
Customer services strategy	Improved responsiveness	24/7 access to answers	Queries resolved more quickly
Finance strategy	Greater certainty revenue predictions	Fewer refunds	Fewer credit notes
HR strategy	Workforce with relevant skills	Upskill staff in latest technologies	Align people resources to complex tasks

Technique – Inputs/Outputs diagram   Use an Inputs/Outputs diagram to enable all those involved to recognize that when their process changes, and their outputs are different, this will impact another team because their outputs become the inputs for another part of the process.

Example   I have a colleague who uses the Input/Output diagram to initially establish and continually review the common objective with those creating the tangible changes and those who will have to work differently. These are some of the questions she asks and the points she makes:

- Have we agreed on what we mean by input and output? Don't forget, even the updating of one piece of data is still an output.
- Do you know everyone in this flow – are there things we can do to get to know more about each other's work?
- Is this a complete flow of business functions to achieve this end goal – are there any areas of the business we should be including in this change?
- Is this a complete picture of all the inputs and outputs we create – have we mapped everything, however small?

REDUCE MISMATCH BETWEEN REALITY AND EXPECTATIONS – FROM BIG TO SMALL

The bigger the change, the harder it is to describe it in detail. This means there are more opportunities for misunderstandings about what is expected.

FIGURE 11.9

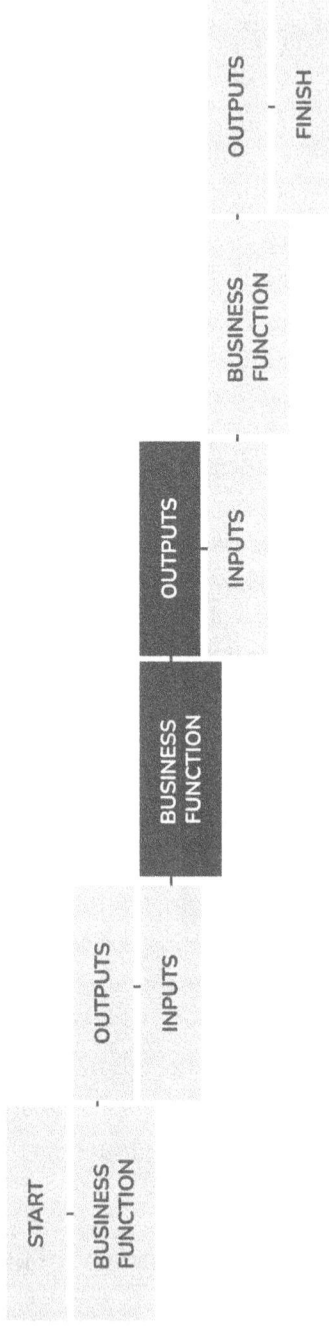

START – BUSINESS FUNCTION – OUTPUTS – INPUTS

BUSINESS FUNCTION – OUTPUTS – INPUTS

BUSINESS FUNCTION – OUTPUTS – FINISH

Change affecting a specific business function

Transformation affecting multiple business functions

FIGURE 11.10

START

BUSINESS
FUNCTION

OUTPUTS

INPUTS

BUSINESS
FUNCTION

OUTPUTS

INPUTS

BUSINESS
FUNCTION

OUTPUTS

FINISH

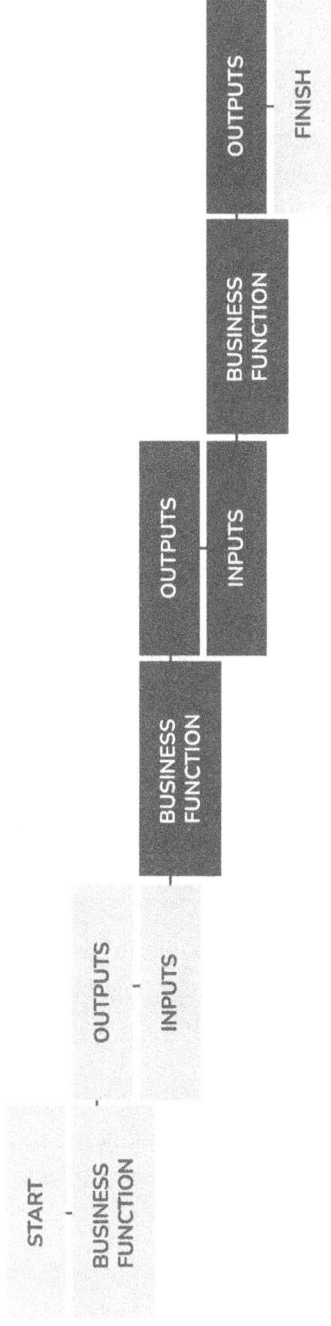

Change affecting a specific business function
Transformation affecting multiple business functions

When what happens does not meet what we assumed would happen, our brain sends us a powerful error signal. This signal makes us stop and assess the situation. Our brains are telling us to be cautious, the mismatch is a threat and it is not safe to proceed.

To minimize misunderstandings and manage expectations, be prepared to break the scope of your change into a series of smaller goals. This will help to overcome two potential areas for misunderstandings:

1 Your role requires you to hold a broader strategic view of the change. Using your strategic view, you might assume that elements of the change needed to support other changes and priorities within the organization are being considered and acted upon by all those involved in the change.

2 Those affected by the change have a deeper, tactical view of the change. They might assume you have the same knowledge, so you understand the full impact of the change on their work, and that you agree to all these changes.

Technique – Iterative plan/breakdown technique   For more details about how to use this technique, refer to the guidance on iterative planning earlier in this book. Reduce misunderstandings by asking for an iterative plan, where the end goal of the change is broken into smaller, more specific outcomes. Give the team permission to deliver one outcome at a time, focusing on the development, delivery and adoption of each outcome over a short period of time.

Your contribution to this planning is to ensure alignment between this outcome and the scope of your change. Make sure everyone involved is clear about the answer to this question: 'This outcome contributes to the change by enabling the organization to....'

Collaboratively review and agree the initial order of these outcomes at the start of the change and at review and re-plan this order at regular intervals throughout the duration of the change.

Example – Breakdown of scope to become a premium supplier   My friend is sponsoring the creation of a new, high-quality product range. Her organization has many competitors for their current products, leading to pressure on the prices they can charge and their profit margin:

> I assumed everyone appreciated that these new products were just the start of a move towards positioning ourselves as a premium supplier, able to charge more and differentiate ourselves from the competition. I didn't realize that my team had a different view. They saw the new products as a significant increase

in workload and a reason to streamline their existing processes. This means I assumed they knew I wanted us to revise our marketing messages and our customer services processes, whilst they assumed I wanted greater focus on efficiency.

I overcame this mismatch by breaking the bigger goal of becoming a premium supplier into a series of outcomes.

These more specific outcomes reduced misunderstandings about what we collectively needed to achieve and gave everyone a sense of purpose and a feeling of being part of something significant.

ENERGY SAVING – PROMOTE VISUALIZATION – REDUCE LISTENING TIME

A willingness to use visuals to explain the change you are sponsoring has many advantages. Visuals reduce the processing effort needed by the brain to understand your message. This means your audience has more energy to absorb the message. You do not want them to feel tired when you need them to feel motivated by your change. In addition to reduced processing power, you can use visuals to:

- expand the context of your change, using pictures that explain how your change fits what your organization does, the position of your organization in its industry or marketplace;
- give insight into your understanding of the change via the imagery you use.

FIGURE 11.11 Breaking the change into outcomes

Increase profitability

Gain reputation as premium supplier

Run down existing low margin products

Launch higher-quality products into market

Focus effort on creation of new products

Streamline to reduce effort of delivering existing product range

Technique – Select visuals to match your personal style   Refer to the section above for success criteria for visuals. To increase engagement with your audience, ensure you select or create images that reflect your personal style. Do you like diagrams, graphs, images or photographs?

Example – Using YouTube   My friend finds video content on YouTube that sets an exciting, energetic tone for her presentations. She searches for videos about the future of work, how technology is changing work and the latest innovations in how humans work to find clips that demonstrate her excitement about sponsoring new ways of working.

A colleague working in transformation uses a jigsaw image to explain that the transformation is the completed jigsaw and each of the changes is a piece of the jigsaw.

Creating participation using the PEPE© model

Change only happens if all those affected are involved in creating, practising and adopting new ways of working. As a sponsor, you need to ensure:

1 The right people are involved – this is directly linked to the scope of the change, and as this evolves, those who need to be involved will change.

2 Everyone has the time to be involved – this means asking people to be creative about how they use their time, to ensure a balance between business as usual and the change activities.

3 People are doing the right things – as the change evolves, it is easy for people to be busy, but busy doing the wrong things. Changes that were viewed as essential initially can be superseded by other ideas. Ensuring that things are stopped is as important as creating new ways of working.

4 The atmosphere inspires willing involvement in the change.

REDUCE THE PERCEPTION OF PAIN – BEING VALUED AND RESPECTED
It is hard to feel valued if you feel that the odds are stacked against you. Many affected by change would like to be more involved, but their existing workload prevents this. It is difficult for individuals to resolve this situation for themselves, because they have split loyalties:

- their performance is evaluated against their normal workload;
- the teams responsible for the change initiative will be asking for their help.

Both activities are valuable, so your teams need you to act as an advocate to step in and help them balance these competing demands.

This is a complex area, and you will need a mixture of techniques to enable your limited resources to deliver 'business as usual' and change simultaneously. The challenge is further complicated by the pressure of other changes taking place at the same time, so you will need to revisit the situation regularly to ensure your teams are not overwhelmed and can cope (and thrive) with their workload:

1 Formal recognition of competing demands

2 Good housekeeping

3 Saturation assessment

TABLE 11.3

Dimension	Activity	Technique	Example
Reduce perception of pain	Being valued and respected	• Formal recognition of competing demands	• Accurate role descriptions
		• Good housekeeping	• Eliminating low priority work
		• Saturation assessment	• Using a Saturation Checklist
Reduce perception of pain	Control and autonomy	• Set clear boundaries	• Boundaries when managing multiple changes
Reduce perception of pain	Growth mindset, psychological safety	• Stay curious; do not judge	• Look beyond the initial failure
		• Avoiding a blame culture	• Celebrate where you are now
Increase pleasure	Common goals and objectives	• Look for others	• Who else?
Increase pleasure	Altruistic giving and volunteering	• Buddy learning	• Mini coaching sessions
Managing peaks	Focus on small cycles of change	• Iterative planning	• Clearly defining when help is needed
Save energy	Create habits and routines	• Clear allocation of time	• Weekly schedule
Reduce mismatch between reality and expectations	Focus on incremental/ iterative change	• Stepping-stones	• Use differences to predict the future

(continued)

TABLE 11.3 (Continued)

Dimension	Activity	Technique	Example
Release positive prediction signals	Create a culture of asking for and providing positive feedback	• Actions and achievements	• Finding something to praise
Release positive prediction signals	Create small habits of providing unexpected rewards	• Plan positive interventions Give thanks	• Drop-ins Specific praise
Release energy	Own insights	• Sharing work in progress	• What comes after/ What comes before?

Technique – Formal recognition of competing demands   Too often, staff performance is evaluated against their existing workload, and ignores the significant effort they are making to achieve the change. Alongside their day-to-day responsibilities, they are sharing their knowledge of existing working practices, participating in designing new processes, testing systems, attending training and making alterations to data, documents and communications to customers and suppliers.

Recognize this balance in their role description and ensure their contribution to the change is included in their performance review.

Example – Accurate role descriptions   A few years ago we worked on a change that had initial support, but over the months needed to make the change happen, the contribution from those affected reduced. Progress slowed and we were missing important deadlines. When we talked to those involved they explained that they were coming up to their annual appraisals and any backlog in workload would be criticized, so they had to halt their involvement in the change. They explained that they would be criticized for any performance reduction in 'business as usual' because these were the metrics that formed the annual reports to the executives. They were angry that their efforts to help make the change happen were not recognized but they did not feel they had any power to do anything about it.

I worked with the HR Director to address this problem at source. We had a meeting with managers conducting the performance reviews to ask them to praise the change efforts and to recognize how much discretionary time people were volunteering on top of their day jobs.

We also commissioned a working party to help us identify new responsibilities that could be added to the role descriptions to reflect the balance of role-specific work and change-related work. These changes took nearly a year to put in place, but it has benefited not just that change, but all changes since then.

It has also helped to shape the culture of the organization, because it has raised the profile of change and helped to ensure every job is formed of 'business as usual' and change activities.

Technique – Good housekeeping   Help your teams streamline their work. As senior leaders, your willingness to identify less valuable tasks and eliminate them or put them on hold for now demonstrates your support.

Focus on 'good housekeeping' to help your teams find all the half-finished projects and ideas that are taking up their time and their focus. Create a culture that discourages 'hoarding' – the holding on to old working practices, team structures, documentation, meetings and priorities that do not reflect the new ways of working.

This is an area your role-modelling can significantly impact. Demonstrate your willingness to de-clutter by cancelling less important initiatives, reducing the number of meetings in your schedule and getting rid of old files and paperwork. Make a big show of doing these things, so that everyone realizes that removing things is an important aspect of the change.

Actively encourage and support your teams to:

- review their existing work to find low-priority tasks that can be abandoned, either temporarily during the change or removed completely;
- remove tasks that add little value or that duplicate the work of others

Start by agreeing the definition of low priority. For example:

- Not a legal requirement
- Does not immediately generate revenue or reduce costs
- Does not immediately contribute to customer satisfaction
- Does not immediately improve the situation
- Any actions we take 'just in case' because they are not essential, they protect us from possible harm in the future, but if there are problems in the future, they can be dealt with then

The use of the word 'immediately' is important, because a lot of what we spend our time on will be valuable eventually – for example, projects that simplify the file structure so everyone can find information more easily, or updating process manuals to make sure they fully reflect how things are done.

The value of these tasks will be felt in the longer term but more immediate benefits can be gained by freeing up time to participate in the change.

Example – Eliminating low-priority work   At a transportation company, I helped the senior leadership team implement a decluttering approach to their portfolio of initiatives, cancelling projects that were no longer needed. We defined a set of criteria to assess the value of the initiative compared to the resources required to deliver it, and used this to rank the projects from highest to lowest importance.

This was so successful that we then invited department managers to apply the same approach to initiatives that their teams were involved in.

Technique – Saturation assessment   We often talk about 'change fatigue', recognizing that our teams can become exhausted by the volume and pace of change taking place at work. Increasingly I find this term unhelpful because the word fatigue implies that someone is tired, and that this is their fault. Saturation is a better word because it means 'no more can be absorbed'. It is a less judgemental word, recognizing that it is the volume of change that means no more can be absorbed, not making a personal judgement on the effort of those involved.

Use a saturation checklist to assess how people are feeling about their workload before asking them to become involved in more change. If you don't know they are feeling overwhelmed, you cannot address it.

Saturation checklist:

- Not turning up for meetings
- Not being prepared, not engaged with the subject before the meeting
- Stating outright that they are too busy to do something
- Not volunteering for additional pieces of work
- Overly emotional – quick to anger, frustration or tears
- Commenting negatively or pessimistically on things that would not normally trigger this response
- Distracted, not giving their full attention to the task

Example – Using a saturation checklist   My friend uses this checklist as a reminder to herself of things to look out for, in her own behaviour and in her team:

> This checklist enables me to assess the emotional state of the team using the same questions each time, so there is a structure to the assessment, and I can compare the results from week to week. I do not ask the questions directly, but I look at the list at the start of my team meeting to help me remember things to look out for. I use the checklist again on a Friday morning when I am reviewing how the week has gone. It is often at this point that I have my insights about how the team is really feeling because I can think back on their behaviours during the week, not just their attitude at our weekly meeting.

Another senior leader told me:

> Most of the time new ideas are met with even more ideas. We share the things we are going to do, how we can build on the initial task to make it even better. When this stops, and is replaced by questions, concerns, identification of risks or worse, no comments at all, I know we have reached saturation. My job at this point is to take a decision. Is the new piece of work more important than finishing what we are already involved in or can I put it on hold? If it is more important, what can I stop to reduce the workload and make it easier for people to find the time to get involved?

REDUCING THE PERCEPTION OF PAIN – CONTROL AND AUTONOMY

To inspire your teams, give them as much control over their work as possible. Make it clear where the boundaries are for what you need to know, and what decisions you are responsible for. Outside of these requirements, make it clear you trust them to achieve the required results using their abilities and expertise in any way they feel is necessary.

Technique – Set clear boundaries   You can achieve this by focusing on the outcomes of the change, and not the specifics of how they achieve these outcomes. As they have not 'promised' you exactly how they will work, it enables them to experiment and try new things, which is essential for any change. After all, change means making something new and different, so it is not possible to predict everything that will happen, as it has never been done before.

This requires you to consider your place in the decision-making hierarchy, so that you can be clear where their authority ends and yours begins.

As the sponsor of the change, you are responsible for taking decisions about the scope of the change, the timing and budget and the commitment of resources, both internal resources and external suppliers. To fulfil these responsibilities you probably need to know:

- How the work is organized within the team
- What the expected outputs will be and when they are available
- Any criteria used by the team to decide on priorities

Ask for high-level plans; make it clear that you need to see the plans that define what the team are going to create, but you don't need to see the details of every activity and technique they will use to achieve their new ways of working.

By asking for the expected outcomes, you are setting a clear boundary for what you need to know. People are more likely to experiment when they have these boundaries, as it reduces misunderstandings and the anxiety and stress that they might unintentionally do the wrong thing.

Use the diagram in Figure 11.12 to establish three levels of responsibility. Using this visual will ensure everyone hears a consistent message. For each of the areas of responsibility, you can provide specific examples relevant to your change.

Example – Boundaries when managing multiple changes   A colleague sponsors multiple changes that involve teams from her company and external suppliers and uses a version of Figure 11.12s to manage to give as much control to her teams as possible whilst remaining involved in the key decisions. As she explains:

> If I do not make clear what I need to be involved in, I can be left out of important decisions, or decisions about which I have relevant information. At the same time, there is the risk that I am asked to review and decide on too many situations that I become a blocker, as I am not responding quickly enough and people waste time waiting for a decision from me.
>
> As I am responsible for so many change initiatives that need my attention and sometimes my intervention, I find using this approach for each of them gives me back some control and helps me use my time effectively.
>
> As a rule, these are some of my requirements:
>
> - I must be notified immediately if we are doing anything that has an impact on external parties. This includes changing any requirements for our suppliers, changing what, when or how we deliver products to

FIGURE 11.12 Levels of responsibility in change

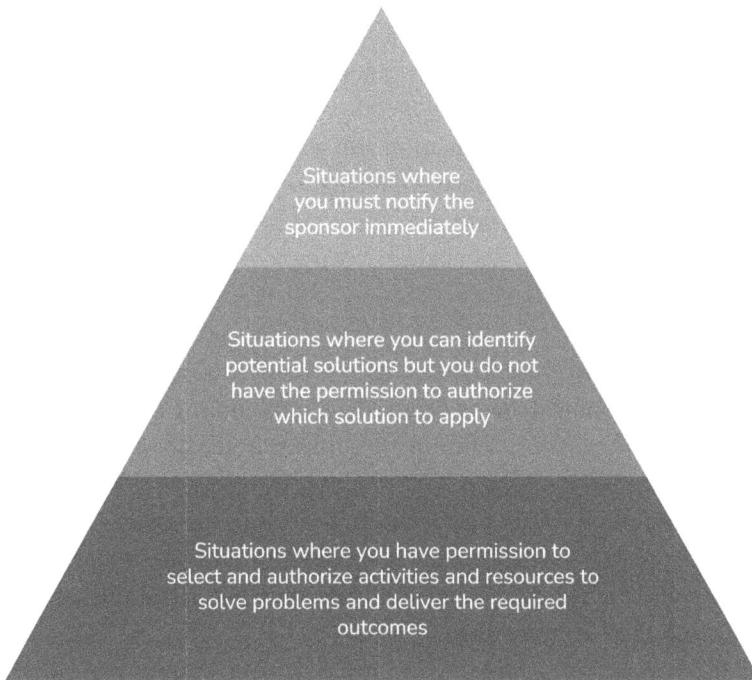

Situations where you must notify the sponsor immediately

Situations where you can identify potential solutions but you do not have the permission to authorize which solution to apply

Situations where you have permission to select and authorize activities and resources to solve problems and deliver the required outcomes

customers or anything that is likely to trigger the attention of our regulators.

- I must be involved in any decisions where we are changing our performance metrics, or if we are building interfaces with other systems or making demands on other teams not previously identified and agreed in the original scope.

- I do not need to be involved in your decisions on what techniques to use, who from each team is going to carry out the work or the detailed tracking of progress against the plan.

REDUCE THE PERCEPTION OF PAIN – GROWTH MINDSET AND PSYCHOLOGICAL SAFETY

By adopting the growth mindset we value the experience of changing as much as we value the achievement of the change and the benefits it creates. We perceive the change as a challenge and any failures as an opportunity to learn and to improve.

As a sponsor, your behaviour can encourage the adoption of this mind-set in others, as they seek to emulate your approach. Your seniority and career achievements mean you are a role model for others. By adopting a growth mindset, you encourage the adoption of this openness and flexibility in others.

This openness to new information and willingness to learn creates a safe and encouraging space for sharing information. This builds an environment of psychological safety, encouraging everyone to share their ideas and experiences as all information is a chance to learn so there is no need to criticize what is said.

Technique – stay curious; do not judge   To apply this way of thinking, try to intercept your immediate judgement of a situation with an open question. For example, asking and celebrating the answer to the question, 'What have we learnt so far?'

This question establishes positive intent, because it assumes that whatever has happened, we have learnt something. By adding 'so far' at the end of the sentence, we imply we are not at the end, but are in the middle of a journey, and there is more learning to come.

As the volume of changes taking place in your organization increases, change must be viewed as an opportunity to build on what already exists. If not, those making an effort to improve their current ways of working will be demotivated by the fear that their achievements will be overturned when the next change takes place.

Applying the growth mindset is a perfect fit for this situation, as it requires us to seek out the learning from situations, and to continually adapt our approach, building in new information, ideas, techniques and solutions.

Example – Look beyond the initial failure   My friend was sponsoring the digital transformation of the marketing department in her organization. Her team alerted her to their concerns that the original scope of the change could not be delivered as originally planned. Switching over to a new CRM system was impacting processes within marketing, sales and finance. The team managing the transfer of data to the new CRM identified lots of missing fields, duplications and other errors within each of the departments. This has triggered the need for re-work, and the original deadlines and the changes to how people work will not be made this year.

With a fixed mindset, my friend would have emphasized the failure and the negative impacts of failing to change how work is done to make the

FIGURE 11.13 Impact of sponsor mindset

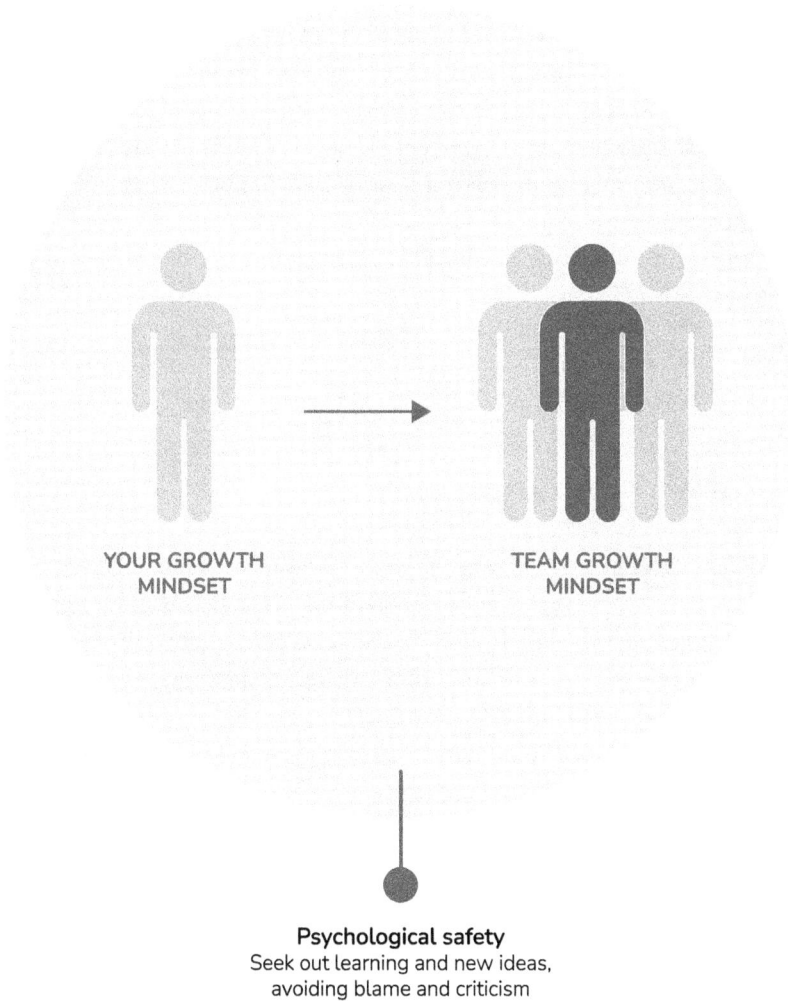

YOUR GROWTH
MINDSET

TEAM GROWTH
MINDSET

Psychological safety
Seek out learning and new ideas,
avoiding blame and criticism

greatest use of the system. With a growth mindset, she was able to celebrate that the CRM initiative identified a much-needed cultural change to a data-driven culture, adopting new behaviours that encourage and reward accuracy and completeness.

Technique – Avoiding a blame culture   Creating a 'no blame' culture is not easy. We must suppress our emotional reaction to problems and try to move past our initial desire to criticize and blame when things go wrong. A technique for doing this is to reframe the problem or failure as the current position.

This recognizes that we cannot change what has happened in the past, so we need to adopt the belief that 'we are where we are'. We can control how we respond to this situation and focus on what actions to take now to create a feeling of trust. By not looking back for opportunities to criticize and blame, we encourage those involved to share a more detailed and probably more honest statement of the current situation. Celebrate the achievement of this understanding because it reduces the risk that next steps will be based on incorrect assumptions.

Ask open questions to promote discussion on activities that will move you towards a solution:

'Where do we go from here?'

'What have we not tried?'

'What else do you think we can do?'

'What do we think are the next steps?'

Example – Celebrate where you are now   At a recent team meeting, it was clear that progress was much slower than expected because the work was more complex. The general view of the team was that whilst they were producing good work, each time they created something, it triggered the need for other things.

The sponsor stepped in to summarize the current situation, emphasizing what had been achieved and congratulating the team for increasing the quality of the project with their dedication to finding answers and adding to the scope of the work. The sponsor explained how this additional level of quality created the opportunity to sell the final product at a higher price.

By setting this new baseline of progress and celebration, the atmosphere in the meeting shifted from pessimism to a high-energy debate on what to do next, how to solve problems and increase the rate of progress.

FIGURE 11.14 Avoiding a blame culture

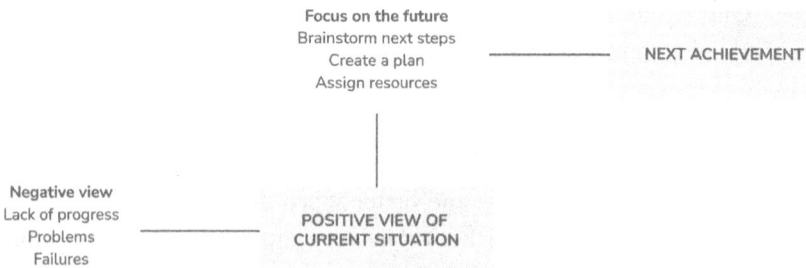

Focus on the future
Brainstorm next steps
Create a plan
Assign resources

NEXT ACHIEVEMENT

Negative view
Lack of progress
Problems
Failures

POSITIVE VIEW OF
CURRENT SITUATION

After the meeting, the sponsor shared his view of the meeting:

> I was frustrated; after all I am the one who must put a positive spin on this
> with the executives. But the team cannot work any harder and if I just criticized
> them, we would not have found solutions and the motivation of the team would
> have slowed things down.

INCREASE PLEASURE – COMMON GOALS AND OBJECTIVES

As a sponsor, you can help your teams feel connected. By focusing on team
spirit, your actions help team members generate oxytocin, the neurochemical that creates feelings of trust and the pleasure derived from the company
of others.

Whilst it is important to create a common goal across the wide range of
disparate interests involved in the change, there is also the danger of too
much bonding.

Highly connected teams can view others as a threat to their performance.
This inhibits their ability to collaborate as they are quick to defend the opinions and achievements of their own team members, whilst ignoring or
disparaging the contribution of members of other teams.

As a sponsor, you want to maximize the contribution of all those responsible for and impacted by the change.

Technique – Look for others   To minimize the risk of any team becoming
too insular, ensure a constant widening of the resource pool contributing to
the change. Create the habit of seeing everyone as part of a wide network of
connections.

When discussing the involvement of any individual or team, consider
who they could benefit from working with. Share these questions with your
team to encourage them to continuously expand their connections. For each
existing relationship, identify:

- Who does this person report to?
- Who are their key decision-makers?
- Who are the suppliers for this team?
- Who are the customers for this team?

Example – Who else?   One of my colleagues is excellent at building connections between large groups of people within her organization. Her mantra
when anyone proposes a meeting, workshop or social gathering is, 'Who
else can we include?'

As she explains, the results are always helpful:

> The answer to this question usually identifies someone unexpected. Perhaps
> someone new to the organization, or a representative from the business we had
> not recognized until now is affected by the change. Whoever we find, they are
> grateful that the impact of change on their work has been acknowledged, and
> they will often willingly join any events we invite them to.

INCREASE PLEASURE – ALTRUISTIC GIVING AND VOLUNTEERING

To produce the motivation for taking part in change, framing people's
participation in the change as an opportunity to help others is a powerful
way to generate oxytocin, which is pleasurable.

The interpretation of how the change can benefit others comes from
understanding the change and having a chance to review it from different
perspectives. It is a product of a moment of insight, an 'aha' moment where
your team can identify a reason why the change matters to them.

Many of our changes are internal to how our organization is managed,
and it would be too ambitious for us to describe these changes as a selfless
concern for others. However, we can create opportunities for team members
to willingly help each other.

Technique – Buddy learning   For experienced staff, provide the opportunity for them to share their previous learning with others who know less
about this type of change. This ensures they feel valued and respected as
they share their past career history and examples of situations they have
been involved in and lessons learnt.

For less experienced staff, give them the opportunity for reverse mentoring, offering their skills to others. This ensures they feel valued and respected
for the things that they know, even though their level of experience might
be less.

Example – Mini-coaching sessions   We have a colleague who begins each
new initiative with a description of the learning environment she wants to
achieve during the work. She talks about the opportunities to help each
other and to create something that is more than the change itself:

> I know we are all busy, and the idea of volunteering for extra work seems
> counter-intuitive but hear me out! If we help each other to develop new skills
> we will experience personal benefits from this change, alongside the benefits we
> are creating for our organization. When we share our learning, we relive our

FIGURE 11.15 Identifying those involved in your change

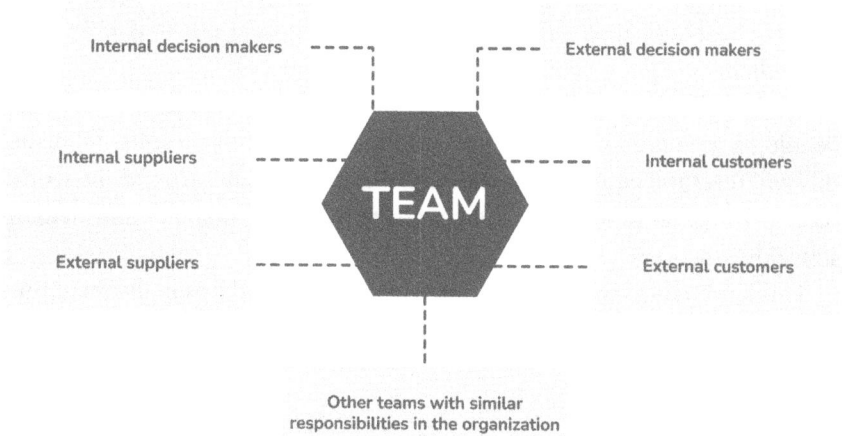

knowledge and skills which deepens our understanding of what we know. When we share what we know, the questions we are asked make us think and deepen our knowledge. Everyone has something to contribute, so I want each of you to think about something you are willing to share with someone else in the team. Let's build in time every week for mini coaching sessions.

MANAGING PEAKS – FOCUS ON SMALL CYCLES OF CHANGE

Working in smaller cycles of change makes it easier to involve others in the change, as you are asking for a shorter, more focused time commitment.

This helps to create cross-functional groups to develop elements of your change, minimizing the risk that what is delivered does not meet the needs of everyone impacted by the change.

Technique – Iterative planning   Use the iterative plan described earlier in this book to encourage your team to work in short cycles:

1 Iterations that last from 8 to 14 weeks, which bring together a number of small changes that taken together create an ability to do something new.

2 Short sprints last one to three weeks to deliver small, clearly defined changes in ways of working.

The scope of an iteration or sprint is used to identify what specialist resources are needed, when and for how long. This increases the probability they will participate because the obligation to contribute to the change is not open-ended.

Example – Clearly defining when help is needed   To make it clear when people are needed, my friend uses the iterative planning technique to reassure those whose help she needs that this additional effort is only for a short time.

She is leading a team in the head office of a global organization who are defining a new product launch process for all future innovations. To ensure this will meet the needs of the sales and marketing teams around the world, they identify the times when they want to consult, co-create and demonstrate their process.

This has enabled them to schedule a series of workshops in different time zones, maximizing the involvement of everyone who will be involved in future product launches.

SAVE ENERGY – CREATE HABITS AND ROUTINES

As described earlier in this chapter, we must help people find the time to participate in change. Help those involved to balance their existing workload alongside their involvement in the change as a routine activity.

The brain expends energy imagining what is going to happen next. We can cut this energy usage by establishing certainty over what work to do when. Create regular timeslots for each type of work so that switching focus between existing workload and change activities becomes an established routine.

Technique – Clear allocation of time   Encourage the team to identify when to focus on each type of work, so that during the life of the change, they build a new habit – for example, knowing that every Wednesday afternoon they will be in a workshop to design, develop or practice new ways of working. This enables them to manage expectations for other colleagues and their customers for when they are available and when their other work will be completed.

Example – Weekly schedule   I worked for an organization that specializes in complex scientific information. Staff need a lot of concentration, often reviewing documents for several hours at a time. Any interruption loses concentration, meaning they must repeat their review to make sure they haven't missed important information.

The change was causing them considerable stress, as they experienced a lot of interruptions because of the requirements created by the change activities. For example, they needed to attend meetings and workshops and some of the consultants asked questions at their desks. The consultants were also frustrated because they could not get the information they needed when they needed it.

I proposed a schedule where existing work was completed between 9 am and 3 pm each day and all workshops and meetings related to change took place from 3 pm to 5 pm. The sponsor encouraged this approach, and with their support, we set up this new routine. This helped to manage expectations of workload and gave everyone the chance to focus on their tasks. After the cut-off point each day, we found that the key people we needed to work with on the change were focused and committed to creating new ways of working, and productivity improved.

In another team, I had a similar experience. This team were subject experts who supported other colleagues with complex work. They never knew when they would be needed so change activities would often be cancelled at the last minute as they rushed to support colleagues in the business.

After discussions with the sponsor, we were given permission to restructure their time. It was agreed that they would run specific 'surgery' hours when the business knew they could be contacted, and at other times they could safely attend meetings and workshops without interruption.

This worked so well that the schedule has remained in place even though that original change took place seven years ago!

REDUCE MISMATCH BETWEEN REALITY AND EXPECTATIONS – FOCUS ON INCREMENTAL/ITERATIVE CHANGE

One of the most brain-friendly things you can do as a sponsor is to reassure everyone that you do not expect them to know everything at the start. This reduces hesitancy and an unwillingness to get started because everyone is waiting to achieve a 'perfect' level of understanding before they make their contribution.

By encouraging an iterative approach, you can inspire earlier action, as teams try out small elements of the change and learn the true impact on their ways of working. This gives them the chance to test and refine their assumptions, reducing the difference between what they expect and what happens.

Technique – Stepping stones   To encourage an iterative approach, make it clear that you are flexible and open to change and that all outcomes, whether intended or unintended, form part of the learning. For example, discuss the end goal of the change, describe your vision and ask for plans that identify the key outcomes that will achieve this vision. Once you are happy with this

'stepping stone' view, focus the energy of the team on planning and delivering the first outcome but no more. Agree that detailed plans for subsequent
outcomes will be created after the delivery of the previous outcome. This
removes the wasted energy of trying to predict in detail exactly what is
needed months from now, when circumstances might have changed anyway.

The added advantage of this approach is that you are demonstrating you
are going to be actively involved throughout the change, which provides
reassurance that the team have senior-level support for making this change.

Example – Use differences to predict the future   My friend uses a high-
level plan of expected outcomes as the basis for all her team meetings. She
asks the team to describe the outcome they have just delivered and the one
they are currently working on in terms of how closely it matched their
expectations. She uses their identification of the differences to discuss what
this means for the achievement of the change and all the remaining
outcomes:

> These differences are an important piece of information, because we can use
> them to question what will happen next. I do not regard these differences
> as anything other than useful information. They are not failures. Things are
> different to what we expected because our environment changes very fast, and
> we cannot predict everything that will impact us. The only certainty is that
> everything is always changing, so we need to keep checking our understanding
> so that our predictions can be as close to reality as possible.

RELEASE POSITIVE PREDICTION SIGNALS – CREATE A CULTURE OF ASKING FOR AND PROVIDING POSITIVE FEEDBACK

A blocker to providing positive feedback is the desire for 'real' achievement
as the basis of the feedback. Real achievement is often perceived as the
successful completion of a piece of work, or the realization of a measurable
benefit. If we only provide feedback when we reach this point, staying silent
until we reach this 'perfect' moment, then we create a vicious circle.

Technique – Actions and achievements   Overcome this negativity by
providing positive feedback on actions and achievements. For example, give
positive feedback on how people are working, including examples of collaboration with others and the supportive environment for asking questions and
challenging the status quo, identifying and sharing what has been learnt.

FIGURE 11.16 Iterative plan of outcomes to achieve end goal: stepping stone view

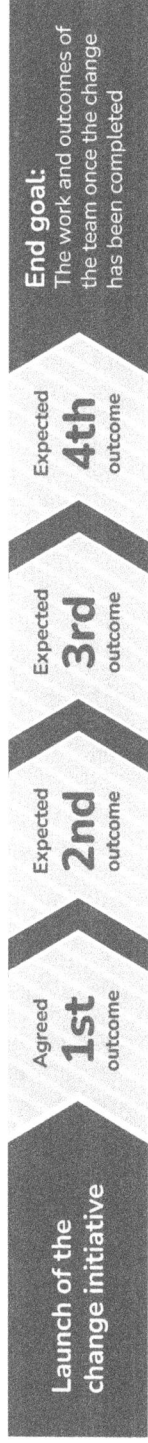

Launch of the change initiative

Agreed **1st** outcome

Expected **2nd** outcome

Expected **3rd** outcome

Expected **4th** outcome

End goal:
The work and outcomes of the team once the change has been completed

FIGURE 11.17 Negativity created when feedback is not sought early enough

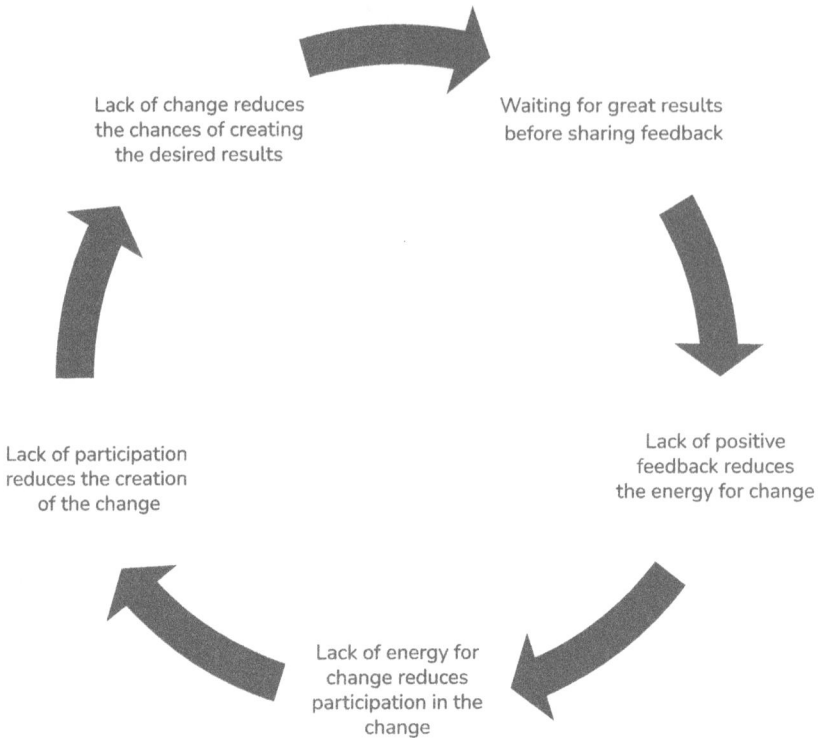

Lack of change reduces the chances of creating the desired results

Waiting for great results before sharing feedback

Lack of positive feedback reduces the energy for change

Lack of energy for change reduces participation in the change

Lack of participation reduces the creation of the change

Factors to consider to increase your range of positive feedback opportunities include:

- Examples of help being provided from one team member to another
- Examples of curiosity and willingness to challenge current ways of working to find new ideas
- Insights and observations that generate a new perspective or help people consider things in a different way
- Bringing new examples and sources of information to the team
- Quality of the work; even when the work is still in progress we can comment on attention to detail, accuracy or how well it is presented
- Willingness to volunteer for extra tasks
- Energy and commitment of team members

Example – Finding something to praise   One of my friends has a way of following up after a visit that provides positive feedback and acts as a celebration. When she is meeting lots of different people, hearing their views, asking them questions about the impact of the change, she takes extensive notes, including the name and job title of who she was speaking to and at what time.

At the end of the visit, often on the train or the plane home, she reviews all her notes and creates a personal email to each person she spoke to, outlining one thing from their conversation that she found insightful, helpful or interesting.

For example, she told me about a 15-minute meeting with someone who during that time had described a new service he had developed. It wasn't this that had caught her attention. As he described the pricing policy, he shared his assessment of the economic factors. He made a remark about the UK focusing on a cost-of-living crisis, whilst across Europe the emphasis was on investment and productivity. It was a pertinent remark for other pricing discussions I was having at the time, and I drew this to his attention and thanked him.

RELEASE POSITIVE PREDICTION SIGNALS – CREATE SMALL HABITS OF PROVIDING UNEXPECTED REWARDS

As a senior leader, a high proportion of your time at work is scheduled and arranged, often weeks in advance. This leaves you little time for spontaneity. However, you can have an immediate and positive impact on your team if you do something unexpected, especially if it is kind or helpful.

Technique – Plan positive interventions   As you plan your schedule for the week, include 15 minutes to answer the question, 'What will I do that will bring my team pleasure this week?'

Think about things that will surprise your team and will show them that you are actively involved with the change, so that they know you are committed to your role. For example, turn up at team meetings to hear their progress or spontaneously congratulate someone for their insight or ideas.

To select an appropriate action, use empathy. Consider the pressures and concerns that a person has. Consider what they are trying to achieve, who they are working with and what their priorities are.

Whilst this section is headed 'unexpected' rewards, we need to be clear that they are unexpected for the recipient but are likely to have been authorized by you. Encourage your change manager to develop a 'celebration strategy' that will trigger dopamine, which builds the energy for more achievement and endorphins, which create positive feelings, reinforcing the willingness to continue involvement with the change.

Consider these three types of celebration:

- Organizational rewards – formal awards, originating from performance management, and often involving a financial element in the form of cash bonuses or thank you vouchers.

- Team-level rewards – these might include some financial rewards but also social rewards via team-wide acknowledgements of achievements, which creates oxytocin.

- Individual rewards – specific to an individual, but while this boosts their endorphins it does not create the oxytocin delivered by team rewards.

Example – Drop-ins   A CEO friend of mine worries that her role isolates her from those affected by the changes she is pursuing. She reviews her diary every week and books in time for 'look-sees' and 'walkies'. These are her terms for getting out of her office and going for a wander around the building, dropping in on people at their desks. Now that her organization permits a hybrid of office and home working, she asks managers for details of any virtual events where they feel an appearance from her would be beneficial. She doesn't dominate these meetings, she tells people she is there to listen, to understand and to answer any questions they have. If they think that she can help remove any of the blockers they are experiencing, they should ask for help, and she will do what she can:

> These sessions energize me so much. I am inspired by the hard work and creativity I see happening all around me. I know I am helping to motivate and to resolve issues, but my walkies always inspire me too.

Technique – Give thanks   You can use positive feedback to create an unexpected reward for those involved in the change. This will boost their feelings of reward and reduce stress. Careful choice of words to highlight a specific characteristic can enable someone to reset their view of themselves away from the negative to the positive.

We are all subject to an inner negative voice, which for some can be very powerful. This voice criticizes our performance, finding faults that others have not noticed and comparing ourselves unfavourably with others.

When senior leaders offer praise, the strength of the compliment is amplified by their seniority.

Example – Specific praise   I work with someone who has no idea how excellent her customer service skills are. By taking the time to specifically praise the quality of her emails to customers, especially with complex issues, I am giving her the evidence that she writes well. I am providing evidence to counter her negative inner voice, so I ensure I am specific in my praise, pointing out phrases she has used and how these connect to the needs of her audience.

RELEASE ENERGY – PROVIDE A CULTURE OF PEOPLE COMING UP WITH THEIR OWN INSIGHTS

It is impossible to demand insights, as these are discoveries that happen as we process information and have new thoughts. They cannot be forced but we can create an environment that increases the probability of this creativity.

We have already described the value of psychological safety in encouraging people to speak up and share their thoughts. We can go further by giving them a starting point and inviting them to build upon it by sharing part-completed work.

To understand why this works, consider what happens when we present a 'complete' idea, solution or argument. If you present every aspect of the change as a complete thought, you have removed the chance for others to contribute. If something is already finished, we have no choice but to accept or reject it. We cannot add to it or make alterations because it is already complete.

Technique – Sharing work in progress   Create the habit of sharing part-completed work. Explain what you are trying to achieve, why it is important, how it connects to other work and who is involved, as customers and suppliers.

Outline your initial ideas. Share your sources of information and assumptions you have made, and then facilitate a discussion on 'Where do we go from here?' Make this session inclusive by emphasizing that this is a group activity, and contributions are welcomed from everyone. To get things started, consider:

- Highlighting gaps and asking for ideas on how to fill them
- Describing your ideas as a range of options and asking others to rate them in order of preference, value, difficulty etc
- Drawing visuals of what you are thinking and inviting others to add to the diagram

Example – What comes after/what comes before?   My colleague sponsors a team of AI developers. She is not an expert in AI but she understands what customers need and working out what will be popular in the future. When she commissions work she knows that she is presenting incomplete thoughts:

> I like diagrams, so I will often draw something up as I am speaking, showing the first few steps. I then ask if the team agree with these steps and ask them what they think comes next. Sometimes I work backwards from these steps, identifying the things I think have happened prior to them, demonstrating my assumptions about work that has already taken place.

> We collaborate on this picture until there are no more ideas flowing and then we agree our next steps. Sometimes I am asked to host a focus group with customers, sometimes the team will decide to build a prototype or research more about the subject ready for another ideas session.

> By sharing my ideas I can get them to the team quicker than if I held on until I was more definite in my thinking. Also, this approach always generates more ideas, challenges assumptions and finds new criteria than I was thinking about, so the quality of our work is better.

Creating information using the PEPE© model

Much of what the PEPE© model teaches us is to apply empathy when engaging with others. There are many techniques in this section that enable you to ask for and listen to the feedback from those directly affected by the change.

These techniques inspire those affected by the change to share their experiences with you, so that you can update the scope of your change in response to the effects of the change, as it is implemented incrementally and iteratively.

REDUCE PERCEPTION OF PAIN – PSYCHOLOGICAL SAFETY

Two-way dialogue relies on psychological safety. It is hard to speak up when there is the fear of being criticized or blamed. As a sponsor, a failure to establish this safety creates the risk that people will only tell you what you want to hear. In change situations, this is especially dangerous, because change means experimenting and trying new ideas. The source of these ideas comes from as many people as possible sharing their assumptions, concerns and past experiences to identify potential next steps.

Technique – Creating a safe space   Creating a safe space means remaining open to new information without jumping in to shut down the discussion

TABLE 11.4

Dimension	Activity	Technique	Example
Reduce perception of pain	Psychological safety	• Creating a safe space	• Let others speak
Release positive signals	Create a culture of asking for and providing positive feedback	• Share the reasons	• Empathetic explanation
Release positive signals	Manage expectations from the beginning and at every stage	• Describe your role • Reduce the rumours	• Instructions for use • Establish a feedback loop
Save energy	Provide the right amount of information at the right time	• Little and often	• Sponsor message board
Save energy	Make it local, personalize it	• Ask, don't tell	• Avoid 'royal visits'
Release energy	Provide opportunities for people to come up with their own insights	• Tell your story	• Sharing your truth
Release energy	Create anticipation and promote hunting	• Visual timeline	• Team timeline
Managing peaks	Promote curiosity	• Engagement strategy	• A 'day in the life of' event

because you are being told things you don't want to hear. This requires self-control, to pull back from your immediate emotional reaction and give a more considered response that acknowledges what you are being told, encouraging the sharing of more details.

To create this self-control, give your brain an action to take when others are giving you feedback. Put yourself in the role of note taker and capture the key points. Become an analyst and follow up with open questions to discover more. This gives your brain time to move from the immediate emotions, which might include anger or rejection of what you are being told, to acceptance and a willingness to hear more.

Example – Let others speak   A friend of mine recognizes that she is impatient, and is often irritated when her ideas are questioned. When she is describing changes that need to be made in her department, she knows she needs to engage the thoughts of others, but too often she feels this delays progress, so she wants to close down the debate and ask people to get moving and get things done:

> It takes a lot for me to listen to others, so I use props to make sure I encourage a two-way flow of ideas. Firstly, I have a checklist of open questions to remind myself to ask for feedback, as I tend to move from announcement of the task to scheduling what needs to be done. Secondly, I always have a notepad and pen with me, to remind myself to take notes when others are speaking. Thirdly, and something that works well for me, is to make sure that as soon as someone has shared an opinion, I open up the conversation to everyone else, by asking specifically for people to add their thoughts. I create an environment where whatever someone has said, it is expected that others will build upon it by adding, removing or amending the scope or the techniques for achieving it.

RELEASE POSITIVE SIGNALS – CREATE A CULTURE OF ASKING FOR AND PROVIDING POSITIVE FEEDBACK

Hearing about change can create anxiety because the requirement to do things differently implies that what people are currently doing is not good enough. This creates a 'threat response' in the brain, characterized by high levels of adrenaline and cortisol. This reduces the energy available for change and inhibits willingness to change.

To overcome this, include positive feedback about current ways of working in your announcements and presentations about the change. Providing this feedback creates a sense of celebration and inspires people to do more, because they are being told they are successful, so they want to achieve more success.

Technique – Share the reasons   Use your empathy to recognize that an announcement of change is a message that what is currently happening is not right. This can trigger self-blame as those involved believe that their current ways of working are not good enough. This is less likely if the change has emerged from within the team, and your sponsorship is helping to give it the resources and authority that it needs.

Overcome these negative assumptions by being as open as possible about the reasons for the change. Share details about the original discussions that led to the idea for the change, who has been involved in these discussions and any sources of information that triggered these ideas.

Example – Empathetic explanation   One of my friends is a senior manager in an organization that she joined straight from school. She has worked her way up the management grades over the last 25 years so she has a good understanding of how it feels to be the person who must change, and not the person imposing the change. When I was doing more junior roles, any change felt like a criticism:

- When I was told 'we are restructuring' I believed the reason was because we were not productive or efficient enough.

- When I was told 'we are changing the software' I believed we were moving to a new system because our work was not accurate enough.

- When I was told 'we are changing our processes' I believed it was because we were working too slowly.

I use these memories to ensure I begin any announcement of change with a clear explanation of where the idea for the change has come from. This decision to commission the change is rarely because of these perceived criticisms, so I want to make that clear at the start.

I explain how the change originated from a look at the longer-term impact of continuing to work as we do, including an assessment of what our competitors are doing, what our customers are telling us that they want, and what others in different industries are doing. I explain the latest technological innovations that are creating new possibilities.

I make sure that my description of the change demonstrates that it is an opportunity, that it is borne out of optimism for doing new things in new ways. It is not a criticism of what we do now. In fact, I celebrate what we do now, what we achieve in my opening remarks because I want people to feel praised for their efforts, not fearful that they are about to be told they are not doing well, that they are not good enough.

RELEASE POSITIVE SIGNALS – MANAGE EXPECTATIONS FROM THE BEGINNING AND AT EVERY STAGE

Our brains are very powerful prediction machines. To minimize how much energy they need, our brains constantly make assumptions about what will happen next, based on previous experiences and immediately available information.

To increase the effectiveness of your information provision during change, use techniques to manage these expectations:

- Expectations about your role
- Expectations about the scope of the change

Your team will have an expectation of your role in the change, based on their involvement in previous change initiatives and their relationship with other sponsors. If they apply these assumptions, it is likely that they will not fully reflect your expectations. You can create positivity and reduce stress by being clear about what you see as the remit of your role and what you expect others involved in the change to be doing.

As a seasoned Chief Executive, and as someone who coaches senior leaders, it is worth noting that the more senior our roles, the less likely the details of our responsibilities will be known by those we manage. Too often there is an assumption that 'we are in charge' but this blanket description creates inaccurate assumptions.

Technique – Describe your role   Be clear about the actions you will take, when you will take them, the information you will share, who you share information with and how people can contact you. Give examples of the situations you expect to become involved in, and situations that you expect the teams to manage for themselves.

Do not deliver this as a statement of fact, but as an initial idea that you want to complete collaboratively.

Example – Instructions for use   We know a talented sponsor, admired and liked by his teams because of his honesty. His name is Matt so he runs a session called 'Matt instructions for use!' We think this is because he loves *The Big Bang Theory* and Sheldon's friends often say that he came with an instruction manual.

In this session Matt presents this diagram (Figure 11.18), and asks the team to help fill it in.

Technique – Reduce the rumours   Expectations about the scope of the change, when unchallenged, can spread as rumours. These are often negative, as the brain is biased towards negativity, so the assumptions that spread rapidly through an organization focus on what might go wrong, or how unworkable the change is.

Use the authority conferred by your role to address these rumours and put across facts that refute them or give a more positive perspective to counteract the negative messages.

To do this, it is important that you establish a structure to source feedback:

- Inclusive – from everyone affected by the change.
- Comprehensive – from every event, formal and informal, where the change is discussed.
- Direct – individuals can share their views without having to escalate through a management hierarchy to be heard.
- Easy – using media that is already in use and understood in your organization.

Use Figure 11.19 as a guide to your mechanism.

Example – Establish a feedback loop   A colleague has used the diagram to formalize the responsibility for gathering and processing information about the changes taking place in her organization. She has made the Portfolio

FIGURE 11.18 Describing your role

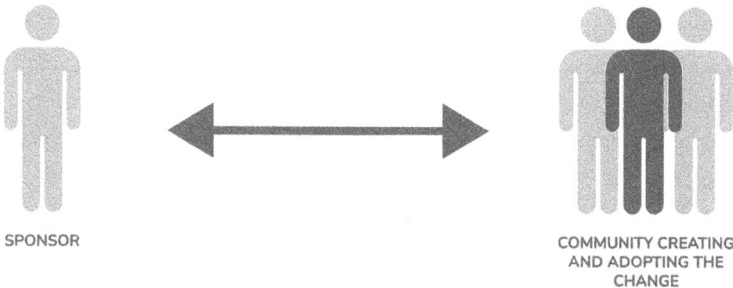

SPONSOR

COMMUNITY CREATING
AND ADOPTING THE
CHANGE

You provide to your team:
Strategic context, reasons why the change is important
and is needed now
Information about other initiatives
Examples of how I am changing my behaviour
Encouragement and support for the team
Celebrations of achievement

You need from your team:
Regular updates on progress and achievements
Requests for my assistance when there are blockages
that my seniority/expertise can remove

FIGURE 11.19 Sourcing and managing feedback

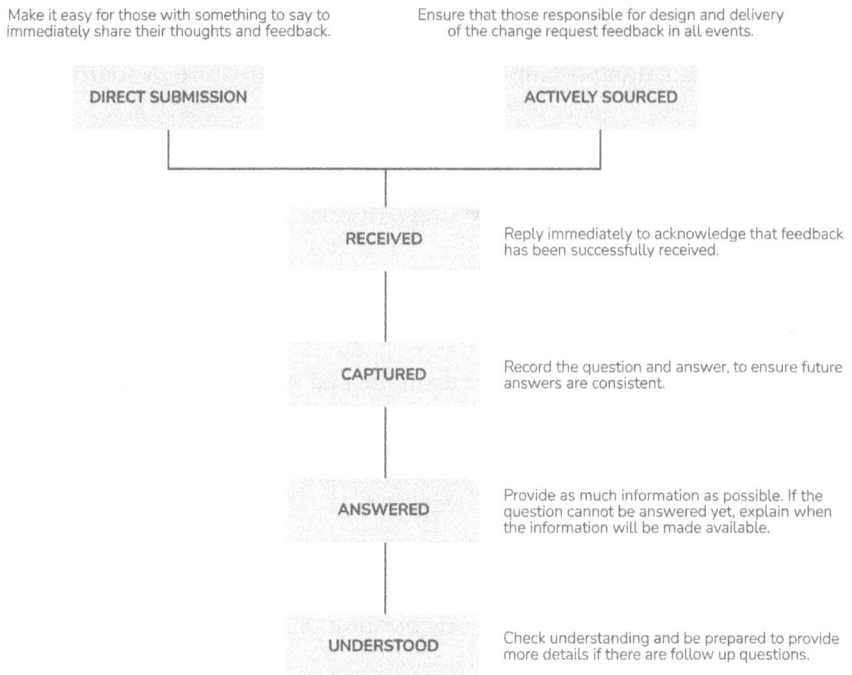

Make it easy for those with something to say to immediately share their thoughts and feedback.

Ensure that those responsible for design and delivery of the change request feedback in all events.

DIRECT SUBMISSION	ACTIVELY SOURCED

RECEIVED — Reply immediately to acknowledge that feedback has been successfully received.

CAPTURED — Record the question and answer, to ensure future answers are consistent.

ANSWERED — Provide as much information as possible. If the question cannot be answered yet, explain when the information will be made available.

UNDERSTOOD — Check understanding and be prepared to provide more details if there are follow up questions.

Office responsible for this work, because they have oversight of every change initiative.

They have established a process for capturing feedback using conference management tools to host poll questions at every formal presentation about the change. They also have a chatbot running on their intranet site, so that anyone involved in or affected by the change can ask questions or share an opinion.

They initially allowed staff to give feedback anonymously, but found that this generated lots of criticisms but did not allow them to find out more and solve the problems.

These internal feedback loops have been extended to customers and suppliers, which has been welcomed, although account managers are encouraged to ask questions about satisfaction levels directly with customers. This approach has been extended to include procurement and finance staff who have relationships with supplier organizations:

> The only reason we have been able to widen out this feedback loop is because of technology. We have created an AI-driven chatbot connected to a vector database so we can ask a wide range of questions about the feedback and find answers immediately.

SAVE ENERGY – PROVIDE THE RIGHT AMOUNT OF INFORMATION AT THE RIGHT TIME

Obviously, as the sponsor you have a lot of information about the scope of the change, the reasons why the change is needed and the expected benefits of the change. You can also provide useful information about how the change aligns with other initiatives taking place across your organization. However, providing too much information can be counterproductive, because this increases the amount of energy the brain needs to process the information. Sharing too much information all at once means your audience will feel overwhelmed; they will lose concentration as their brains form assumptions and imagine scenarios, which diverts focus from your core message.

Technique – Little and often   The simplest way to overcome this is to look ahead and identify the best time to communicate key messages throughout the life of the change. Let your audience know that your approach to communication is 'little and often' and share the likely events and/or dates when you will update them.

This demonstrates that you are going to be supporting them throughout the change, which counteracts a common assumption, that senior leaders only appear at the start and end of a change initiative.

This also frees your audience to concentrate on the message you are providing now, knowing there is more to come.

Example – Sponsor message board   A friend of mine shows the same picture every time she makes strategic announcements about changes in her organization. It is a simple visual that sets out what she calls the 'core updates' (see Figure 11.20).

This visual clearly shows I am going to be around and I am going to be involved. It takes the pressure off me because I don't have to wait until I have lots of information before I make my first announcement and as things are changing all the time anyway, by staying close to the team I can keep them up to date with new developments as they happen.

SAVE ENERGY – MAKE IT LOCAL, PERSONALIZE IT

If you only describe the change from the strategic perspective, it will be difficult for those impacted by change to connect with it. This is because, for the most part, their perspective concerns the practical application of the change. They have a responsibility to identify and adopt changes to what

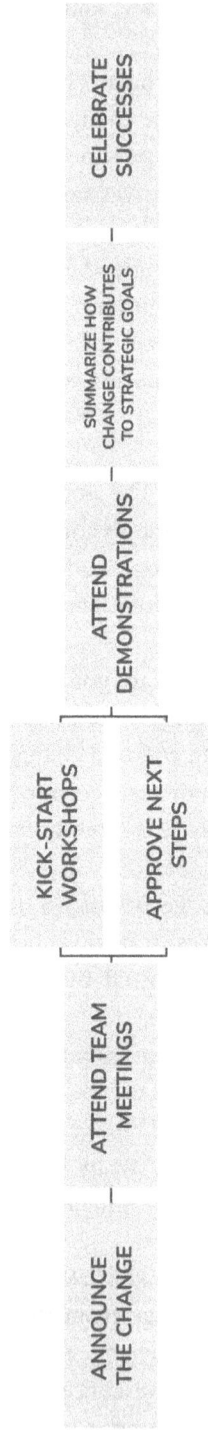

FIGURE 11.20 Core updates throughout a change

they do, how, when and with whom. Describing how the change helps to achieve the overall objectives of the organization might be useful for some, but for many it is not meaningful enough to generate motivation to make it happen.

Technique – Ask, don't tell   Accept that you do not have a full understanding of how the change will be experienced by those you are asking to work differently. You cannot personalize or localize your message sufficiently to capture the full impact.

Instead of trying to create a perfect explanation of the change, focus on asking questions about what the change means for others, how they are affected and what their concerns are:

- Ask how those affected by the change will need to work differently
- Ask for demonstrations and walk-throughs of their processes
- Follow up on their answers, so that you can demonstrate that you heard what they had to say

Some of your follow-up will involve the immediate removal of blockers to their progress. Other actions will require the involvement of others and potential compromises. In some cases you will not be able to resolve their issues.

Whatever the outcome, ensure that you reply, summarizing their key points and what actions you took. Failure to do so means that those you talked to will have gone from being heard to feeling that they wasted their time. This means they no longer feel valued, creating resentment and turning what was positive intervention into a negative.

Example – Avoid 'royal visits'   A friend who is a senior leader in a large global organization describes visits to offices and customer service centres around the world as 'royal visits'. He says it feels as if the King is visiting: 'Everyone is on their best behaviour. I am given a tour of the facilities, and a high-level summary of current issues. No one wants to share any details.' To overcome this, he asks to sit beside people at their desks and he stands beside people on the production line and asks them to show him exactly what they do:

> It is in those sessions that I can ask detailed questions about how their work will change as a result of our new strategic objectives. I get to see how the changes will affect the business at a very detailed level.

Over the years, I have refined my approach, so I now ask for these sessions to be planned so that I meet people from the start to the finish of an activity. This includes meeting someone from each step in the process of managing a customer enquiry or the fulfilment of an order in our distribution centre.

I have refined my questions so that I specifically ask how the change affects their work, what they think will be easier and more difficult, and what else they wish was changing. It is this last question that generates insights into blockages, disconnects and duplications of effort that we just do not see from a strategic view.

RELEASE ENERGY – PROVIDE OPPORTUNITIES FOR PEOPLE TO COME UP WITH THEIR OWN INSIGHTS

You can encourage people to have insights or moments of clarity by sharing your perspective. This gives them useful inputs to compare against their own assumptions, challenge their thinking and have ideas.

Technique – Tell your story   To inspire people to ask questions and seek out more information, demonstrate that you have information to share! During your career, you will have been involved in lots of changes. You will have been affected by change, and you will have sponsored changes. You might have experienced similar changes to the one you are now sponsoring.

Use your knowledge to tell a story about the journey that staff are about to go on. As with any story, include a description of the feelings you experienced at each step. This demonstrates that the change is not just a series of tasks, but that change is emotional.

Example – Sharing your truth   A friend always starts her change initiatives with a story about the last change she was involved in. She describes how it started, and the excitement she felt at the new opportunity but the fears she had about the workload, and the difficulties of doing something that she had not done before.

She describes the extra effort she had to put in on top of her day job, and the frustrations when things took longer and were more complicated than expected. She describes the need for resilience when everything feels like it is going wrong but it is still important to keep going.

She always ends her story with an assessment of the skills she learnt, the people who inspired her and the achievements she is most proud of.

When asked for her advice for this book she said:

I am not a natural storyteller. I am an engineer and I like facts and I like solutions. However, I find this story easy to tell because it is my truth, it is how

I experienced change and I find when I tell it I end up feeling proud of myself, which is nice. But I don't tell it for me, I tell it so that others can imagine their own journey of change, and have ideas about what they will do, or how they need to prepare themselves.

I always get lots of questions at the end, and these tell me that people are having insights about how they will manage themselves and the new situation. For example, I always get questions about the impact on my work/life balance during the change; what coping mechanisms I used and who I turned to for advice when I was worried.

RELEASE ENERGY – CREATE ANTICIPATION AND PROMOTE 'HUNTING' ACTIVITIES

Anticipating the successful outcome of our work gives us energy and the resilience to keep going when we face problems. As a sponsor, you can increase the anticipation of your team by sharing details of expected outcomes across the organization.

This sends powerful messages to the team:

- They are not the only ones experiencing change
- Their work is an input to other things happening
- There is a lot happening, their organization is energized and is committed to change

Technique – Visual timeline Create a simple visual that identifies other changes, expected benefits, product launches, opening of new offices etc. Use one year as your timeline, because less than this and you may have fewer items to share, longer than this and your audience will find it harder to connect to the immediacy of what you are sharing.

Think about how to break up the ideas. If you do this by business function, it is harder to show cross-functional outcomes. If you are a global organization or a conglomerate of multiple brands it might be helpful to show the outcomes by different continents or different legal entities.

Alternatively, show all the changes that are impacting different groups. You can increase the customer-centricity of your explanation by demonstrating how many other changes each customer group is experiencing in the next year.

Example – Team timeline   A friend of mine has been using this diagram for years (Figure 11.21), and has refined her thinking. As she told me:

> I use this to generate excitement about our organization, and not just for the changes I am sponsoring. I want to make it fun, so I include personal events, because when we picture the future, we do not confine our thoughts only to business outcomes.
>
> I like to include the holiday periods, so we have something outside of work to get excited about – the enjoyment of a summer break, or the chance to celebrate the new year watching the fireworks with family and friends.
>
> A way to learn more about each other is to include significant home events including births, graduations, significant birthdays, wedding anniversaries or retirements. Some of my team like to include significant sporting events (my US team always adds the Super Bowl!) and some have suggested the inclusion of major religious festivals as these often coincide with holiday periods, as long as everyone agrees.
>
> Another tip is to make sure that I show the whole year, but start from whatever month we are in the first time I show it, so it feels as if we are all starting the journey at the same time.

MANAGING PEAKS – PROMOTE CURIOSITY

To be effective, information is a two-way process. Any announcement needs to generate a response. This response is a result of curiosity. If people are questioning the information they receive, they are engaging with it, assessing its relevance to them and thinking through its implications. This two-way exchange is vital to ensure the success of your change. You cannot sponsor in a vacuum; you need this engagement to ensure the right changes are made at the right time.

Technique – Engagement strategy   As a sponsor, your perceived seniority within the organization can inhibit people from sharing information. To overcome this, develop your own engagement strategy that reflects your personality and how you like to work. This strategy includes:

- Deciding upon the frequency, format and guest list for regular sessions with those affected by change
- Identification of communication channels that reach your audience and that you are confident using

FIGURE 11.21 Team timeline

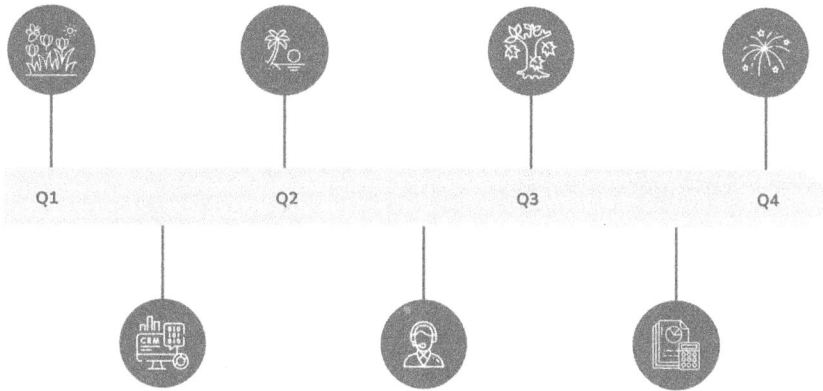

Example – 'A day in the life of' event   A friend of mine has an effective technique for encouraging curiosity from his workforce, who for cultural reasons are unlikely to ask questions in a big presentation. The culture is respectful of seniority, so asking a question of a senior manager is viewed as impertinent. This makes it difficult to really understand how people are reacting to the change, or to provide them with the information they need.

He has overcome this reluctance by holding smaller meetings between staff on the frontline of production, distribution, sales and marketing, customer service and corporate services (HR, finance, procurement, etc).

He will ask managers to bring a group of staff covering all grades and levels of experience to the meeting. He asks his own management team to attend. The seating is arranged so that members of the management team sit amongst the rest of the staff, himself included. The first session he runs, before any formal presentations of the change, is a 'day in the life of' discussion. Everyone gets together in small groups of two or three people, and they share details of their working day.

This has two important effects:

1 It creates the realization that everyone is the same; whatever their job, they still have to commute to work, balance childcare with work, or make time to get the shopping or go to the gym after work.

2 People describe what they are working on, what takes up most of their time, what their priorities are, things that are difficult and things they enjoy. This enables them to learn more about each other's contribution to the company.

This session is a warm-up; it builds bonds, it creates trust. I cannot expect people to speak up, share their opinions and critique the change if they are fearful of 'the suits'. I need them to know we are all the same despite the job titles and implied seniority. We all work for the same company, we all make a contribution and we are all valuable.

Building the capability for change

In your strategic role as a senior leader of your organization, you have a responsibility to successfully implement the change you are sponsoring, whilst at the same time building capability for change. This capability for change is the ability of your organization to maintain achievement of all 'business as normal' activities whilst simultaneously re-imaging what this normal is.

This capability involves commissioning, implementing and benefiting from transformation, where transformation is formed of a spectrum of activity from large-scale change programmes to continuous improvements.

Capability scales up the successful achievement of a single change into an environment that enables the organization to systematically and reliably implement and realize the benefits from multiple, simultaneous changes.

There are many cultural, behavioural and tangible elements that form this capability, generated by the prevailing business conditions and the contribution of each change. As a sponsor, you can make a significant contribution to this capability by ensuring that the activities you select throughout your leadership of the change maximize these four factors:

- Optimism
- Skills
- Confidence
- Empowerment

OPTIMISM
Optimism is the expectation of the best possible outcome. It is a willingness to seek out the most hopeful aspects of a situation. Optimism creates an environment of positivity, which has specific benefits during change. By expecting the best:

- we are more open to new information, as we see this as an opportunity to learn and improve our outcomes;

- we are more willing to consider other views and a wider range of possibilities;
- we are kinder and less judgmental of others because we assume they have positive intent.

If we are optimistic, each successful implementation of change builds the view that change enhances results. This good news can be used to increase optimism by providing examples of when things go well. This helps to overcome the cynicism described in the previous chapter.

SKILLS

Skills are the ability to do things well. Change offers many opportunities to build skills outside of the restrictions of a specific role, because during change we experience new situations and have the chance to innovate, doing new things in new ways. Developing skills in your team increases the ability of your organization to self-manage future changes without relying on the contribution of external resources. As well as reducing the cost of future changes, this also makes sense because of the high volume of change. To match this increasing volume of change, there is a need Without the skills to plan, manage and adopt change.

An important consideration from a neuroscientific perspective is the need to enable skills development by allowing time for reflection. Review the section later in this chapter about promoting valleys for ideas on how to do this.

CONFIDENCE

Confidence is feeling sure of yourself, belief that you have the necessary skills and abilities for the situations you face. This is an inner belief, a form of self-reliance as you have the certainty that you know how to do things. Building the collective confidence within your team generates a broader capability for the organization for future changes. This is because their belief in their abilities means they will volunteer for more change, safe in the knowledge that they know what to do and how to do it. Confidence increases the willingness to coach others and role-model new behaviours, essential elements of a change organization.

EMPOWERMENT

Empowerment is a willingness to take control of a situation rather than relying on the authority of others to dictate events. Empowerment creates increased engagement and motivation, as this self-direction and personal decision-taking generates dopamine and endorphins. The brain experiences each decision we take as an achievement, which triggers the production of these positive brain chemicals. An engaged and motivated workforce will volunteer for more change situations, creating a workforce willing to innovate and change how they work.

Elements of a successful change

An obvious definition of a successful change is one that achieves the desired benefits. After all, the objective of organizational change is to improve the current situation. These improvements lead to increases in productivity and revenue whilst reducing costs. However, in an environment of high volumes of change, it makes sense to widen this definition to include a positive experience of change.

IMPACT OF A POOR PERFORMANCE

A negative experience generates costs that reduce or even eliminate any benefits generated by the change. A poor experience in the short term leads to withdrawal of effort, which lengthens the time required to adopt the change, pushing out the point at which a return on investment can be achieved.

In the medium term, a poor experience triggers exit plans, as those affected seek out employment with lower stress and greater reward. In the longer term, a poor experience of change makes it less likely that future changes will be successful, as the impact of a poor experience is to foster negativity in the form of cynicism. As we learnt earlier, cynicism is a contagion that easily affects others.

Figure 11.23 shows the need to maintain a balance between experience and achievement. It provides success criteria for achievement and experience. At any point in the change, refer to this diagram to assess which aspects of the change to emphasize.

Example   A colleague uses these criteria to create the agenda for his weekly team meetings:

> I am under pressure to deliver the outcome of the change. My performance is assessed against revenue and cost targets so it is easy to get caught up in driving the team to get things right. This table helps me remember that creating bonding moments, focusing on relationships and the quality of our experiences at work is as important. It certainly makes work more enjoyable, and it represents the type of leader I want to be. I just wish there was more emphasis on these factors in my annual appraisal.

FIGURE 11.22 Change and capability

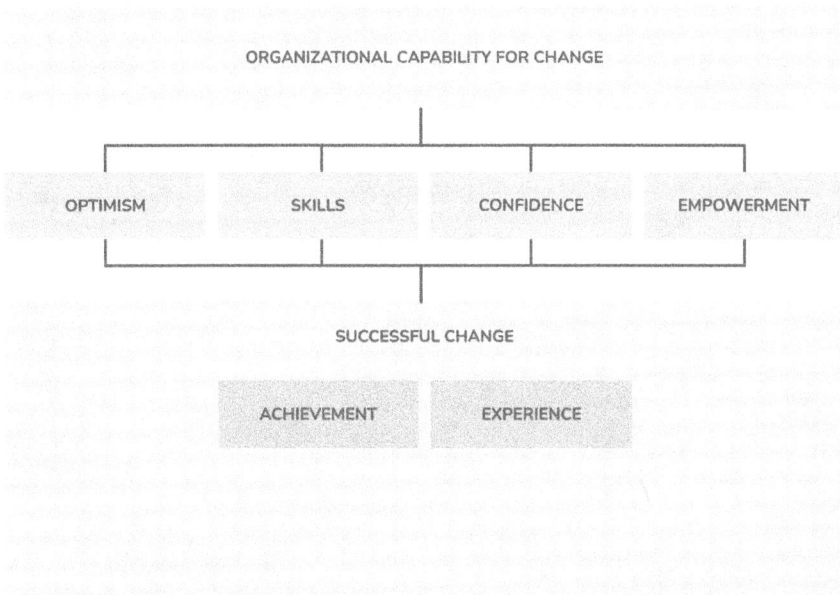

Creating a positive experience of change

Previously in this chapter, we gave examples from the PEPE© model that will increase the probability of a successful outcome. The rest of this chapter focuses on activities that will increase the probability of a positive experience.

Peaks and valleys

Using the Peaks and Valleys domain of the PEPE© model, we can increase the probability of a successful change experience. This increases the probability of realizing the benefits and of contributing to the organizational capability for change.

Our brains operate at their best when levels of brain chemicals fluctuate. These fluctuations lead to heightened focus and concentration, the generation of new ideas and high performance. If we have prolonged exposure to one state (highs or lows) we can experience lower motivation, shorter attention span and poor memory.

During the change lifecycle we need to encourage peak working whilst balancing this with periods of rest and reflection. Creating and maintaining this balance means the sponsor role is incredibly demanding, especially because your level of authority amplifies the impact you can have on the reactions of those involved in the change.

FIGURE 11.23 Balancing experience and achievement

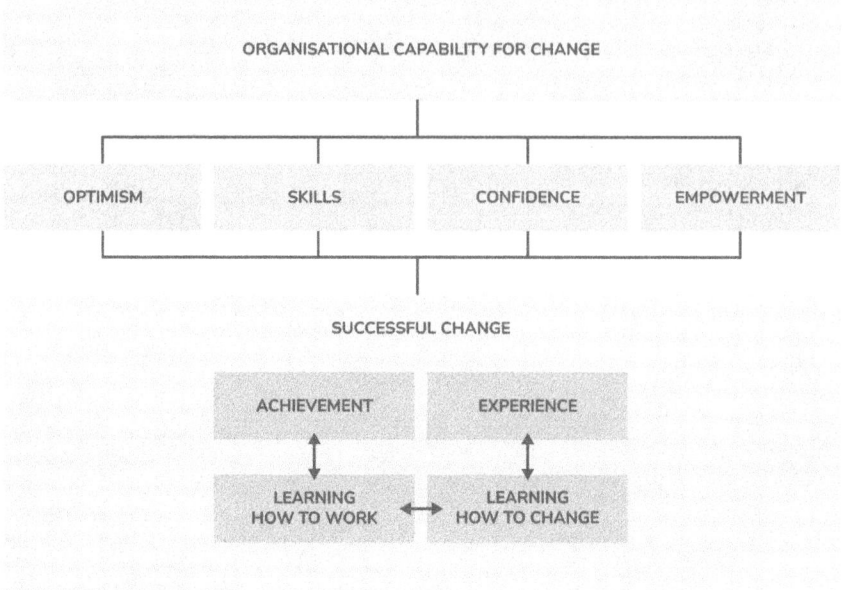

```
                    ORGANISATIONAL CAPABILITY FOR CHANGE


   OPTIMISM          SKILLS          CONFIDENCE        EMPOWERMENT


                         SUCCESSFUL CHANGE


            ACHIEVEMENT            EXPERIENCE


             LEARNING              LEARNING
            HOW TO WORK           HOW TO CHANGE
```

Being aware of this impact will help you to understand when and what to adjust to energize your team or create a period of rest before the next peak.

As a sponsor, you have an almost automatic ability to create the 'threat' response, which triggers the release of adrenaline. This is because:

- your seniority within the organization creates the belief that your requests must be complied with, generating a sense of necessity and urgency to cooperate;
- team members perceive that they are not in control, because they are following your instructions.

Whilst some adrenaline is helpful in getting work started, too much and for too long means there will be a lack of progress as fear and anxiety impede creativity and motivation.

Your actions can also have a disproportionate influence on the creation of valleys, because your requests for reflection and celebration can encourage your team to stay too long in this restful state, limiting their progress and achievement of the new ways of working.

Earlier in the chapter, we described many activities you can use to deliver a successful change. Use the descriptions below to understand how these activities can be drawn together to create peaks or valleys and use the success criteria to understand if your interventions are having the desired effect.

Managing peaks

Create a regular rhythm for the work by encouraging your teams to work in small cycles of change. Each cycle begins with a focus on the goal to be achieved and the work required, as this will create energy through the stimulation of dopamine and adrenaline.

This regular rhythm creates a sense of comfort, as our brains can see the pattern of repeating tasks. This saves energy and reduces the threat response in the brain, even if the goal for each cycle of change is ambitious.

Establish success criteria to clarify what good looks like. These criteria provide the indicators along the way that the team can check for, to understand their progress. This creates energy as they are able to anticipate their success.

Focusing on the goal and discussing it with colleagues creates oxytocin, increasing the pleasure associated with the work. This stops the energy people feel for the work becoming overwhelming, where this feeling of stress inhibits rather than encourages progress.

Identifying specific tasks and encouraging team members to volunteer for them increases the control they have over their work, which increases their feelings of autonomy, associated with the release of endorphins which reduce pain.

This volunteerism increases the pleasure we associate with work, as we are choosing things that mean something to us, work that we enjoy doing, that we think is valuable or that we believe will help us develop our skills.

Encourage people to volunteer for work that provides some stretch and helps them to move outside of their comfort zone. This personal risk-taking will generate energy via the creation of dopamine.

CRITERIA FOR SUCCESSFUL PEAKS

- There is a common understanding of the goals to be achieved and the work needed for these goals.
- There is a clear plan, with milestones and measures of success created using the subject expertise of all the team members.
- Individuals feel energized by the work – there is a buzz, people are asking questions, sharing ideas and information.

- There is a sense of personal responsibility for the work:
  o People are volunteering for tasks without having to be asked.
  o They are self-managing when, how and for how long they work.
  o They are willingly sharing their progress.
  o When there are problems, they are contributing potential solutions.
- There is a collaborative environment:
  o Teams are forming spontaneously as needed for the work.
  o People are sharing their skills through coaching others.
- There is a willingness to take risks and try new things.
- There is debate, people are demonstrating curiosity and a willingness to challenge the status quo.
- There are high levels of ideas generation.

Promoting valleys

Once the work is completed, facilitate a move into reflection and celebration, which creates endorphins, enabling your team to feel pleasure. As we learnt at the start of this book, releasing acetylcholine enables individuals to be more open to learning and to adapt positively to change. There are no specific activities identified to produce acetylcholine, as it develops over time. The best way for you to stimulate this neurotransmitter is to provide time for reflection. There are more details about this in 'Peaks and Valleys', specifically 'promote the valleys'.

REFLECTION

Too often, no time for this reflection has been included in the change initiative, because the focus is on the delivery of the tangible change, often to a tight and unyielding deadline.

As a sponsor, you have the authority to adopt a different approach. Instigate 'official' periods of reflection as part of your iterative change plan.

Encourage team members to put time aside for personal reflection. For ideas on this, see the 'practical application' section later in this chapter.

Reflecting on the achievement will produce endorphins, generated by a feeling of pride that work has been completed. Encourage collaborative reflection that focuses on the achievement of the change and the experience of the change.

- Discuss the success of the work in terms of the quality criteria, new ideas that were added and new techniques used to create the work.
- Share examples of the support received from colleagues and the enjoyment of helping others, sharing skills and knowledge and ensuring everyone feels part of the team. This creates a sense of belonging which generates oxytocin.

By sharing thoughts and feelings, this creates energy as people have 'aha' moments, realizing what they have learnt, or how the results of their work connect together to form a bigger picture.

Focusing on learning increases a feeling that people are valued and respected, which increases the pleasure associated with the work.

Reflection is not merely a nice gesture. It has considerable business value, as this diagram shows. Periods of reflection before commencing further work enable us to drive the most value out of what has already been changed. It enables everyone to recognize that the change has delivered a

FIGURE 11.24 Iterative plan without time for reflection

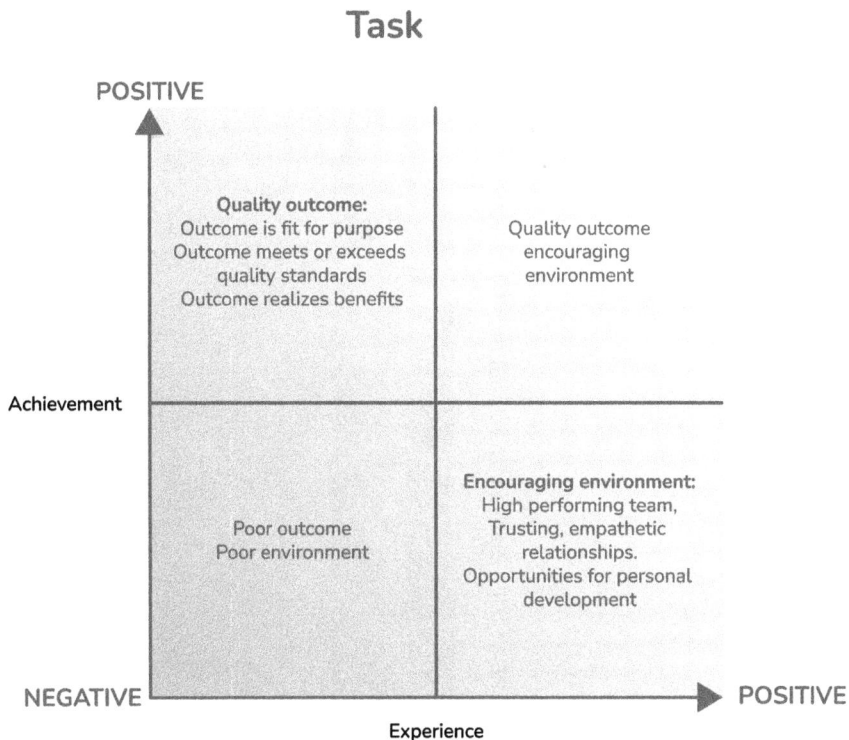

Task

POSITIVE

Quality outcome:
Outcome is fit for purpose
Outcome meets or exceeds quality standards
Outcome realizes benefits

Quality outcome encouraging environment

Achievement

Poor outcome
Poor environment

Encouraging environment:
High performing team,
Trusting, empathetic relationships.
Opportunities for personal development

NEGATIVE   POSITIVE

Experience

FIGURE 11.25 Iterative plan without time for reflection

new capability. This means your organization can do more than it could do before, so question how you can further exploit this ability. What difference will this capability make and who will benefit from it? Answering these questions encourages curiosity and generates insights about what other changes to make.

Try to encourage identification of where things went better than expected. Talk about things that were easier or took less time than everyone assumed. Highlight where there were fewer mistakes or failures than everyone anticipated. Each of these is a bonus, an unexpected reward that triggers the creation of endorphins as we feel pleasure from the enjoyment of the reward.

Use this reflection on what has been achieved to create a new baseline. Ensure everyone has a common understanding of what has been achieved and what this means for the organization. This increases certainty, by defining the journey so far and the rest of the route to be travelled. Certainty increases pleasure and reduces stress.

Create a diagram or other visual to represent this journey. The visual reduces the energy needed by the brain to understand the information being communicated.

This will create dopamine, which energizes your team as they identify the achievements, and endorphins as they enjoy the satisfaction derived from their achievements.

Make time for sharing positive feedback so that the brain creates endorphins. If there is suspicion that positive feedback will be packaged with 'areas for improvement' the brain will be waiting for this negativity which will inhibit the creation of the positive brain chemicals.

CRITERIA FOR SUCCESSFUL VALLEYS

- Reflections are spread out over time, with opportunities for team members to consider their experiences and develop their own insights.
- People are given the opportunity to 'tell their story' so they can explain to their colleagues the techniques they used, what they learnt, the skills they developed and how they are feeling about their progress.
- Team members are encouraged to formally capture these so they gain recognition for their new abilities.
- Time and resources are dedicated to socializing and creating informality amongst the team.
- Success is celebrated at a leisurely pace, with a chance to talk through the successes and enjoy the moment.

FIGURE 11.26 Reflection

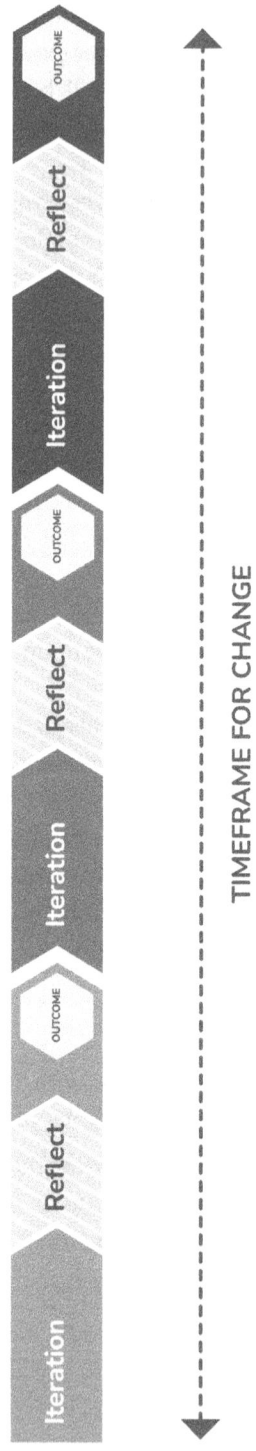

TIMEFRAME FOR CHANGE

FIGURE 11.27 Impact of reflection

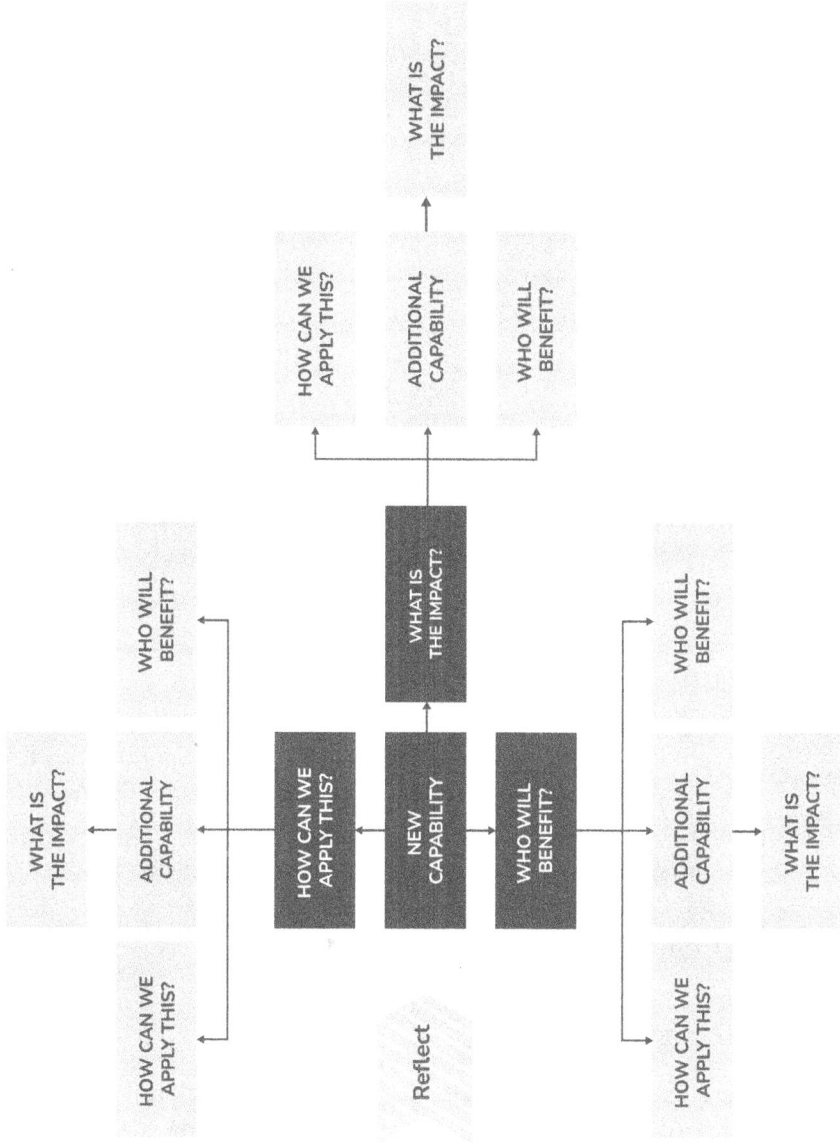

FIGURE 11.28 Example of visually representing the new state after your change

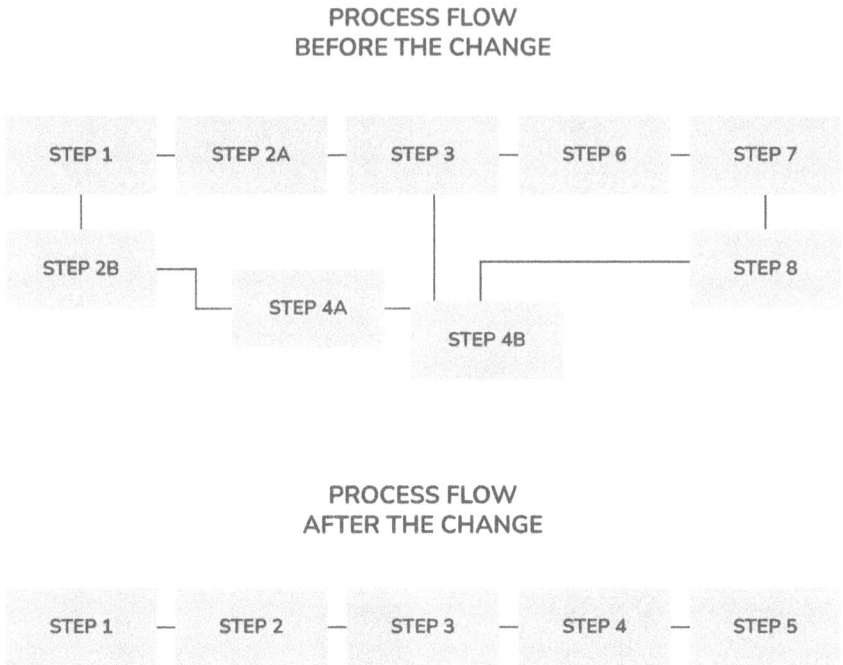

PROCESS FLOW
BEFORE THE CHANGE

PROCESS FLOW
AFTER THE CHANGE

TIMING

It is not possible to specify how exactly how long we need to spend in each state, as some people need more time in the valleys than others. However, generally speaking we should allocate more time to peaks than to valleys to maintain motivation, focus and peak performance.

In our experience, very little time, if any, is formally allocated to the promotion of valleys in change initiatives, so any progress in this area is an improvement.

Practical application

We are encouraging the creation of peaks and valleys throughout the lifecycle of each change, so that it becomes part of the ideal environment for effective change.

At the same time, sponsors should encourage individuals to build habits that manage their work using this concept throughout the day and week to minimize the risk of stress and burnout.

FIGURE 11.29 Example 'ideal day'

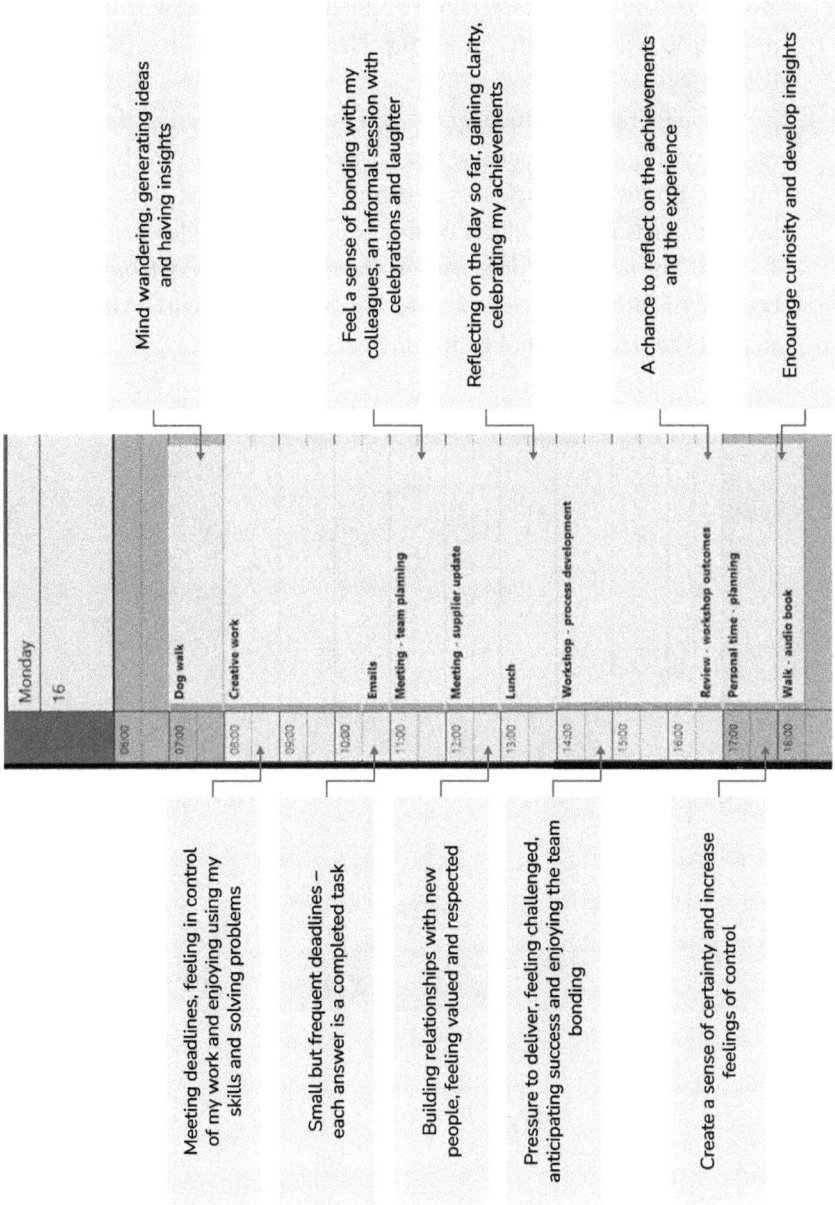

Monday	
16	
06:00	
07:00	Dog walk
08:00	Creative work
09:00	
10:00	Emails
11:00	Meeting - team planning
12:00	Meeting - supplier update
13:00	Lunch
14:00	Workshop - process development
15:00	
16:00	
17:00	Review - workshop outcomes
	Personal time - planning
18:00	Walk - audio book

Mind wandering, generating ideas and having insights

Feel a sense of bonding with my colleagues, an informal session with celebrations and laughter

Reflecting on the day so far, gaining clarity, celebrating my achievements

A chance to reflect on the achievements and the experience

Encourage curiosity and develop insights

Meeting deadlines, feeling in control of my work and enjoying using my skills and solving problems

Small but frequent deadlines – each answer is a completed task

Building relationships with new people, feeling valued and respected

Pressure to deliver, feeling challenged, anticipating success and enjoying the team bonding

Create a sense of certainty and increase feelings of control

Of course, the best way to do this is to role-model your own peaks and valleys approach. By applying these ideas to your own work, you can empathize with others about the experience. For example, in writing this book alongside demanding careers, we applied what we know from neuroscience to develop what we refer to as our 'ideal' schedule, on a daily and weekly basis.

We deliberately include valley activities, interspersing them throughout each working day to increase our chances of working in the optimum way for our brains. This helps us remember how easy it is to achieve peaks, because needs and deadlines from our clients and colleagues keep the pressure up. The skill is to detect when we are falling away from peak working because of too much stress, and to take time for activities that enable us to step off the treadmill and gain some perspective.

12

Supporting neurodiversity

Neurodiversity is a concept that recognizes and celebrates the natural diversity of the human brain and the various ways individuals experience and process information. It describes the idea that people experience and interact with the world around them in many different ways; there is not a single 'correct' mode of thinking, learning or behaving and the differences are not viewed as disabilities.

Even though neurodiversity may sound like a term used in brain science, effectively it emerged in the late 1990s from a social justice movement and social science research and was coined by sociologist Judy Singer.[1] It offers a new perspective on the differences in the human perception, behaviour and communication styles, focusing on the strengths each individual has to offer, as well as the need in terms of collective effort to adopt new processes, tools or environments so neurodivergent individuals can flourish and society and organizations can optimize the unique strengths that neurodiversity can bring for the benefit of all.

From a neuroscience perspective, neurodiversity describes the vast variation in human neurocognition, communication, brain functions and how the brain is wired. The concept has evolved to incorporate a range of neurological differences, including autism spectrum disorder (ASD), attention deficit hyperactivity disorder (ADHD), dyslexia, Tourette's syndrome and dyspraxia (DCD) among other neurodevelopmental differences.

From a brain science perspective, neurodiversity is often used to identify and label a deviation from the typical statistical representation of neuronal and behavioural traits (sometimes referred to as 'neurotypical'). Research has demonstrated around 15 to 20 per cent of the population fall under this 'atypical' range of categories of neurodiversity. It is important to emphasize here that the terms typical and atypical are just used for statistical purposes and are neutral terms, which means they are not better or disabling but simply denote a probability of expression. The term 'neurominorities' should be used recognizing that it is used for purely statistical purposes rather than in any way to express exclusion, social expectation or achievements.

It definitely should not be pathologized or viewed as a condition that needs a 'cure' or 'repairing'. In fact, neurodiversity actually exists across the entire population, even though only around 15 to 20 per cent of the population show a greater deviation from the 'typical' range. Unfortunately, there are still a huge number of misconceptions and stigmatization around neurodivergent individuals and a great effort is needed to switch perceptions at the social, psychological, medical and organizational levels.

Even though neuroscience research has progressed enormously in uncovering the underlying reasons and biological measurements of the neurodiverse population, still there is much need to discover and explore the genetic and neurodevelopmental basis of neurodivergent individuals[2] as well as the benefits from an evolutionary perspective.

Neurodiverse people often possess unique strengths, such as exceptional attention to detail, innovative problem-solving abilities or heightened analytical skills, which can be incredibly beneficial to organizations, particularly during times of change. At the same time each neurodivergent configuration can have its own challenges. For instance, individuals with autism might have difficulties with social communication, a need for routine and be more inclined to compromised well-being but may excel in pattern recognition, attention to detail and memory, which can be particularly advantageous in roles requiring analytical precision or innovative problem-solving. Those with dyslexia might struggle with traditional reading and writing, stress management and organizational skills but often exhibit strengths in spatial reasoning, big-picture thinking, creativity and entrepreneurism. Similarly, individuals with ADHD can have difficulties with time management, concentration, attention to detail or self-regulation but they have heightened creativity, dynamic problem-solving skills, passion and courage.

This perspective challenges the traditional view of neurological differences as deficits or disorders to be fixed or cured, promoting instead an understanding of these differences as a valued form of diversity, much like biodiversity or cultural diversity. The intention is not only to better understand these variations but also to apply this understanding to develop more effective educational strategies, workplace accommodations and social support systems that embrace diverse neurological conditions, promoting inclusion and well-being for all individuals.

Some research, medical experts and the 'lived' experience of individuals have led to the introduction of a new term, 'neurominorities', to emphasize the statistical perspective rather than the diversity of the brain itself. It's an umbrella term to not only include neurodevelopmental neurological conditions such as ASD, ADHD or dyslexia but to also include 'acquired brain wiring differences' and mental health difficulties due to brain plasticity such as PTSD (post-traumatic stress disorder), depression and anxiety.[3] Again, the term 'neurominorities' should be used, recognizing that it is used for purely statistical purposes rather than in any way to express exclusion, social expectation or achievements.

Change, as explained in earlier sections of the book (see Chapter 1), interferes with how our brain is wired as it goes against our principles of survival and reward. We are not wired for change, but instead to resist first. However, due to the impact of brain plasticity, we are wired in any case to 'adapt'. In this case, the price of the adaptation to change could represent a very high cost to the brains and bodies of individuals as it could result in maladaptation, stress, addiction, non-helpful behaviours or illnesses. In the case of organizations, the maladaptation could lead to lack of innovation, motivation, disengagement, major financial losses and failure to achieve results from a proposed change.

Neurominorities face unique challenges during periods of organizational change, a time characterized by shifts in structure, strategy, processes or culture within an organization. Such changes can create environments that are particularly challenging. One significant difficulty is the disruption of routine and predictability, which are often crucial for individuals with autism, ADHD and other neurological variations. These individuals may rely on consistent schedules and familiar processes to manage their day-to-day tasks effectively. Organizational changes lead to uncertainty and ambiguity, which can be particularly stressful and disorienting for neurodiverse employees, potentially exacerbating anxiety and affecting their work performance.

Also, communication during organizational change often becomes more complex, rapid and sometimes less clear. Neurodiverse individuals, especially those with autism, might find complex, subtle or indirect communication challenging to interpret, leading to misunderstandings and feelings of exclusion. Changes in reporting structures or team dynamics can also bring difficulties for those who struggle with social interactions, making it harder for them to adapt to new groups or managers.

Moreover, changes in job roles or responsibilities can be particularly daunting for neurominorities. Individuals with dyslexia or ADHD, for example, may have developed specific strategies to manage their tasks effectively. When these tasks change significantly, it can require a period of adjustment and additional support to develop new strategies, during which their performance may temporarily decline.

Accommodations that might have been previously in place may also be overlooked or disrupted during times of change. It is vital for organizations to maintain a commitment to inclusivity, ensuring that accommodations are adapted as necessary to support neurodiverse and neurominority employees through the change.

Proactive measures, such as clear and direct communication, maintaining some level of predictability, offering additional support and ensuring continued accommodations, can significantly mitigate the extra challenges of change faced by neurominority populations, fostering an inclusive environment where all employees can have higher well-being and thrive.

The introduction of the PEPE© model into leadership, organizational change management and as an approach to change, represents a transformative step towards creating brain-friendly practices and strategies that not only accommodate but also celebrate neurodiversity. By integrating insights from neuroscience, the PEPE© model offers a structured approach to understanding and leveraging the strengths of neurodiverse individuals, enhancing well-being, active resilience, positive adaptation and innovation.

The PEPE© model, with its emphasis on the four domains that from a brain perspective impact change resistance and positive adaptation to change, provides a framework for developing leadership and change management strategies that are sensible of the extra neurological and psychological needs of neurodivergent individuals. By reducing the perception of pain and discomfort associated with change, saving and releasing energy in sustainable ways, managing the emotional highs and lows (peaks and valleys) and minimizing the mismatch between reality and expectations (error detection), the model offers a holistic approach to supporting all employees – especially those who are neurodivergent – during times of change.

Integrating the PEPE© model into a brain-friendly framework for neurominorities during times of change

Understand pain

Many neurodivergent individuals experience atypical sensory processing. This can mean they are either hypo-sensitive (less sensitive) or hyper-sensitive (more sensitive) to pain compared to their neurotypical peers. For example, someone with autism might not respond to a pain stimulus that would typically cause distress to a neurotypical person, or they may find certain stimuli overwhelmingly painful. Individuals on the autism spectrum often experience 'pain' in the form of sensory sensitivities, social misunderstandings and environmental unpredictability. On the other hand, individuals with ADHD might have difficulty focusing on the pain signal in the middle of other distractions, or they may hyperfocus on the pain, making it feel more intense. Emotional regulation challenges can also amplify the distress associated with pain.

Communicating about pain can be particularly challenging for some neurodivergent individuals. For example, non-verbal individuals with autism may not use words to express pain, relying instead on behaviour changes or physical cues that require careful interpretation. Likewise, research indicates that acquired PTSD can alter brain chemistry and the nervous system, affecting the way pain is processed and perceived. Changes in the brain areas responsible for processing stress and emotion can make individuals with PTSD more sensitive to pain.

Leveraging the practical strategies arising from both dimensions of the 'pain domain' within PEPE© model (reducing perception of pain or increasing pleasure) could have a big positive impact within neurominorities. Focus on:

ASSURANCE

The goal of assurance is to provide information, or the context of information, to help them navigate transitions more smoothly, for example by following up individually to explain how the change specifically impacts their role and routine, and address any concerns they may have. Assign a mentor or a 'buddy' who can offer guidance and support during the transition. This person can be a consistent point of contact for any questions or concerns, helping to reduce feelings of uncertainty and isolation and providing more reassurance.

PSYCHOLOGICAL SAFETY

This is paramount for neurodiverse populations as it fosters an environment where individuals feel accepted, valued, and understood. Neurodiverse individuals may have unique cognitive styles and communication preferences, making it essential to create a supportive atmosphere free from judgment or stigma. When individuals feel psychologically safe, they are more likely to express themselves authentically, contribute their diverse perspectives and fully engage in collaborative efforts. This not only enhances their well-being and sense of belonging but also promotes creativity, innovation and productivity within the organization. Overall, psychological safety empowers neurodiverse individuals to thrive and reach their full potential.

BEING VALUED AND RESPECTED

Customizing workspaces is a major sign of inclusion, being valued and respected for neurominorities. For example, implementing adjustable lighting, noise-cancellation options, quiet zones and personalized workspace arrangements can significantly reduce sensory discomfort for individuals with ASD and DCD. Similarly, providing clear instructions and visual aids can help those with dyslexia and ADHD better understand and process information.

INCREASE SENSE OF BELONGING

Oxytocin, often referred to as the 'social bonding hormone', plays a major role in building trust, empathy and social connection, which for neurominorities are essential. Most importantly it is a powerful hormone that our brain releases when we feel we are part of the 'in-group', helping to reduce stress, cortisol and anxiety and helping us to move out of pain during times of change. In the case of neurominorities it is essential to implement practices that promote a sense of belonging, so we can leverage the power of oxytocin. For example, organize team-building exercises that cater to a wide range of interests and abilities, ensuring that activities are accessible to everyone. Instead of high-energy competitive games, consider group activities that require collaboration and problem-solving, which can be more inclusive for individuals with different neurological profiles. These activities encourage cooperation and mutual understanding, fostering a sense of unity.

Another strategy could be celebrating neurodiversity by implementing regular events or meetings dedicated to sharing and celebrating the strengths that neurodiverse individuals bring to the team. Encourage employees to share their experiences, challenges and successes related to their neurodiversity. This not only educates the team on diverse ways of thinking and processing but also highlights the value of these differences, reinforcing the idea that everyone belongs and contributes uniquely to the organization's success.

CELEBRATE OFTEN AND BRING LAUGHTER

Research has demonstrated that celebration and laughter can release endorphins, which are our natural painkillers. For those with ASD or PTSD, environments that foster laughter and positivity can help lower stress and anxiety levels by leveraging the power of our natural painkillers, making social interactions and adaptation to change more manageable.

Recognizing and celebrating achievements can bolster self-esteem, motivation and a sense of belonging, which are beneficial for all employees, including those with ASD. However, it's crucial to tailor these celebrations to suit the sensory sensitivities and social preferences of individuals with ASD. Some may prefer private acknowledgement over public celebrations, which can be overwhelming. Instead of large gatherings, which might be stressful, consider smaller, more intimate settings for celebrating achievements. A one-on-one congratulatory meeting or a small team gathering can be less intimidating and more meaningful. Likewise, ensure that any group celebrations are held in sensory-friendly environments. Avoid loud music, bright lights or other sensory stimuli that could be uncomfortable or overwhelming.

Understand energy

Energy management and brain energy are critical concepts when considering the workplace integration and productivity of neurominorities due to their unique brain wiring and cognitive functioning patterns. These significantly impact how individuals manage their energy levels and how their brains metabolize energy during cognitive tasks and manage their energy levels when active and at rest.

Managing brain energy efficiently during times of change is crucial for maintaining focus, processing information, engaging in productive work and avoiding chronic stress as a vast amount of the energy the brain consumes is used in various cognitive processes such as attention, memory, language processing, making sense of unfamiliar patterns and sensory perception – areas where neurodiverse individuals might experience differences in efficiency or processing styles.

Likewise, neurominorities often experience pronounced fluctuations in energy levels throughout the day. For instance, individuals with ADHD might have periods of high energy followed by significant drops, affecting their ability to maintain consistent productivity. Tailoring work schedules to align with these natural fluctuations, allowing for flexible work hours or task allocation based on current energy levels, can significantly enhance performance and well-being.

Tasks that align poorly with an individual's neurodiverse traits can create excessive cognitive load, leading to rapid depletion of brain energy and mental fatigue. For example, a person with dyslexia may find extended reading tasks particularly draining. Employers can mitigate this by providing assistive technology, such as text-to-speech software, or by diversifying the types of tasks assigned to reduce cognitive strain.

For individuals on the autism spectrum, sensory processing differences can impact energy management. Environments with high sensory inputs (e.g. loud noises, bright lights) may accelerate energy depletion. Creating sensory-friendly workspaces or allowing the use of noise-cancelling headphones can help conserve brain energy for core tasks and responsibilities.

Utilizing the practical strategies derived from both dimensions of the 'energy domain' within the PEPE© model (either 'save energy' or 'release energy') could potentially yield significant positive outcomes for neurominorities. Focus particularly on:

CREATING HABITS AND ROUTINES

Establishing predictable habits and routines can significantly reduce the cognitive load on neurodiverse employees, especially individuals on the autism spectrum or with PTSD where unpredictability can be a significant energy drain. Establishing consistent routines and providing extra advance notice of any changes can help conserve cognitive energy. Structured environments where expectations are clear and communication is straightforward can minimize the mental effort spent on navigating social and sensory complexities. Leaders can support this by developing structured workflows and providing consistent feedback to reinforce these habits and routines, thereby facilitating smoother transitions for neurodiverse employees.

ADD CLARITY – FOCUS ON QUALITY CONVERSATIONS

Providing clarity and engaging in quality conversations are critical components of an inclusive workplace that supports neurodiversity. Clarity in communication eliminates ambiguities that can lead to confusion and anxiety, particularly for individuals with ASD, ADHD, dyslexia and PTSD. For example, individuals with ASD rely on predictability and clear, unambiguous communication and therefore it is crucial to provide detailed explanations of what changes are occurring, why they are necessary and how they will affect daily routines, or providing agendas in advance of meetings. Likewise, individuals with PTSD may find the uncertainty associated with change particularly stressful and therefore transparent, empathetic communication that acknowledges potential concerns and offers clear information on support mechanisms can help mitigate anxiety. Leaders should offer regular, scheduled updates to provide stability within change.

These strategies not only benefit those with neurodiverse conditions but also enhance the overall communication culture within the workplace, leading to improved collaboration, innovation and employee satisfaction.

PROMOTE VISUALIZATION – REDUCE LISTENING TIME

Offering information in multiple formats, such as charts, graphics or bullet points and reducing verbally dense or prolonged communications can have a major impact on brain overload and therefore on reducing change resistance in neurominorities, especially individuals with ADHD who may struggle with attention and retention of details. For example, highlighting key points and action items using flow charts or bullet points can save a huge amount of energy for all individuals but especially in individuals with ADHD or dyslexia. Using contrasting colours will positively enhance the ability to see all aspects of an image.

PROVIDE OPPORTUNITIES FOR PEOPLE TO COME UP WITH THEIR OWN INSIGHTS

As reviewed earlier in Chapter 5, when individuals arrive at an insight on their own, the brain releases dopamine (the neurotransmitter associated with excitement and motivation). This not only boosts energy levels but also encourages a positive association with problem-solving and creative thinking. For neurodiverse individuals, who may face daily challenges in traditional learning or working environments, these dopamine boosts can be particularly reinforcing.

Moreover, individuals with ADHD are known for their creativity and ability to think outside the box; individuals with dyslexia often develop unique problem-solving skills and innovative thinking as they navigate a world designed for linear processing. Those with ASD often have deep, specialized interests and an exceptional ability to focus intensely on subjects of interest.

Providing platforms, contexts and opportunities for this neurodiverse force to come up and share their insights is a powerful strategy within organizations to increase innovation, motivation and release positive energy. For example, create problem-solving groups or projects around areas of interest, facilitating brainstorming sessions where individuals with ASD can dive deep into topics they are passionate about, and encouraging them to share unique insights and solutions with their peers. Or implement rapid ideation sessions where individuals with ADHD can freely express their ideas without fear of judgment. Use tools like mind maps or idea boards that allow for dynamic interaction and visual representation of thoughts, capitalizing on their spontaneous creativity and high energy levels.

Providing time and space to a neurodiverse force is one of the most powerful management tools during times of change, transformation and innovation.

Understand peaks and valleys

The concept of peaks and valleys emphasizes the natural fluctuations in motivation, energy and emotional states that all individuals experience. From a brain perspective, understanding and managing these peaks (high-energy, high-focus periods) and valleys (low-energy, rest or reflective periods) is crucial for optimizing the changing workplace environment, workflows and well-being of neurodiverse teams. For neurodiverse individuals, these cycles can be more pronounced or differently paced, affecting their work and engagement levels. Understanding and accommodating these differences can lead to a more inclusive and productive work environment, especially during times of change.

For example, individuals with ASD may experience intense focus (peaks) on areas of interest; often autistic people report that the time spent in those intense periods of focus is fundamental for their well-being as it helps to clear their mind from persuasive thoughts and is a way of coping with everyday life.[4] Therefore, it is important to create more structured downtime (valleys) to avoid sensory overload or burnout. In this case it could be implementing a flexible work schedule that allows for deep focus work periods followed by quiet, sensory-friendly relaxation zones where individuals with ASD can unwind without sensory disturbances.

As a consultant, I have worked with a few technology and data science organizations to help them create brain-friendly practices as part of their transformation programmes. Some of their actions have been: 1) creating outside quiet space within the office (terraces) for individuals to go to either have time off or to work in these areas for a period of time, and 2) creating areas dedicated to mind games, such as puzzles or other stimulating games – usually very attractive and effective for ASD individuals.

On the other hand, individuals with ADHD often have periods of hyper-focus (peaks) but may quickly shift to states of distraction or disengagement (valleys). In this case, you might consider utilizing short, varied tasks that align with natural attention spans, interspersed with physical activity breaks or engaging, interactive tasks that can serve as a reset, helping to manage the peaks and valleys of focus and energy.

For those with PTSD, managing stress levels is crucial. High-stress situations (peaks) can trigger symptoms, requiring strategies to facilitate calm and recovery (valleys).

Implementing practical strategies from both aspects of the 'peaks and valleys domain' in the PEPE$^{©}$ model – aimed at either 'managing the peaks' or 'promoting the valleys' – could lead to notably beneficial results for neurominorities. Especially focus on:

PROMOTE FLOW

Achieving a state of flow, as defined by psychologist Mihaly Csikszentmihalyi, occurs when an individual is fully immersed in an activity, experiencing a sense of focus, engagement and fulfilment. As reviewed earlier in this book, research has demonstrated that during a state of flow all the neurobiology markers rise to peak levels, allowing one to perform at peak. For neurodiverse individuals, including those with ASD, ADHD or dyslexia, entering and maintaining a state of flow can offer significant benefits for productivity and well-being, but it also requires tailored strategies to accommodate their unique processing styles and challenges.

For example, someone with ASD might find flow in tasks that align with their specific interests or routines. In the case of those with ADHD, finding flow might be a bit more challenging due to the difficulty of focusing and filtering out internal and external distractions; however, they might achieve flow in dynamic, fast-paced activities that match their energy levels.

Recognizing and leveraging these preferences is key to facilitating flow.

BALANCE ANTICIPATION AND PLEASURE

Balancing anticipation and pleasure involves understanding the nuanced interplay between dopamine and endorphins in the brain. Dopamine plays a key role in anticipation and motivation, driving individuals to pursue goals and engage in activities that promise rewards. Endorphins, on the other hand, are linked to the experience of pleasure and pain relief, contributing to a sense of well-being and satisfaction after engaging in enjoyable activities or achieving goals.

For some neurodiverse individuals, such as those with ADHD, ASD or dyslexia, the dopamine-driven motivation system can function differently, affecting how anticipation and goal-directed behaviours are experienced. Similarly, the release of endorphins after achieving a goal or participating in a pleasurable activity can vary, impacting the sense of satisfaction and well-being.

For example, in the case of ADHD there is a consensus in the literature that suggests there is a dysfunction in the 'brain reward cascade', especially in the dopamine system, causing a low dopaminergic trait, which may require more constant short boosts of dopamine.[5] Setting short-term, achievable goals can create frequent opportunities for dopamine release associated with anticipation. Celebrating these small achievements can then stimulate endorphin release, enhancing pleasure and satisfaction.

Another example is that for those with dyslexia or PTSD, physical activities that are enjoyable and provide clear, immediate feedback (like team dynamics, celebrations or sport) can offer a balance of dopamine-driven anticipation and endorphin-fuelled pleasure.

Practices such as meditation or yoga can help regulate the brain's response to stress and anticipation, mitigating the anxiety that can sometimes be associated with dopamine-driven anticipation. These practices can also enhance endorphin release, promoting a sense of calm and well-being. Incorporating and providing space for guided meditation practices during a workday for the neurotypical and neurominorities can help to regulate emotional states and promote a healthy number of fluctuations in the mental states.

PROMOTE MINDFULNESS

Mindfulness, the practice of being present and fully engaged in the current moment without judgment, has shown promising benefits for neurodiverse individuals, particularly in the context of organizational change. For example, for individuals with ADHD, mindfulness practices can improve focus, reduce impulsivity and enhance self-regulation.[6] In the case of PTSD, it can help to manage symptoms such as hyperarousal, intrusive thoughts and emotional numbness.[7] And for those with ASD, mindfulness can aid in managing sensory overload and improving social skills and emotional understanding.

Encouraging the incorporation of mindfulness practices into daily work routines, such as mindful breathing before starting a task or mindful listening during meetings, can help foster a culture of presence and attentiveness.

Hosting workshops or bringing in experts to teach mindfulness techniques can equip employees, especially neurominorities, with tools to manage stress and remain focused during periods of change.

Understand error

The concept of the 'error signal' in the brain revolves around the discrepancy between expected outcomes and actual results, a phenomenon that plays a crucial role in learning, adaptation to change and motivation. This mechanism is particularly significant in understanding neurodiverse individuals, who may process these error signals differently due to variations in their neural pathways.

In neurotypical individuals, a match or slight positive mismatch between expectations and reality can release dopamine, promoting feelings of satisfaction and motivation. However, a significant mismatch can result in negative emotional responses, demotivation or cynicism. For neurodiverse populations, the sensitivity to and processing of these error signals can magnify the impact on their adaptation to change and overall well-being.

For example, individuals with ASD might have difficulty with unexpected changes or outcomes, leading to heightened stress or anxiety when reality diverges significantly from expectations. Their strong preference for routines and predictability means that error signals associated with unexpected changes can be particularly distressing.

People with ADHD may exhibit a higher threshold for stimulation, seeking novel and varied experiences. This quest for novelty can mean that they are more accustomed to experiencing and navigating the discrepancies between expectations and outcomes, potentially making them more resilient to negative error signals but also more prone to seek out situations with uncertain outcomes.

Individuals with PTSD are often in a heightened state of alertness to potential threats, meaning that error signals, particularly those associated with negative outcomes, can trigger stress responses. Managing these signals and the expectations around them is crucial for minimizing stress and anxiety.

Implementing practical strategies from both aspects of the 'error domain' in the PEPE© model – aimed at either 'reduce the mismatch between reality and expectation' or 'releasing positive signals' – could benefit neurominorities. Especially focus on:

INCREMENTAL/ITERATIVE CHANGE
Implementing small, incremental changes can help reduce the intensity of negative error signals by minimizing the gap between expectations and reality.

For neurodiverse individuals, this approach allows for gradual adaptation, reducing stress and anxiety associated with change. Regular feedback loops can help adjust expectations and provide a sense of progress and control.

In the case of ASD, introducing new tasks or changes in routine in small, manageable steps can really help reduce the size of the error signal in the brain. For example, if implementing a new workflow, start with one small aspect of the change, provide ample time for adaptation and use visual supports to outline each step of the process.

People with ADHD may struggle with organization and following through on tasks. Large-scale changes can exacerbate these challenges, making it difficult to adapt. Incremental changes can help by providing clear, focused steps that are easier to manage and execute, reducing the feeling of being overwhelmed. Break down projects into smaller, clearly defined tasks with specific deadlines. Using tools like task managers or apps that allow for tracking progress on micro-tasks, offering immediate feedback and a sense of accomplishment can also help to release short boosts of dopamine in the brain of ADHD individuals.

For individuals with PTSD, sudden changes can trigger stress responses or flashbacks. Gradual changes, introduced in a controlled and predictable manner, can help minimize these triggers, providing a sense of safety and control during periods of transition.

BRING FAMILIARITY AND PATTERN RECOGNITION

This plays a critical role in supporting individuals with ASD and other neurominorities, particularly during periods of change within organizations. Familiarity releases prediction positive error signals, providing a sense of security and predictability, which can significantly reduce anxiety and stress for neurodiverse individuals who may find unexpected changes challenging. Pattern recognition, on the other hand, leverages the natural propensity of those with ASD to identify and understand patterns, making it easier for them to navigate and adapt to new situations.[8]

When managing changes, use formats and structures that are already familiar to neurodiverse employees. For example, if a new software tool is introduced, customize its interface to mirror that of a tool the employees are already comfortable with.

Even in the midst of change, maintain elements of the daily routine that do not need to be altered. This could include keeping the same meeting schedules or break times, providing a stable framework that neurodiverse employees can rely on.

When possible, relate new information or changes to existing knowledge or processes that neurodiverse employees are already familiar with. This approach can make new concepts less intimidating and easier to grasp.

Likewise, when training neurodiverse employees on new processes or tools, structure the learning materials in a way that highlights patterns or sequences. This method can facilitate quicker learning and adaptation by tapping into their strengths in pattern recognition.

CREATE A CULTURE OF ASKING FOR AND PROVIDING POSITIVE FEEDBACK

For people who identify as neurodivergent, positive feedback can significantly modulate the intensity and perception of error signals, fostering a more supportive and motivating environment to facilitate change. Positive feedback can be particularly impactful for those with ADHD or ASD, as it may directly influence their dopamine systems, enhancing motivation and focus. For individuals with ASD, who might have heightened sensitivity to social cues, positive feedback provides clear, reinforcing signals of success, helping to navigate social and task-related expectations more effectively.

In the brain, positive feedback following an unexpected success can reduce the negative impact of error signals, which are typically associated with the brain's prediction error mechanisms. By acknowledging and rewarding efforts and achievements, positive feedback helps shift focus from what went wrong to what was accomplished, reinforcing learning and adaptation.

Tailor the mode of recognition to suit the individual's preferences and needs. While some may appreciate public acknowledgement, others, particularly certain individuals with ASD or social anxiety, may prefer private recognition.

Notes

1   J Singer. Odd people in: the birth of community amongst people on the autistic spectrum, University of Technology Sydney: Sydney, Australia, 1998

2   H Goldberg. Unraveling neurodiversity: insights from neuroscientific perspectives, *Encyclopedia*, 3(3): 972–80

3   N Doyle. Neurodiversity at work: a biopsychosocial model and the impact on working adults, *British Medical Bulletin*, 2020, 135(1): 108–25

4   National Autistic Society, https://www.autism.org.uk/ (archived at https://perma.cc/693R-M2D8)

5 K Blum et al. Attention-deficit-hyperactivity disorder and reward deficiency syndrome, *Neuropsychiatric Disease and Treatment*, 2008, 4(5): 893–918

6 JT Mitchell, L Zylowska and SH Kollins. Mindfulness meditation training for attention-deficit/hyperactivity disorder in adulthood: current empirical support, treatment overview, and future directions, *Cognitive and Behavioral Practice*, 2015, 22(2): 172–91

7 JE Boyd, RA Lanius and MC McKinnon. Mindfulness-based treatments for posttraumatic stress disorder: a review of the treatment literature and neurobiological evidence, *Journal of Psychiatry Neuroscience*, 2018, 43(1): 7–25

8 B Crespi. Pattern unifies autism, *Frontiers in Psychiatry*, 2021, 12: 621659

13

Creating your change plan

Successful adoption of change requires moving ourselves and others through the experience of change. Some will voluntarily move themselves along this journey, because they are motivated to make the change happen. Others will need to be encouraged. Some will move quickly; others will be slower or will get stuck and need help to move to the next step.

Change plan

The effort to achieve this transition is captured in a Change Plan, which identifies the activities, the schedule for when they will take place and the resources needed to make them happen. The activities described in the PEPE$^©$ model can be used to form the basis of this plan.

Using the steps of the change lifecycle described earlier in the book as the basis of the plan, we can identify:

- the criteria that describe the successful completion of each step;
- the contribution of each of the domains of the PEPE$^©$ model;
- suggested activities from each of these domains.

Instead of trying to provide an exhaustive list of activities for each step, we have used an example change situation that includes the most common challenges that occur during organizational change. This situation provides you with a practical example of how to assess and select relevant activities for each step of the lifecycle.

We want to emphasize that your Change Plan will be different, because your plan reflects the type and scale of your change, the reasons for the change and the culture of your organization. However, this example will give you a guide to get you started.

FIGURE 13.1 Lifecycle of change

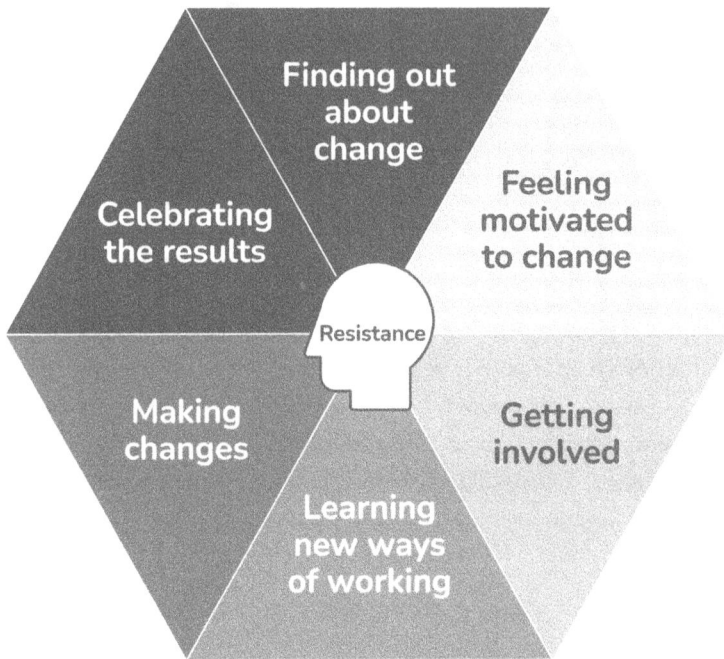

Change example

The change is organization-wide, to address growing concerns about sustainability. Impacts include changes to the company travel policy; a move to collaborative online tools (away from printing documents); recycling programmes; changes to supply chain, to include more sustainable suppliers; a new energy policy to reduce greenhouse gas emissions; and application of smart building technologies.

This change is a typical example of 'imposed' change. It has been decided strategically that improvements in sustainability are needed to achieve the strategic objectives of the organization. It is not entirely unexpected because prior to this point, there were discussions amongst staff as sustainability affects us all and many people want to work for a responsible organization. However, at the start of this change there is limited understanding of the scope and eventual impact of the change and little motivation to achieve the outcomes.

Some of the ideas circulating in the organization have been included, but the scope goes further than people were expecting. Some people will be

FIGURE 13.2 Range of responsibilities for change

Changing how you work

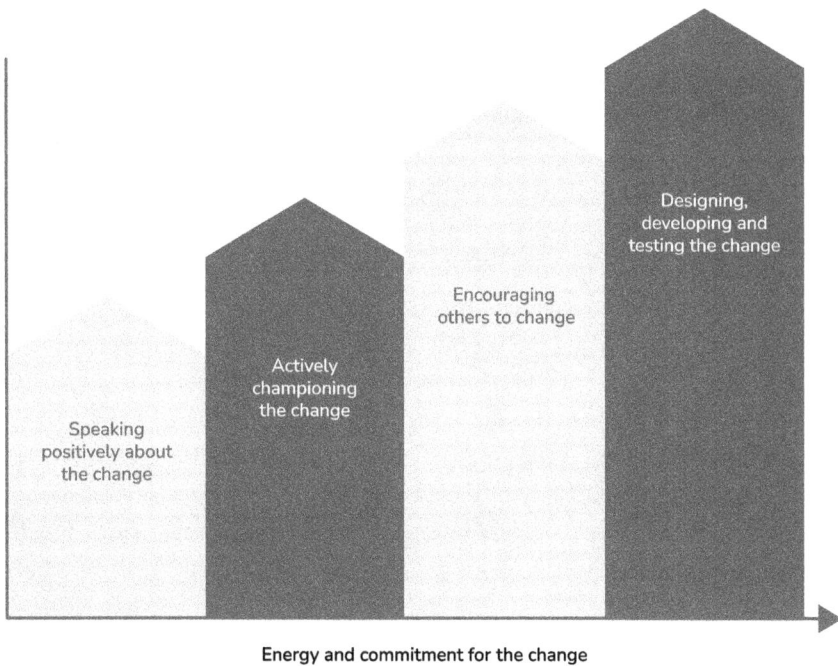

Designing, developing and testing the change

Encouraging others to change

Actively championing the change

Speaking positively about the change

Energy and commitment for the change

pleased, others irritated by the changes. Some people will experience significant changes to their work, and others will notice very little difference.

At any point, individuals will feel a range of emotions. Some will feel angry that their established routines are being disrupted. Others will feel threatened that their skills are no longer relevant. Some will feel excited by the changes and others overwhelmed by the work required.

The activities included in this example Change Plan are not targeted towards any specific role in the change. This is because change only happens if everyone associated with the change supports it and takes part in making it happen, irrespective of their job title. Involvement in change ranges from encouraging others to change to taking action to adopt new ways of working.

To generate the necessary support, each step in your Change Plan must engender the right outcome. In the early stages of change, the focus is on achieving understanding and acceptance that the change is going to happen. Next, the emphasis moves towards creating acceptance of and positivity about the change, leading to motivation to make it happen. This need for motivation continues throughout the lifecycle, but in the later stages it is accompanied by the need to create resilience.

Resilience is critical because change requires endurance. Altering how we work requires repeated actions over a considerable period of time, until these actions become routine and move from change to normality. Resilience also gives us the ability to overcome adversity, which is prevalent in change. Doing things for the first time rarely works as expected, and we identify mistakes and failures that need to be put right. It is our resilience that ensures we do not give up and roll back to our old ways of working when we encounter these problems.

From the brain perspective, this means that early in the lifecycle, we need to minimize the pain triggered when the change is first announced. We then need to focus on releasing the energy needed to make the change happen. As we experience change, we need to reduce the mismatch between what we think is going to happen and the reality. We need to encourage peak working, but balance this with the creation of the valleys to enable those involved to reflect on the current state of their ways of working, form a new baseline and enjoy a period of rest before re-engaging with the change effort. Finally we want to generate pleasure as we celebrate everything that has been achieved.

Understanding what the brain needs at each step of the change provides criteria that you can use to select appropriate activities. We have illustrated this with our selection of the most relevant domains from the PEPE© model. Use Table 13.1 as a guide to identify your priorities for each step of the change lifecycle.

We are not looking to get rid of all pain; to stimulate change we must feel some sense of challenge. As described earlier in this book, we are aiming to create the 'sweet spot' between threat and reward but in doing this we must assess how those affected are feeling and select those activities that boost the pleasure and energy for change whilst reducing the anxiety and stress.

Too little challenge and the energy for the change will be too low. The impact ranges from, in the worst case, no progress, as the change is unlikely to generate the necessary support and motivation to make it happen, to, in the best case, progress but at a speed that is not acceptable to the organization.

Too much challenge and whilst the energy for change is high, it is too high. Those involved will feel pressured, leading to stress or, in the worst cases, burn-out.

Use these criteria to decide what actions will create the optimum brain reaction.

TABLE 13.1

Step in the lifecycle	Criteria for success
Finding out about the change	• Pain – Focus on minimizing pain experienced when people hear about change for the first time • Energy – Create the energy needed to feel change is possible • Error signal – Address the potential mismatch between what people were expecting and what will change
Feeling motivated to change	• Pain – Highlight the opportunities created by the change to create pleasure and a desire to change • Energy – reduce the perception of how much energy is required for the change to increase positive feelings about it
Getting involved	• Pain – reduce the pain associated with the change, so that it is a more appealing opportunity and people are more likely to volunteer to participate • Energy – Create the energy to volunteer to participate in the change • Error – clarify what is involved to minimize any confusion about the effort and involvement that is required
Learning new ways of working	• Pain – reduce the pain associated with learning something new and increase the pleasure of taking part in a collaborative effort • Error – provide relevant information and work in small cycles of change to reduce misunderstandings and conflicting expectations about what the change will achieve • Peaks and valleys – allow the brain to work optimally by encouraging peak activity and providing rest and reflection
Making changes	• Pain – reduce pain and increase pleasure to maintain motivation for the change • Energy – focus on creating energy and enthusiasm to stimulate actions to create the change • Peaks and valleys – allow the brain to work optimally to produce the most change in the shortest time
Celebrating the results	• Pain – focus on the pleasure of achievement to increase the motivation for further change • Energy – reduce the perception of the energy required for change, to increase the motivation for further change

Below is a summary of the outcomes for each step of the lifecycle, with criteria for successful completion of the step and examples of how to apply the PEPE© model to achieve that success. For a more detailed understanding of the change lifecycle, please refer to the first chapter of this book.

Finding out about the change

The outcome from this first step in the lifecycle is an acceptance that change is happening. No one can move to the next step and begin to feel motivated about something that they do not believe is real.

This example shows an initial announcement. This will need to be repeated many times as those affected by the change start to 'tune in' to what is being said. Some will take notice of the information immediately and move through to the next steps of the lifecycle. Others will ignore the announcements because they do not feel it is relevant to them, or they are too busy with other work to give it their attention. Your Change Plan will need to include multiple explanations at different times using a range of communication channels until you have captured the attention of everyone who needs to act.

Success for this step in the lifecycle relies on reducing the pain triggered by realizing that things cannot continue as they are. Effective messaging will minimize the amount of energy required by the brain to process the information, by making it easy to consume. The brain will experience error signals as what was expected to happen is now changing, so address these differences in expectations.

PAIN – TELLS US SOMETHING IS WRONG, WHICH WILL ACT AS A BARRIER
SO WE MUST MINIMIZE THIS SIGNAL BY REDUCING PAIN

Initial announcements of the change trigger pain because we are losing our existing routines and habits, and will have to learn new ways of working. This creates threats as we risk getting things wrong, finding it hard to learn or losing our status as someone who knows what they are doing.

Overcome this pain barrier through:

- Being valued and respected – an announcement of change can leave people thinking that how they currently work is not valued. This makes them regretful about all the effort they have put into their work and can cause them to doubt their self-worth and value to the organization. To minimize this pain, thank everyone for their hard work in creating the current ways of working that have built powerful foundations upon which to build the change, so they do not feel their previous efforts have been wasted.

FIGURE 13.3 Example communications for finding out about change

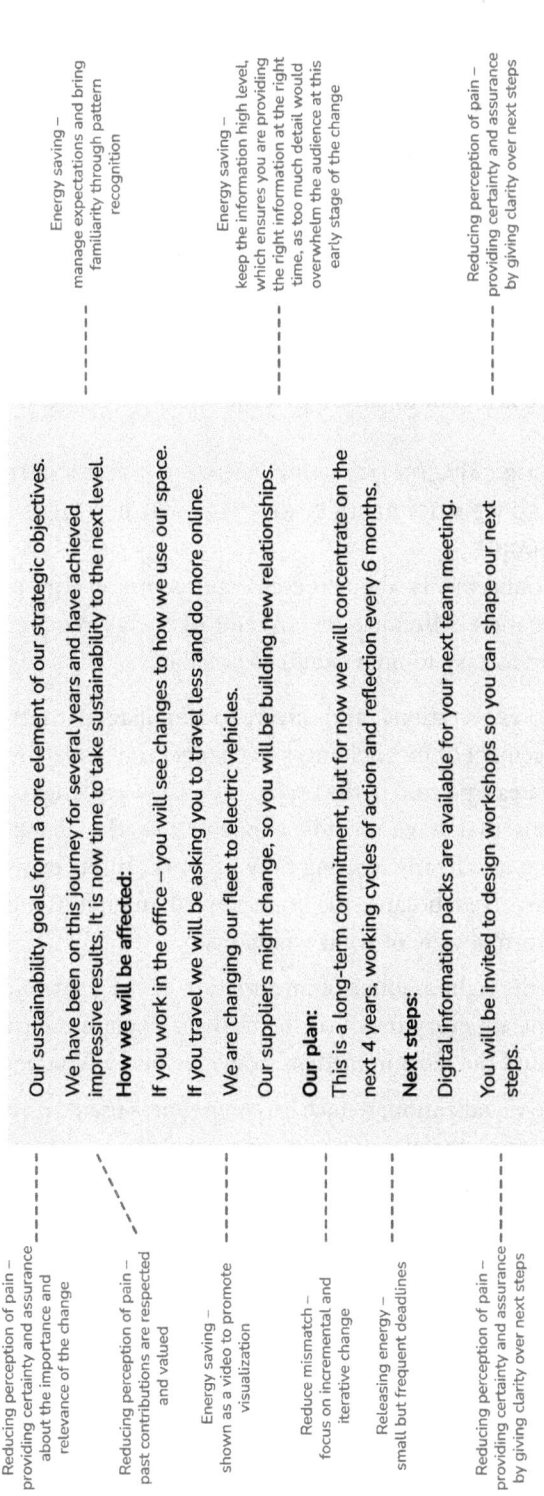

Reducing perception of pain –
providing certainty and assurance
about the importance and
relevance of the change

Reducing perception of pain –
past contributions are respected
and valued

Energy saving –
shown as a video to promote
visualization

Reduce mismatch –
focus on incremental and
iterative change

Releasing energy –
small but frequent deadlines

Reducing perception of pain –
providing certainty and assurance
by giving clarity over next steps

Energy saving –
manage expectations and bring
familiarity through pattern
recognition

Energy saving –
keep the information high level,
which ensures you are providing
the right information at the right
time, as too much detail would
overwhelm the audience at this
early stage of the change

Reducing perception of pain –
providing certainty and assurance
by giving clarity over next steps

Our sustainability goals form a core element of our strategic objectives.

We have been on this journey for several years and have achieved
impressive results. It is now time to take sustainability to the next level.

How we will be affected:

If you work in the office – you will see changes to how we use our space.

If you travel we will be asking you to travel less and do more online.

We are changing our fleet to electric vehicles.

Our suppliers might change, so you will be building new relationships.

Our plan:

This is a long-term commitment, but for now we will concentrate on the
next 4 years, working cycles of action and reflection every 6 months.

Next steps:

Digital information packs are available for your next team meeting.

You will be invited to design workshops so you can shape our next
steps.

- Certainty and assurance – changing ways of working creates uncertainty, as people are not sure how they will be affected, what they will be doing, who they will be working with and whether this new situation will benefit or disadvantage them. Provide information that creates a sense of certainty. For example, explain how the change aligns to the purpose and values of the organization and the strategic objectives. Explain that the change aligns to other changes taking place within the organization and in your industry or in society in general. Provide enough information about the change for people to feel it has been carefully thought through and there is a plan to ensure that the effort requested will not be wasted.

ENERGY – OUR CAPACITY FOR WORK, WHICH IF INSUFFICIENT ACTS AS
A BARRIER SO WE MUST REDUCE THE ENERGY WE BELIEVE IS REQUIRED
FOR THE CHANGE

Initial announcements about the change require energy to process all the new information. Minimize the amount of energy required by making the information as easy to understand as possible:

- Manage expectations and create a familiar pattern – connect the announcement of more changes to changes that have already taken place. This creates a pattern in the brain, as the new activities connect to a series of actions that have already happened, so the change appears to be extending an already existing flow of work. It sets expectations of what will be involved, because the brain can use an understanding of the recent past to form a view of what will happen.

- Provide the right amount of information at the right time – do not try to communicate every detail of the change. Explain the overall aim of the change and the most immediate activities that will take place.

- Promote visualization, reduce listening time – use pictures, videos, graphs and diagrams throughout your announcement as these convey a lot of information in an immediately accessible way. For example, the use of video in this announcement to explain different impacts of the change will help people imagine themselves working in the new way.

ERROR SIGNAL – ADAPT BEHAVIOUR WHEN THERE IS A MISMATCH BETWEEN
OUR EXPECTATIONS AND WHAT IS ACTUALLY HAPPENING

Initial announcements of the change trigger an error signal because our expectations are always to continue as we are. This is because our brain likes the certainty provided by continuing to do what we are already doing. The announcement of the change will come as a shock to our brain, because it is being asked to do something different. Minimize this 'threat' response:

- Focus on incremental and iterative change – acknowledge that the change is a long-term commitment but encourage the brain to focus on the next immediate change.

Feeling motivated to change

The purpose of this step is to ensure that all those who need to commit effort and energy to making the change happen believe in its value, its relevance and its necessity, leading to a willingness to get involved.

Success for this step in the lifecycle enables everyone impacted or affected by the change to find a sense of meaning and purpose. This includes their personal motivation by identifying how the change affects their work, their work-life balance, their career progress and levels of ability. It might include their view of the importance and usefulness of the change to their organization, their industry or their community. Whilst these more altruistic reasons will trigger endorphins, they lack a personal connection to the change. We cannot ignore the need to answer the question, 'What is in it for me?' so ensure you repeatedly communicate messages describing the personal benefits of the change.

PAIN
To create motivation, we need to signpost potential benefits, improvements and advantages that will be created by the change:

- Informal meetings – minimize the formality of the organization structure for the change, to encourage people to network and become excited by the opportunities for working with new people and learning from others.
- Increased sense of belonging – a feeling that everyone is being treated the same, and that this will be an opportunity to work with others, form relationships and enjoy this social aspect of work.

ERROR SIGNAL
- Create habits of unexpected rewards – in this case, the reward is the financial commitment that the organization is making for individuals to benefit from the change. Extra money is nearly always unexpected, so will generate endorphins, creating feelings of pleasure and enjoyment.

FIGURE 13.4 Example communications for feeling motivated to change

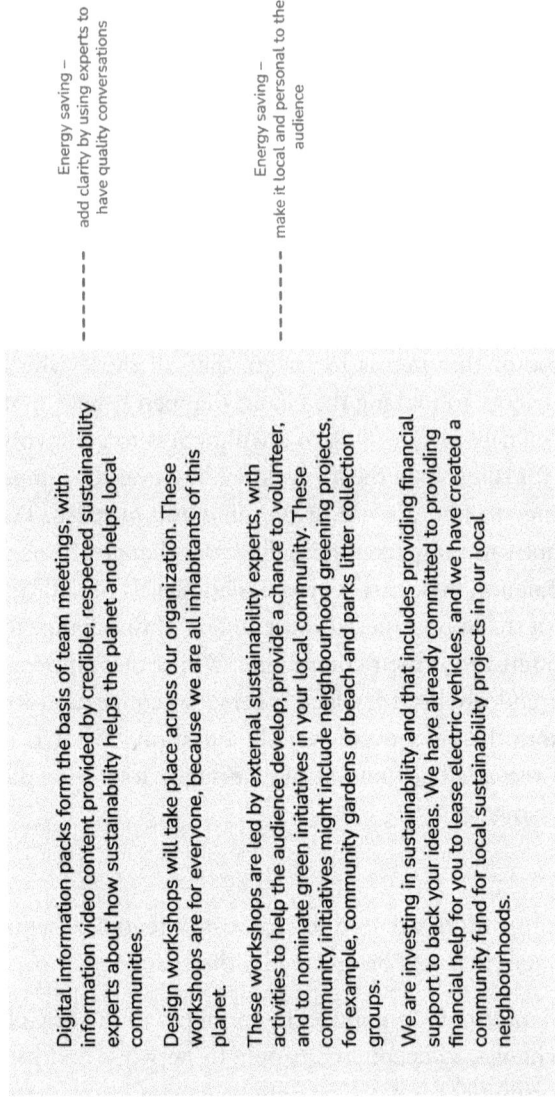

Energy saving –
add clarity by using experts to
have quality conversations

Digital information packs form the basis of team meetings, with information video content provided by credible, respected sustainability experts about how sustainability helps the planet and helps local communities.

Design workshops will take place across our organization. These workshops are for everyone, because we are all inhabitants of this planet.

Energy saving –
make it local and personal to the
audience

These workshops are led by external sustainability experts, with activities to help the audience develop, provide a chance to volunteer, and to nominate green initiatives in your local community. These community initiatives might include neighbourhood greening projects, for example, community gardens or beach and parks litter collection groups.

We are investing in sustainability and that includes providing financial support to back your ideas. We have already committed to providing financial help for you to lease electric vehicles, and we have created a community fund for local sustainability projects in our local neighbourhoods.

Increase pleasure –
informal meetings and an
increased sense of belonging, as
everyone can attend, whatever
their role or seniority and can
enjoy being together

Error –
release positive signals by
providing unexpected rewards

CREATING YOUR CHANGE PLAN   281

ENERGY

- Add clarity – focus on quality conversations – to generate motivation, have focused, engaged conversations about the benefits of the change. The aim is to reduce waffle and meaningless platitudes and to give people specific and credible information. Use of experts means the brain will categorize the information as high quality and safe to build expectations from.

- Make it local – personalize it – to feel motivated, we need to create a feeling of 'What is in it for me?' which is specific to us. In this case, the sustainability change is being linked directly to where people live, by using the word neighbourhood. This word immediately triggers a visualization of where we live and how it will be more enjoyable if we fix environmental issues, including litter clearing and the planting of green spaces. The announcement also provides examples that will trigger ideas for those listening about things they could do, making the announcement personal to them.

Getting involved

The outcome from this step is voluntary action. We need those affected by the change to identify two types of involvement:

1 How they are going to include change activities into their current workload.
2 Their involvement in the change activities, including workshops, demonstrations and supporting their colleagues.

Success at this step of the lifecycle is the mobilization of a 'volunteer army' of people who are committed to making the change happen. They are energized by the motivation they discovered in the earlier step, and are starting to identify ways in which they want to contribute to the change.

PAIN

To get involved, those affected by change need to maintain the motivation that they have already developed. This means continuing to reduce the pain of the change and to maximize the pleasure associated with it.

Generate certainty and assurance by clearly defining the roles available for those who want to volunteer. Increase their feelings of certainty that they will be able to participate by identifying the need for their involvement.

FIGURE 13.5 Example communications for getting involved

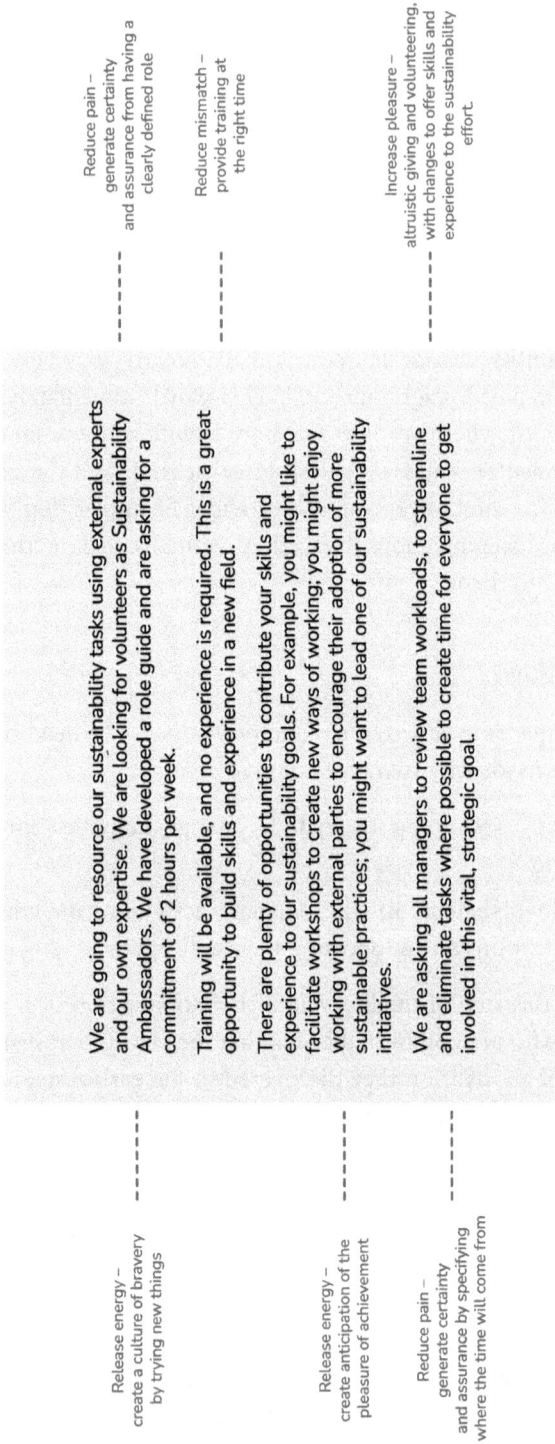

Release energy –
create a culture of bravery
by trying new things

- - - - - -

We are going to resource our sustainability tasks using external experts and our own expertise. We are looking for volunteers as Sustainability Ambassadors. We have developed a role guide and are asking for a commitment of 2 hours per week.

- - - - - -

Reduce pain –
generate certainty
and assurance from having a
clearly defined role

Training will be available, and no experience is required. This is a great opportunity to build skills and experience in a new field.

- - - - - -

Reduce mismatch –
provide training at
the right time

Release energy –
create anticipation of the
pleasure of achievement

- - - - - -

There are plenty of opportunities to contribute your skills and experience to our sustainability goals. For example, you might like to facilitate workshops to create new ways of working; you might enjoy working with external parties to encourage their adoption of more sustainable practices; you might want to lead one of our sustainability initiatives.

Reduce pain –
generate certainty
and assurance by specifying
where the time will come from

- - - - - -

We are asking all managers to review team workloads, to streamline and eliminate tasks where possible to create time for everyone to get involved in this vital, strategic goal.

- - - - - -

Increase pleasure –
altruistic giving and volunteering,
with changes to offer skills and
experience to the sustainability
effort.

Back this up with practical support to increase the credibility of the message. For example, making it clear managers have a responsibility to streamline existing workloads makes the opportunity feel more believable and therefore more certain.

Increase pleasure by offering opportunities for altruistic giving and volunteering, with chances to offer skills and experience to the sustainability effort.

ERROR SIGNAL

- Reduce a mismatch in expectations by providing training at the right time. Training provides accurate information, so it is less likely that the brain will imagine responsibilities and outcomes from the role that do not exist.

ENERGY

- Implement a culture of bravery and risk-taking – take a risk by volunteering for a new role and trying out things that you have not done before.

- Create anticipation and promote hunting – use the anticipation of learning new things and achieving change to encourage your involvement in the change.

Learning new ways of working

The outcome of this step in the lifecycle is to understand the new procedures, systems, policies and priorities for working in the new way and start to build the necessary skills.

PAIN

Learning new ways of working creates pain because it requires us to put aside things we already know and to open ourselves up to new information, some of which might be difficult to understand. We are vulnerable to making mistakes, which causes us pain:

- Growth mindset – encourage everyone to apply the growth mindset to this change, to focus on learning and the acquisition of knowledge and understanding as a valuable outcome of the sustainability change.

- Psychological safety – trainers, managers and experts are encouraged to welcome questions and encourage everyone to ask questions and share their views. Make it clear there are no stupid questions and encourage

FIGURE 13.6 Example communications for learning new ways of working

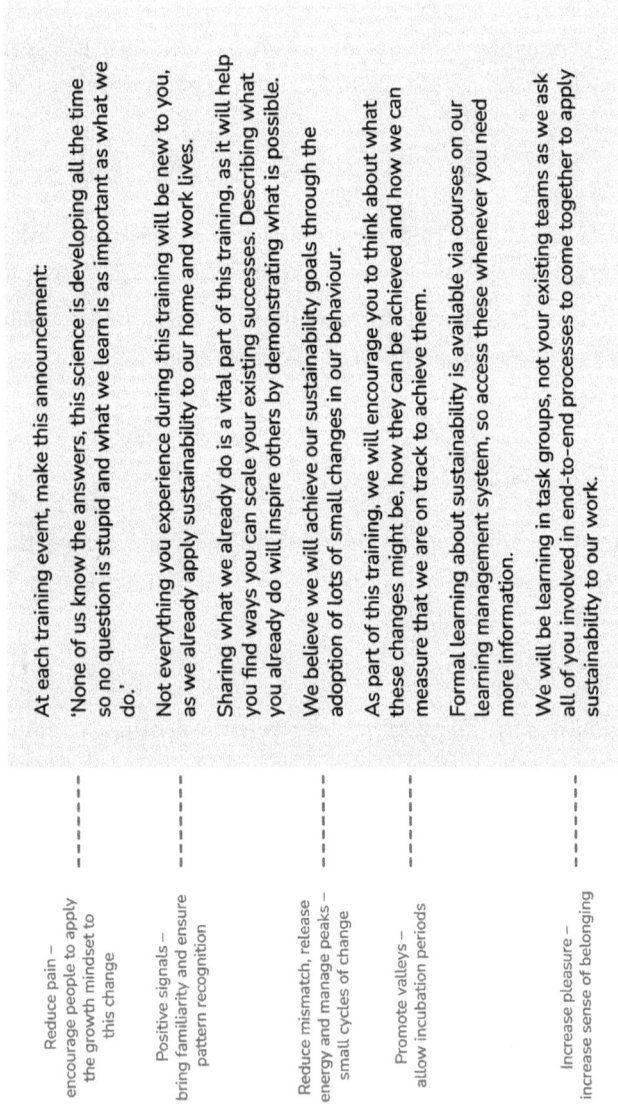

At each training event, make this announcement:

'None of us know the answers, this science is developing all the time so no question is stupid and what we learn is as important as what we do.'

Not everything you experience during this training will be new to you, as we already apply sustainability to our home and work lives.

Sharing what we already do is a vital part of this training, as it will help you find ways you can scale your existing successes. Describing what you already do will inspire others by demonstrating what is possible.

We believe we will achieve our sustainability goals through the adoption of lots of small changes in our behaviour.

As part of this training, we will encourage you to think about what these changes might be, how they can be achieved and how we can measure that we are on track to achieve them.

Formal learning about sustainability is available via courses on our learning management system, so access these whenever you need more information.

We will be learning in task groups, not your existing teams as we ask all of you involved in end-to-end processes to come together to apply sustainability to our work.

Reduce pain –
encourage people to apply
the growth mindset to
this change

Positive signals –
bring familiarity and ensure
pattern recognition

Reduce mismatch, release
energy and manage peaks –
small cycles of change

Promote valleys –
allow incubation periods

Increase pleasure –
increase sense of belonging

Reduce pain –
encourage an environment
of psychological safety

Positive signals –
create a culture of asking
for and providing
positive feedback

Energy saving –
provide the right
information at right time

people to share their ideas and insights by welcoming their contribution and avoiding criticism.

- Increase sense of belonging – opportunity to belong to task groups, making it clear that you are part of a specific team to achieve sustainability. This helps the brain create oxytocin as you feel supported by other members of the task group who are interested in the expertise and experience you can contribute.

ERROR SIGNAL

Learning new ways of working can create many moments where our expectations are not met. Some of these are positive, because we expect things to be difficult to learn and they turn out to be easier. Negative experiences come from the realization that we do not understand something that we thought we had already learnt:

- Bring familiarity and ensure pattern recognition – connect the new sustainability activities with other experiences of sustainability as this sends a message to the brain that there is no change of direction, that this change is merely an extension of an existing pattern. It creates the reassurance that not everything is changing.

- Create a culture of asking for and providing positive feedback – this will encourage further learning. As people share their sustainability experiences, identify positive outcomes from these behaviours as this will boost their engagement and create a feeling that they want to do more.

ENERGY

Learning means our brains are creating new connections which requires a lot of energy. Where possible we should minimize the energy required for learning:

- Provide the right amount of information at the right time – ensuring that training is available when it is needed and when someone is ready to learn minimizes the amount of information that the brain needs to retain, reducing the energy needed for the change. Adults learn best when there is relevance to what they are learning, so it should connect to their job and the tasks they must perform.

- Small changes – this will minimize the energy required, reduce any possible mismatch in expectations and enable people to work at their peak.

PEAKS AND VALLEYS

Learning creates a peak in our energy, which we need to maintain long enough to absorb new information. We need to balance this with valleys, where our brains can absorb the new information and reflect on what we have learnt.

- Allow incubation periods – we need time to reflect on what we have learnt. Make it clear that part of the training is to think about the changes and to develop your own ideas.

Making changes

The outcome of this step is the adoption of new ways of working. Adoption means that individuals have used their understanding of new procedures, systems, policies and priorities and are applying their new skills to create new habits and routines.

Those impacted by the change consistently apply these new ways of working, and with repeated use enable the situation to shift from being a change to being normal.

PAIN

To get involved, those affected by change need to maintain the motivation that they have already developed. This means continuing to reduce the pain of the change and to maximize the pleasure associated with it:

- Control and autonomy – enable people to decide for themselves how to incorporate the changes into how they work.
- Certainty and assurance – create certainty by encouraging everyone to plan their change activities.
- Increase sense of belonging – knowing everyone is participating makes people feel they are part of a unique volunteer network. This is reinforced through the support of Sustainability Champions and the chance to work with a buddy.

ERROR SIGNAL
- Reduce 'manage expectations' from the beginning and at every stage.
- Create small habits of unexpected rewards.
- Create a culture of asking for and providing positive feedback.

FIGURE 13.7 Example communications for making changes

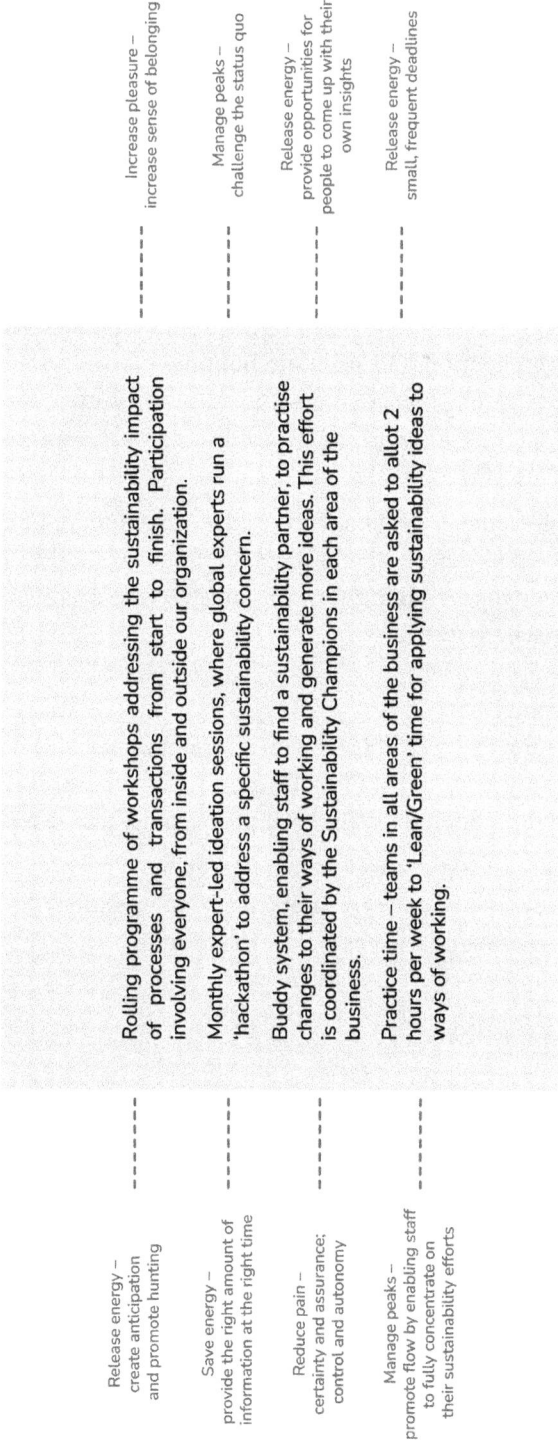

Release energy –
create anticipation
and promote hunting

- - - - - - - -

Rolling programme of workshops addressing the sustainability impact of processes and transactions from start to finish. Participation involving everyone, from inside and outside our organization.

- - - - - - - -

Increase pleasure –
increase sense of belonging

Save energy –
provide the right amount of
information at the right time

- - - - - - - -

Monthly expert-led ideation sessions, where global experts run a 'hackathon' to address a specific sustainability concern.

- - - - - - - -

Manage peaks –
challenge the status quo

Reduce pain –
certainty and assurance;
control and autonomy

- - - - - - - -

Buddy system, enabling staff to find a sustainability partner, to practise changes to their ways of working and generate more ideas. This effort is coordinated by the Sustainability Champions in each area of the business.

- - - - - - - -

Release energy –
provide opportunities for
people to come up with their
own insights

Manage peaks –
promote flow by enabling staff
to fully concentrate on
their sustainability efforts

- - - - - - - -

Practice time – teams in all areas of the business are asked to allot 2 hours per week to 'Lean/Green' time for applying sustainability ideas to ways of working.

- - - - - - - -

Release energy –
small, frequent deadlines

ENERGY

- Provide the right amount of information at the right time – a schedule of monthly engagements enables the experts to share relevant information at the point that it can be applied by those involved in the sustainability changes.

- Provide opportunities for people to come up with their own insights – buddying with a colleague and being supported by Sustainability Champions creates an environment for discovery and experimentation which will lead to new thoughts and ideas.

- Create anticipation and promote hunting – working through processes from start to finish encourages the brain to identify how sustainability will change ways of working, which is a motivator as the brain imagines the benefits of these changes.

- Small but frequent deadlines – to reduce the amount of energy the brain needs to think ahead and consider different scenarios, make small but frequent changes so that the brain can enjoy the energy released from the sense of achievement.

PEAKS AND VALLEYS

- Promote flow – by establishing an agreed amount of time when staff can focus on their sustainability efforts, they are more likely to lose themselves in the work, increasing their productivity and sense of achievement.

- Challenge the status quo – stimulated by new information from sustainability experts, people are more likely to question the usefulness and appropriateness of current ways of working.

Celebrating the results

The outcome of this step is the motivation to continue to change. Celebration is an important step in maintaining momentum and generating resilience for more change.

PAIN

The emphasis is on enjoying the pleasure created by the experience and the achievements of the change.

- Informal meetings and gatherings – celebrations are a chance to come together and enjoy the benefits of socializing and feeling 'part of your tribe', with the emphasis that everyone is in it together, irrespective of their position in the organization.

FIGURE 13.8 Example communications for celebrating the results

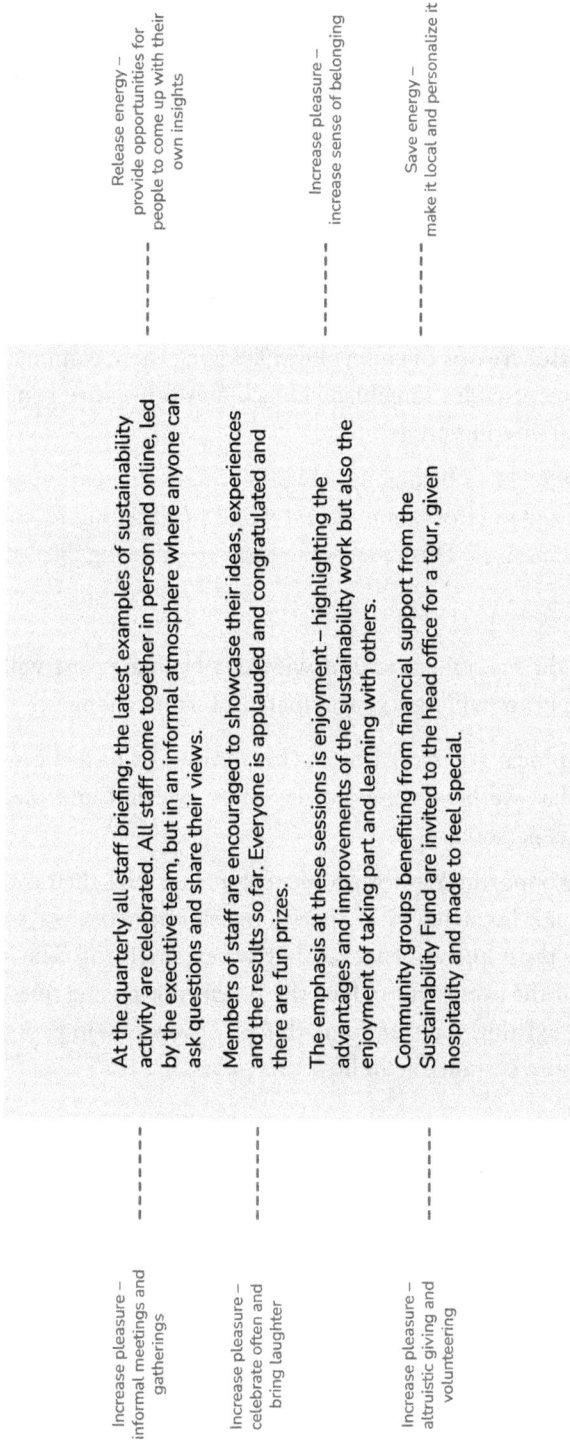

At the quarterly all staff briefing, the latest examples of sustainability activity are celebrated. All staff come together in person and online, led by the executive team, but in an informal atmosphere where anyone can ask questions and share their views.

Members of staff are encouraged to showcase their ideas, experiences and the results so far. Everyone is applauded and congratulated and there are fun prizes.

The emphasis at these sessions is enjoyment – highlighting the advantages and improvements of the sustainability work but also the enjoyment of taking part and learning with others.

Community groups benefiting from financial support from the Sustainability Fund are invited to the head office for a tour, given hospitality and made to feel special.

Increase pleasure – informal meetings and gatherings

Increase pleasure – celebrate often and bring laughter

Increase pleasure – altruistic giving and volunteering

Release energy – provide opportunities for people to come up with their own insights

Increase pleasure – increase sense of belonging

Save energy – make it local and personalize it

- Celebrate often and bring laughter – the release of endorphins enables the brain to associate the change with enjoyment. By talking through positive experiences and being applauded for each achievement, there is a chance to reinforce the good feeling and for the brain to create endorphins. Prizes of any kind create a fun atmosphere, more likely to produce laughter. They also extend the life of the pleasure, because they are an ongoing tangible reminder of the success. Prizes also encourage photographs, which act as a longer-lasting reminder of good times.

- Altruistic giving – doing something for the good it will bring to others is a powerful creator of endorphins. Bringing these community groups into the office provides tangible evidence that others are benefiting from the sustainability initiatives.

- Increase sense of belonging – highlighting participation and involvement in the change effort reminds everyone they belong to something bigger than themselves. This creates the pleasure of being part of a group.

ENERGY

Reducing the energy associated with this change effort will make it more likely people are willing to participate in further changes:

- Make it local – personalize it – for our brains to feel a sense of celebration, what we have achieved has to be relevant and meaningful to our role: it is personal to us.

- Provide opportunities for people to come up with their own insights – ask individuals impacted by change to review their new ways of working and identify the improvement that they are experiencing. The informal atmosphere of the event will reduce the barriers to posing questions and questioning existing ways of doing things. This will help people discover how to be more sustainable in how they work.

COPYRIGHT FOR FIGURES

INDEX

Page numbers in in *italic* denote a figure or table.

Looking for another book?

Explore our award-winning books from global business experts in Human Resources, Learning and Development

Scan the code to browse

www.koganpage.com/hr-learning-development

More from Kogan Page

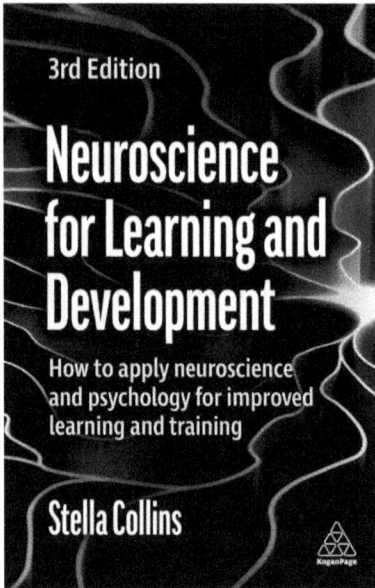

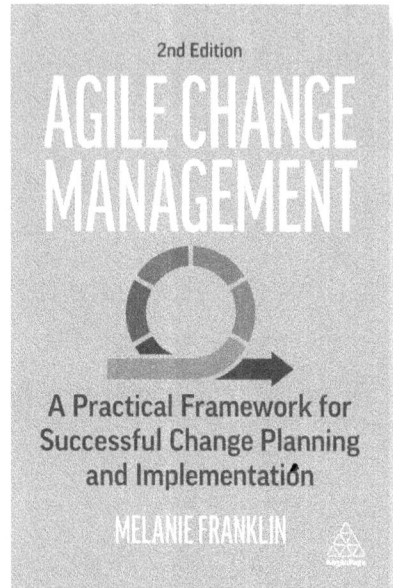

From 4 December 2025 the EU Responsible Person (GPSR) is:
eucomply oÜ, Pärnu mnt. 139b – 14, 11317 Tallinn, Estonia
www.eucompliancepartner.com

www.ingramcontent.com/pod-product-compliance
Lightning Source LLC
Chambersburg PA
CBHW070611030426
42337CB00020B/3759

9 781398 614406